Men and Abortion

Lessons, Losses, and Love

Arthur B. Shostak
Gary McLouth

With Lynn Seng

PRAEGER SPECIAL STUDIES • PRAEGER SCIENTIFIC

New York • Philadelphia • Eastbourne, UK
Toronto • Hong Kong • Tokyo • Sydney

Library of Congress Cataloging in Publication Data

Shostak, Arthur B.
  Men and abortion.

  Includes bibliographical references and index.
  1. Abortion—Psychological aspects—Case studies.
  2. Men—Attitudes—Case studies.   I. McLouth, Gary.
  II. Seng, Lynn.   III. Title.
  RG734.S47   1984   363.4'6   84-4927
  ISBN 0-03-063641-8

Except for the authors, the names of all abortion veterans throughout the text including acknowledgments and appendixes have been changed.

Published in 1984 by Praeger Publishers
CBS Educational and Professional Publishing,
a Division of CBS Inc.
521 Fifth Avenue, New York, NY 10175 USA
© 1984 by Arthur B. Shostak and Gary McLouth

56789 052 987654532

Printed in the United States of America
on acid-free paper

For the men
who wait...
especially the 1,000
who shared with us

"...we know from both women and men that involving the man is important. New avenues and opportunities for involvement of men in pregnancy counseling and abortion need to be adopted. Men will not be a part of what is, in essence, a no-win situation. Men—and women— need roles other than those of victims and villains."

Stephen McCallister,
Abortion Counselor

"We are caught in an inescapable network of mutuality, tied in a single garment of destiny."

Martin Luther King, Jr.

Contents

Preface
Arthur B. Shostak

We said nothing as we trained out of Cleveland for an early morning appointment at a nearby suburban abortion clinic. I guess we both felt there wasn't anything left to discuss, as we had been over all the options, even if very briefly and in a highly tentative fashion. Since our love affair had ended several weeks before, we had no thought of marriage, nor could either of us imagine going ahead with single parenthood.

We had thought long and hard about having our baby and placing it immediately for adoption. A pregnancy, however, would have caused such pain in my friend's life—in her relations with her unsuspecting family, in her career, and in her own mental health—that we felt we had no choice but to decide against the adoption route, too.

The week before the abortion we attended a five-couple group orientation session which lasted about 15 minutes. A clinic staffer chilled me with her assurance that we were only involved with the "disposal of a clump of tissue." But, believing the fetus something more than that, I waited until the others had gone elsewhere before gently urging the young woman to use less flippant language. I also had been disappointed to learn the clinic, widely respected as being sensitive and progressive, had no literature about abortion for males, and no counselor, male or female, with whom I could talk over things. Nor would they allow me to stay with my friend throughout the procedure, or comfort her later during her hour-long stay in the recovery room.

We went for our appointment a week later, silently persuaded our decision was resolute. We were astonished, therefore, when the clinic receptionist, after studying our drawn faces, referred us to the clinic's director instead of to the medical staff. The director, in turn, after assessing our hesitant words, helped us realize we had left much unsaid between us. She thought it best we delay our appointment, and go off together to work harder at discovering what we *really* wanted to do about this pregnancy.

Talking in greater depth than ever about our options, we wandered for hours a few blocks from the clinic. When we finally felt secure about our re-examined (and tear-marked) decision, we returned shortly before the evening closing hour. After we softly thanked the director for our enforced delay, we went ahead with the rescheduled abortion.

Looking back on it now, I recognize I had been little prepared for the complex reality of an abortion. Deeply embarrassed by our contraceptive failure, and privately angry at my partner and myself (she had briefly gone off the pill to relieve headaches), I had confided in no one and had kept my own inadequate counsel. Because I was very upset by my partner's fright and bewilderment, I had rushed to assure her of my total support. But, in the process, I had rushed right past the task of gaining any insight into my *own* confused feelings and ideas.

Since that time, I have remained personally interested in the neglected experiences of men (at least 1,400,000 annually) caught up unexpectedly in the abortion challenge.* In scores of discussions in several American cities, and in related dialogue with abortion clinic personnel from coast to coast, I have learned much about the turmoil, the testing, and the trauma we experience. I have shared the pleasure of men whose love relationships have been strengthened, and the pain of others wounded in their trials. Above all, I have been encouraged to find many clinic staffers as insightful and courageous as the Cleveland area director who intervened in my own case years ago. I have come to appreciate the magnitude of the task they face, that we all face, if males soon are to have the range of high-quality resources that were not available when I needed them the most.

"Abortion," as my friend and writing collaborator Gary McLouth so aptly puts it, "will never be high on our list of things to accomplish." Yet I am more and more persuaded many males can gain much of value from a searching and constructive response to its challenge. I also believe our book can help men *and* women make the best of an experience which tries them as few others may in their lifetimes.

---

*Howard W. Ory, et. al., *Making Choices* (New York: The Alan Guttmacher Institute, 1983), p. 9. Some 74% of the 1.6 million procedures are performed in non-hospital clinics, the setting of our research.

Preface
Gary McLouth

During November 1981, I was working on a short story about a couple's abortion experience. Although it was fictional, the story relied heavily on my own experience—so heavily, in fact, that the essence of my experience, the trauma and numbness, inhibited my efforts to create a workable story.

Coincidentally, the *New York Times* carried a column on the male role in abortion. The article cited sociologist Arthur Shostak as a research expert on the topic. I wrote to Dr. Shostak, asking him to share his findings, so that I could objectify my story enough to rewrite it. I also volunteered to help him with his work. My innocuous offer accelerated the process of unraveling my own abortion experience, begun by my story writing.

Instead of sending information or simply ignoring my letter, Art Shostak called from Philadelphia to ask if I would be willing to appear on the *Today Show* segment with Phil Donahue, to talk about the male role in abortion and, more specifically, my own abortion experience. I had been in the shower when Donahue called. Afterwards, I stood there until the hot water ran lukewarm and then turned cold. I sensed at that moment a chance to accomplish something. I also felt the fear of the unknown potential to make a fool of myself, the chance that I would shame my family or do irreparable damage to my intimate relationships. I knew that opening a previously confidential experience to the public meant revealing it forever in the face of consequences I could not predict or control.

I was not convinced that an appearance with Donahue would do more than fill air time with yet another sideshow of human fallability and frailty. Fortunately, neither the show nor my decision-making process leading up to doing it brought feelings of cheapness and usury. On the contrary, it turned out to be one of the better experiences of my life.

In order to go before millions of TV viewers, I first had to approach my abortion partner with the prospect. Although the abortion had occurred several years before, our discussion was incredibly vivid. It focused on interpretations of events and emotions neither of us previously had discussed. The pain and doubt I had not shared at the time of the abortion surfaced. Things we had avoided or tried to forget were suddenly in the context of the present, and in that context we helped each other work through long established half-truths and misconceptions. We reached a deeper understanding of ourselves and of each other. A warmth, a trust I had missed during the years since the abortion, returned.

During the last two years, I have explored the world of abortion enough to know that men are seriously affected by their abortion experiences and that their memories are extremely sharp and cogent when recalling these experiences. Although there are a variety of social-political responses to the subject of abortion in America, I have been most impressed by the lack of response to the often forgotten partner. Is there need for a response? Can he take care of his needs alone?

Like many men, I suspect, I chose to get my abortion experience over with—behind me. I failed. I hope that my efforts to respond to that failure will help other men and their women partners live with the abortion experience more successfully.

Men and Abortion was not on my list of books I wanted to write; neither was abortion on my list of life's goals. Now that both are part of my life, my greatest hope for them is that they prove useful in times of difficult and lonely decisions for future abortion veterans and that, in some way, veterans of the past will find a perspective and reconciliation . they may have been missing.

Acknowledgments
Arthur B. Shostak

Without the cooperation of 30 abortion clinics in 18 states, we would have no answers from 1,000 of their male visitors, no (unsparing) review by the clinics of their own services for males, and no access to their training manuals and allied material—in short, no book. Our appreciation for their cooperation, exemplifying as it does the highest standards of professionalism, could not be greater.

Early versions of the questionnaire were carefully critiqued by Bob Norris, Herb Lewis, Michael Halperin, and, above all, Lynn Seng, none of whom can be held responsible for its shortcomings. Sociologists who circulated our questionnaire among their college students included Ed Gondolf, Russ Kleinbach, Joe Ruane, Kay Snyder, and Dave Voight, all of whom have our heartfelt appreciation.

Former adult students of mine at the AFL-CIO's George Meany Center for Labor Studies who asked around in the workplace for blue-collar respondents included Randy R. Boulton, Roger A. Burrill, Carl DiMingo, Michael G. Ellis, William Earl Higginbotham, Curtis T. Ezzell, Bill Goetz, Bob Kellerman, Kevin Kistler, "Dutch" Kleywegt, Rocky Morrill, and Larry M. Slay, Jr. (the last of whom also sent a classroom display on Alaska's boisterous abortion rights struggle—prepared by a co-worker's young daughter). A similarly welcomed boost in questionnaire securement came from Gerry Evans, director of Philadelphia's Men's Resource Center.

In the early stages of computer-based research, considerable help was received from Michael Halperin, a Drexel University information specialist. At a critical later stage in the process, another Drexel University specialist, Lou Patridge, of the computer center staff, helped us stay close to schedule. Dee Harper, a Drexel librarian in charge of interlibrary loan arrangements, often facilitated arrangements in a very welcomed fashion.

Especially outstanding was the sustained effort of a Drexel undergraduate, Herb Lewis, who volunteered to manage the complex and vexing task of coding hundreds of questionnaires, and routing 4,500 computer cards through error-free keypunching and computer runs. Michael Baselice, a Drexel senior, converted over 500 questionnaires from a midwest clinic into punched cards, computer printout, and the analysis which appears in counselor Peter Zelles's contribution to Chapter 8.

Over the course of several years, many Drexel undergraduates prepared field research reports on some aspect of this subject. Especially helpful were papers by Susan Anderson, Frances Antolina, Maureen Carr, Nicholas Del Zingaro, Mark Feldman, Chip Gallagher, Theresa Krankel, Marc Marriello, Dennis McCarthy, James McLord, Susan Markowitz, Linda R. Morris, Scott E. Olson, Kathleen Payne, Steve Pugliese, Stephen J. Salvitti, Ed Schickling, William S. Thomas, Wayne Thompson, Kelly L. Willson, Michael Wollfel, and Glen A. Zimmerman.

Special data runs were done for us by *Glamour* magazine, the Drexel University Survey Research Center (directed by Dr. William Rosenberg), and the University of Connecticut's Institute for Social Inquiry (Nancy Barth). Thanks also are owed to the Alan Guttmacher Institute (Barbara Parks) and the Data Users Services Department of the U.S. Bureau of the Census (Dave Lewis) for timely and well-targeted publications.

From beyond the campus, a number of informative publications and letters came from a prominent right-to-life leader, Dr. Olga Fairfax, who has our thanks for sharing her point of view. We also appreciated literature sent by Doris Gordon, National Coordinator of Libertarians for Life. While ours is a decidedly more pro-choice position, we respect the hold the anti-abortion view has on a small minority of waiting room men.

Pro-choice supporters who aided our project included Bill Baird (clinic director and activist; see Chapter 9); Sherrie Berger, Terry Beresford, and Jeremy Levine (Planned Parenthood of Baltimore); Heather C. Green (Hillcrest Clinics, Virginia); Sylvia Hampton (Health Rights Advocate, St. Louis, Missouri); Elaine Levy (former administrator, Albany Women's Medical Center, Chicago, Illinois); and Bruce Rappaport (formerly of the Men's Support Center, Oakland, California). Dan Logan, Washington Executive Director of Free Men, invited us to share ideas in what may have been the first-ever public forum held about men and abortion.

Staffers of *Sociological Abstracts* answered our inquiries about relevant research with impressive (computer-aided) dispatch and thoroughness, for which we are grateful. Novelist William O'Rourke shared his powerful tale—*Idle Hands*—with its gripping abortion account, one that gave us much to ponder. Health education specialists Ione J. Ryan and Patricia C. Dunn, both of East Carolina University (Greenville, North Carolina) generously shared research findings on college student attitudes toward shared responsibility in abortion decision making. Other academic researchers, particularly William Marsiglio (Ohio State University), Anne M. Dimock (Planned Parenthood of Wisconsin), and Esther Benjamin (Northwestern University) made distinct and valuable contributions.

Jan L. Harrington, the project's initial methodologist, made an indispensable contribution with both her craft and her gentle patience. Dr. Joan Spade of SUNY-Brockport joined our two-year long effort in its final two months, and can in no way be held responsible for our use of questionnaire answers. Going beyond the standard call to duty, Joan read and critiqued every paragraph in the entire volume.

My oldest son, Scott, helped considerably with law library research, although busy at Pace University Law School. My younger son, Mark, joined several other college students (Jonathan Levy, Herb Lewis, Timothy Harris) in high-pressure, late-hour keypunch sessions that met critical data-processing deadlines.

Lynn Seng's sons, Matthew and Daniel, made room for this project in their lives, gave their mother the space needed for her substantial contribution, and cheered all three of us with their fellowship, patience, and occasional inquiries about the project.

My parents, Milton and Betty, sent a steady stream of relevant newspaper and magazine items, discussed our findings with their friends, and stood by to help in any possible way.

Our typist, Beth Brown, brought editorial craft, as well as speed, endurance, and experience to her labor. Lynn Seng, our associate, helped us remain alert to our male biases, and guided our appreciation of the woman's point of view. As a college counselor and doctoral candidate in educational psychology, she informed our deliberations about the world of counseling concerns. And, as a talented editor, she strove to keep the writing as clear, cogent, and compelling as possible.

Gary McLouth assumed full responsibility for the interviews that resulted in 25 profiles used throughout the volume. His unflagging enthusiasm, buoyant good humor, and gentle sensitivity contributed at every turn.

Lynda Sharp, our editor at Praeger, encouraged the project throughout, read with valuable discernment, criticized in a constructive way, and nudged us with patience and persistence at just the right times.

Throughout, I assumed final editorial control, including full responsibility for the shortcomings that remain.

Acknowledgments
Gary McLouth

In addition to everyone who contributed insight, talent, and information, I want to specifically thank these fine professionals and friends: Jan Abrams, Doug Bauer, Lee Berry, Joe Bocchi, Rick Claire, Arnelle Coqueran, Harrison Fisher, Stewart Forde, Eugene K. Garber, Mark Hayes, Peter J. Johnson, Anne Johnstone, William Kennedy, Blanche Lansky, Robert Leaver, Eugene Mirabelli, Maureen Murray, Marty Nakell, Rudolf Nelson, Stephen North, and LaVonne Thompson.

To Art and Lynn, more than thanks for what we have done together. Kudos to Matthew and Daniel. And to Dr. Sydney and Virginia McLouth, the greatest acknowledgment of all.

Tables

Chapter 1

Introduction

Of the few hundred men I've seen, I never met one who thought abortion was just 'cool.' People may be relieved after abortion, and utterly convinced of the rightness of the action they've taken, but no one rejoices. Abortion is a difficult experience for everyone concerned. That includes men. A man may escape the physical trauma, but it's unlikely he'll come through unscathed.

> Bruce Rappaport, male counselor, San Francisco, (*Mademoiselle*, April 1981, p. 230).

Although no one seems to give them a thought, as many as 600,000 males annually—from downy-cheeked teens to gray-haired fathers—"do time" in the waiting rooms of the nation's 500 or so abortion clinics.[1]

Generally ill-at-ease, the men sit apprehensively and embarrassed among a much larger group of girlfriends, sisters, and mothers. Striking in their diversity, the men who wait also are set apart by their lack of macho self-confidence and their dour solemnity. ("Nobody, *but* nobody, cracks any jokes in there," a 24-year-old cab driver recalled.)

When we started thinking about them, after having done time ourselves among them, we wondered:

Who are these men? How typical are they of all American males?

Why are they there? What motivates them to come along for the abortion appointment?

How do they feel—about the pregnancy, the decision to terminate, the loss of fatherhood, their role, the female's role, and the future of the relationship?

What do they think of pro- and anti-abortion arguments? Of the nature of the fetus? Of the right to an abortion on request, for any reason whatsoever?

How much power do they want in the decision to terminate a pregnancy?

Whom do they turn to for advice, support, and solace? How many talk to male friends? Parents? Abortion clinic counselors?

What happened at the clinic? How many felt good or bad about it? Why?

Could the experience have been a better one for them? What abortion clinic reforms, if any, do they endorse—and why?

How intent are they on not being abortion repeaters? What sorts of reforms do they think might lower the number of abortions?

We also wondered about the role of "significant others" in this situation:

How does the public feel about the role men should have in abortion decision making? Do men and women think alike here, or do the sexes differ in their viewpoints?

How do lawmakers and jurists treat the role men should have in abortion decision making? What legal rights, if any, do men have in a contested abortion?

Above all, we wanted to learn how the men who wait respond to the *entire* situation—from the news of the conception through the months that follow the abortion; what the range of their feelings was during their ordeal, especially through the obvious fact of relationships strengthened, weakened, or broken by this trial.

Two ensuing years of field research involving 30 abortion clinics from New England to California are now beginning to reveal some provocative answers to these questions.[2]

Of our 1,000 male respondents from the 30 clinics we studied, 60% were single, 18% were married, 12% were "living together," and 10% were formerly married men (87% of the married men, by the way, were accompanying their wives). Even among the singles, the relationships were relatively stable (22% of the single men were engaged and 57% were dating their partner on a steady basis). Thus, it was not surprising that waiting room males show genuine concern about the well-being of their lover, fiancée, or wife, many interrupting clinic staffers with anxious questions about the woman at every opportunity.

The men in our sample also reflected the age distribution of all abortion patients, one-third of which were under 20 years of age (see Table 1-1). The ages of men in our sample were concentrated in the youngest age categories with those 21 or younger comprising 35% of the sample, and those 22–25 making up 30% of the sample. Given their youthfulness, 27% were still in college or a trade school—which is about the average for American males over 18.

Because more financially secure couples tend to use a private physician rather than a public abortion clinic, the waiting room crowd included few professionals, a more representative number of white-collar workers (20%), and slightly more blue-collar workers (35%) than is usually found among males in general. Nearly half were Protestants, a third were Catholic, and 15% reported no

Table 1-1. Comparison of Clinic Male Respondents (1983) with Female Abortion Patients (1980)

	1,000 male respondents	Female Abortion Patients*
Unmarried	82%	79%
White	87	70
Under 20	35	30
Attended or graduated college	45	34
Had a previous abortion	25	33

*Source: Stanley K. Henshaw and Kevin O'Reilly, "Characteristics of Abortion Patients in the United States, 1979 and 1980." *Family Planning Perspectives*, January/February 1983.

affiliation. Finally, in rounding out this profile, the men who wait in abortion clinics reflect the black/white distribution in America (10% and 87%, respectively), while slightly understating the proportion of Hispanics (1.5%) and Asian-Americans (0.8%) (see Table 1-2).[3]

Given these demographic characteristics (which are similar to the U.S. population with the exception of the younger age), as well as the commitment of these men to the relationship and to the female they have accompanied to the clinic—what do *they* think and feel about the unusual situation in which they find themselves? When we gave them a chance to write anything they wished which would capsulize the matter, many took the opportunity to share thoughts like these:

I have two small, great, and beautiful children, but we really can't handle a third right now—it would really hurt us. (*Married, 29, Catholic, white*)

I feel helpless, poorly informed, and put in a "typical" male role. (*Married, 33, Catholic, white*)

I can now understand the importance of birth control. I now have a deeper respect for being able to have sex with a woman. (*Single, 20, Christian, college student, white*)

I wish it wouldn't seem like we're doing something dirty. (*Married, 30, Protestant, white*)

Killing the fetus may be a crime, but child abuse and neglect is a bigger crime, I feel. (*Single, 26, Protestant, engineer, black*)

My strongest concern is for my relationship with my fiancée—emotionally and mentally I believe she will never feel the same about me, herself, children and life in general. I have already experienced some neglectfulness and deep-seated guilt on the part of my fiancée. (*"Living-together," 27, Protestant, electronics technician, white*)

It has opened my eyes to life and love. (*Single, 26, Protestant, machinist, white*)

I think the men should be allowed to be in the room while surgery is being performed. Also, allowed in the waiting room. This procedure is just as important as childbirth, in my mind. Thank you for the opportunity to voice my opinion, because I feel very strong about the procedure. (*Single, 22, Christian, car salesman, white*)

Over and again, in hundreds of such written comments, and in long, vivid personal interviews, we were reminded of the extraordinary nature of this confusing and troubling experience—perhaps the least well known and least understood of any challenges in a man's life.

Barren Bookshelf

For every kind of good reason imaginable, researchers in abortion scholarship have been preoccupied with the female, the fetus, the state, the church, the ethical questions, and other such controversial aspects. Not surprisingly, therefore, when we used a computer search system to assay the content of 279 recent (1963–1984) examples of relevant sociological research on abortion, some 239, or 85%, dealt with women, or the fetus, or the state, etc.—anything except the men involved. Of the 40 articles linked to our subject, nine concentrated on the male experience in countries abroad, and only six (three by Art Shostak, one of this book's co-authors) shared any new field research in the American context.[4] A scholar in 1979 concluded in exasperation that this type of literature "often totally disregarded the male role, reported it in an implicit or covert manner, or at best reported through the perceptions of the man's partner."[5]

Fortunately, a search of unpublished doctoral dissertations, masters theses, and graduate student papers unearthed eight field

Table 1-2. Profile of 1,000 Clinic Male Respondents

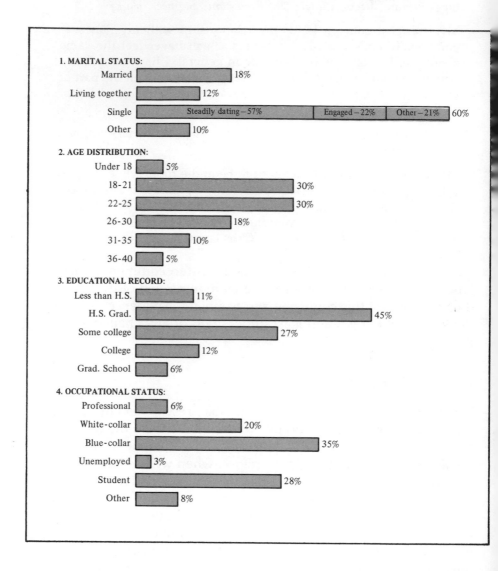

1. MARITAL STATUS:
Married — 18%
Living together — 12%
Single — Steadily dating—57% | Engaged—22% | Other—21% | 60%
Other — 10%

2. AGE DISTRIBUTION:
Under 18 — 5%
18-21 — 30%
22-25 — 30%
26-30 — 18%
31-35 — 10%
36-40 — 5%

3. EDUCATIONAL RECORD:
Less than H.S. — 11%
H.S. Grad. — 45%
Some college — 27%
College — 12%
Grad. School — 6%

4. OCCUPATIONAL STATUS:
Professional — 6%
White-collar — 20%
Blue-collar — 35%
Unemployed — 3%
Student — 28%
Other — 8%

Table 1-2 continued

5. RACIAL DISTRIBUTION:

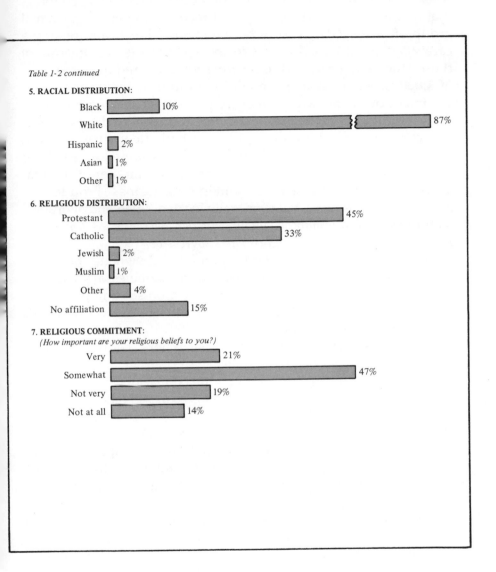

Black — 10%
White — 87%
Hispanic — 2%
Asian — 1%
Other — 1%

6. RELIGIOUS DISTRIBUTION:

Protestant — 45%
Catholic — 33%
Jewish — 2%
Muslim — 1%
Other — 4%
No affiliation — 15%

7. RELIGIOUS COMMITMENT:
(How important are your religious beliefs to you?)

Very — 21%
Somewhat — 47%
Not very — 19%
Not at all — 14%

research reports, all of which we use extensively in the chapters that follow. Each has the strength of focusing in depth on a small group of males (60–126) at only one or two clinics, and testing a carefully honed hypothesis. We incorporate the conclusions of these studies to sharpen the information gathered in our survey of 1,000 males in 30 abortion clinics around the country.[6]

Intent on taking help from every possible source, we expanded our literature search far beyond conventional boundaries. Abortion clinic personnel, for example, who had often never heard of the eight Ph.D. and M.A. field research items, were excited about having read something of relevance in one or another of the major mass-circulation women's or men's magazines. Prodded by leads as vague as these, we eventually located "men and abortion" feature articles in *Esquire, Glamour, Hustler, McCall's, Mademoiselle, New York Times Magazine,* and *The Progressive.*

Characteristically strong on human-interest vignettes but weak on data, statistics, and typologies, the magazine essays were especially valuable for revealing what circulation-seeking publishers believed the public wanted to know about our subject. *Esquire's* writer, for example, advised readers in 1981 that abortion was "a far greater dilemma for men than researchers, counselors—and women—have even begun to realize."[7]

Another useful lead provided by the counselors involved three pamphlets which 62% of our 30 clinics give or sell (at cost) to waiting room males. Authored by current or former abortion counselors, the pamphlets try to sensitize male readers to their *own,* as well as to the women's, varied emotional and spiritual needs in the clinic and in the weeks and months following the abortion. Unique in being based on hundreds of individual and group counseling sessions conducted by their authors, the three pamphlets lack any research data, a deliberate omission in keeping with their nonacademic, practical character. We found them especially helpful as a touchstone of sorts, a validity check on the feedback we were getting from our 1,000 waiting room men. (Two of the pamphlet authors are counselors at clinics cooperating with our study, and both also are contributors to this book.)[8]

Given the preoccupation of abortion scholarship with the world of women, we dared to hope a few items in the bookshelf might pay men at least passing attention. We were not disappointed. Much was written about the thoughts and feelings of abortion patients concerning their boyfriends, lovers, fiancés, and husbands. In the hands of social scientists such as Luker, Zimmerman, Smetana, and Gilligan, these second-hand accounts of what male sex partners were experiencing—as interpreted by their women—shed unique and valuable light on our subject.

Finally, we would be seriously remiss not to mention two very special, very exacting, and very sparse resources that made a distinct contribution.

The first involved the statistical reports of large-scale public polling projects, such as the 1965–1982 set of abortion questions asked of 1,500 Americans by the National Opinion Research Corporation (NORC), and the 1963–1982 abortion surveys of the Gallup Corporation. We also were fortunate in gaining the cooperation of *Glamour* magazine and the University of Connecticut's Institute for Social Inquiry, both of which ran special computer tabulations of their abortion polling data at our request. Similarly, the Drexel University Survey Center included some of our abortion questions in two 1983 phone surveys of the Philadelphia public, and ran the computer analysis for us that we designed. Data of this rich and varied nature helped clarify the attitudes and values of the public in general, and of males and females in particular.

Our second very special, exacting, and all-too-sparse resource involved the fictional and poetic recreation of the male experience. Relevant writers included novelists John Barth (*The End of the Road*), William O'Rourke (*Idle Hands*), Richard Brautigan (*The Abortion*), and Theodore Dreiser (*An American Tragedy*); short-story authors such as Harlan Ellison, Ernest Hemingway, and Alice Walker; and poets Adrienne Rich and Anne Sexton, among others. Evocative and engaging, this small selection of fine writing added soul and substance to the bare numbers of public opinion polls, and augmented the drama we experienced in scores of intense discussions with waiting room men.

Finding Out for Ourselves

Intent on expanding the inadequate research base of knowledge in this matter, we identified six target groups and a data-gathering strategy for each:

1. *Males who accompany their sex partners to an abortion* were invited by staffers at 30 abortion clinics to complete our questionnaire;

1,000 men eventually did so. (The 30 clinics were located through the 1981–82 and 1982–83 directories of the National Abortion Federation, a composite list of 243 providers, all of whom were invited to participate in our research.)

2. *Males who do not accompany their sex partners* were sought through media appeals (radio talk shows, etc.), public forum appeals, and requests for cooperation placed in men's movement newsletters; 18 eventually responded and completed our questionnaire.[9]

3. *Males willing to discuss the aftermath of an abortion* were located through phone numbers they provided on the questionnaires distributed in the abortion clinics; 75 were interviewed by phone or in person.

4. *Clinic representatives* were asked to "guesstimate" the percentage of clients accompanied by sex partners, the percentage of such males who request counseling, and other items on which none usually collect statistics. They also were asked to describe the services available for waiting room males, and their future plans for any such services, a request eventually honored by 26 of our 30 cooperating clinics.[10]

5. *Clinic counselors* were interviewed at length in a dozen locations from coast to coast, and five chose to supplement these focused discussions with essays they wrote especially for this volume.

6. *Abortion activists,* such as Bill Baird of the pro-choice camp and Joe Scheidler of the anti-abortion bloc, were interviewed in person or by phone, and each cooperated in the preparation of a profile on their actions, attitudes, and values.

This six-part data collection effort took the better part of two years, and resulted in our making new friends across the country and gaining a much broader understanding of the man's abortion experience.

At the very heart of the entire project was our main data-gathering tool, a five-sided, three-page questionnaire of 102 questions (see Appendix G). The questionnaire was pretested on small groups of waiting room males whose answers highlighted gaps and ambiguities in our early drafts.

The final version focused on several different areas: We asked the respondents to reconstruct their attitudes and behaviors both when they learned of the pregnancy and during the decision-making period. We then asked questions about the actual abortion, and also had the men look ahead and speculate about the impact of the abortion on their relationships with their female partners. We explored their moral and political views about abortion, and paid special attention to their thoughts about the fetus, the loss of fatherhood, and the allocation of decision-making power between themselves and their partners. We also asked half of our group which, if any, of six possible clinic services for males they would utilize, and why.[11] Finally, we gave the men an opportunity to use their own words to answer two open-ended questions: "How could this entire experience be a better one for you?" and "Do you have any other thoughts you care to add about any aspect of the experience?"

Processing the Data

Each questionnaire was first examined for any handwritten answers or comments (as found in 55%), and then all were turned over to a key puncher for transfer of their 102 answers to a set of five data punch cards. After being rigorously examined for (rare) keypunch errors, the 4,500 cards were run in a statistical program handled by our two methodologists, Jan Harrington, and later, Dr. Joan Spade.[12]

Sharing the Findings

Before beginning our writing, we deliberately sought a hearing from a wide range of concerned audiences and gained much from the lively discussion our data generally provoked. We spoke on TV talk shows and radio "call-in" shows in 15 states (via phone hook-ups), along with pro-choice forums (vigorously attended by anti-abortion activists), a statewide (New Jersey) N.O.W. forum on abortion policies, a Washington, D.C., forum of a national men's organization ("Free Men"), and various campus forums (Hartwick College, West Chester State College, Drexel University, among others). Especially helpful was the time spent sharing findings and reform ideas with the entire staff of two very different clinics, one with an avowed feminist orientation (and a disinclination to help us get surveys done in their waiting room), and the other, a full-service women's health center which was of major assistance to our survey collection effort.[13]

Influenced by these direct exchanges of data, insights, and recommendations with varied groups of adults, we made three policy decisions of major consequence for this book. First, we decided to write for the largest possible audience—the kind we had had in our TV, radio, and forum appearances—as well as abortion clinic staffers, partisans, and the like. Second, we decided to keep the writing as clear and cogent as possible. All statistical tables have therefore been held to a minimum, and the jargon of specialists has been translated into conventional English. Third, we decided to go beyond a cut-and-dried presentation of the findings. Instead, we build on this material to highlight reform posibilities endorsed by many of our 1,000 men—reforms we regard as worthy of sustained trial and sensitive assessment.

Limitations of the Project

As our data come only from males inclined to cooperate with us, we have no way of knowing what the experience meant for others in the clinic waiting rooms too embarrassed, embittered, indifferent, or self-contained to complete our questionnaire. Similarly, while we secured and analyzed 18 surveys from men who did not go along to the abortion appointment, we would have preferred a much larger number—though this is an extraordinarily difficult type of respondent to draw into research cooperation. And while we invited (and re-invited) over 300 clinics (243 NAF members and over 60 non-NAF clinics) to assist in circulating our questionnaire, we would have preferred participation from many more than the 30 that finally joined us.[14] Above all, given the absence of any scientific knowledge of waiting room males in general, and our inability therefore to pursue a random or representative sample of this universe, we have had to settle for a sample of convenience, an "available sample" of a previously unmeasured aggregate. Accordingly, we make no claim for the representativeness of our findings, and urge utmost caution in generalizing beyond the 1,000-male cohort itself.

Summary

We were struck during our own abortion experiences by certain stark and regrettable features of the scene—the absence of any helpful preparation for the experience; the embarrassment and sense of uselessness men felt during their clinic vigil; the wish to talk about it versus the social pressure to tell no one; and the need to appear supportive regardless of one's own ambivalence and heartache. We began to ask if it *had* to be like this, if there wasn't a better way for 600,000 males annually to help their partners and themselves meet the abortion challenge.

Finding very little in the research literature, we spent over two years gathering data, conducting interviews, and exchanging ideas with concerned audiences. Our book shares statistics and human-interest material from 1,000 waiting room men and scores of clinic staffers, data that make clear a remarkable similarity in the attitudes of Catholic and non-Catholic males, a poignant difference in the attitudes of white and black males, a striking increase in postabortion discomfort, and other provocative findings. Guided by front-line insights, we now can make a case for pragmatic and promising reforms of the *entire* situation—from pre- to post-abortion—as it can all be done better, to the substantial gain of men and women alike.

PROFILE

We have chosen Daniel as our beginning interview deliberately and whole-heartedly. His story illustrates much about lessons, losses, and love, even as it is also representative of major concerns of our other men.

Daniel's keen sense of powerless involvement and uncompensated loss forced him to seek resolution. Although he could have chosen resentment and guilt, he sought healthier attitudes of understanding and love. Daniel's level of concern and energy resonated throughout our other personal interviews. These men continually reminded us, indeed, implored us to focus on the human particulars of our material along with our statistical data.

Daniel, like all of our 1,000 men, did not run from his pregnant girlfriend, or from us, or from himself. Unfortunately, many Americans expect a man in his situation to take the easy way out. Daniel chose responsibility, however, and in this society of legally defined choice, such young people model a mature approach to our freedoms and responsibilities.

Daniel had crisscrossed the country from Ohio to Oregon to New York City, alternating college and a variety of odd jobs. In Baltimore he met a woman with whom he began living, and took a job as a full-time chef at a downtown restaurant. He appeared to be enjoying his relationship, his work, and his life when, shortly before Christmas 1982, her pregnancy forced him to reexamine everything.

Daniel:

A lot of it is a blur. I couldn't give you a daily account. I went to work and didn't even know what I was doing. I could have cut myself accidentally . . . I work with knives so much.

It was one of the only times in my life where I realized I was involved, but I didn't have the ultimate say. I wasn't really in favor of it at the time, but I realized it was . . . a woman's decision.

I didn't want to get married, but I wanted to make it comfortable for her, adoption or whatever, but I didn't want to see a life end. Is that it? I'm not sure. I had been against abortion and still am, but a man's position is secondary. It has to be in that decision. It involves someone else's body. That's my primary justification. It makes me feel helpless, having a certain conviction and realizing it doesn't matter in practical terms. It doesn't bother me that people have a choice, but it bothers me because I don't like it [abortion].

My relationship is stronger, better now. It was the first major crisis that tested our feelings. There was initially a sense of resentment on my part, but, again, respecting her right to make the decision made me realize the resentment was a gut reaction.

I resented the fact that I was stuck with the situation and her decision, and the responsibility and commitment to the situation. I resented the fact that regardless of whose body it was in, it was my kid, too.

Working it out was mostly due to what she said and did. She just couldn't face it—the responsibility. If she'd had the child, she couldn't give it up, but the responsibility was too great for her. But, I was willing to lessen the burden as much as I could . . . by taking financial responsibility. I was even toying with the idea of being a single father. I was probably being a bit idealistic at the time. I was willing to give it a try.

In that kind of situation does a man have any rights? To take my baby and bring it up as a single father? If not, it is unfair, especially in this day and age of modern medicine which can prove paternity.

I have only discussed this with my girl, and the guy who gave me the questionnaire, and you. I would talk to more people about it now. I tried to feel like a rational person at the time so I could discuss it, but it was difficult. I didn't want to reveal my emotional state. How would you approach someone to talk about so many mixed emotions?

I have always found it difficult to talk about my deepest personal problems. When I was 14, my father died. It was an incredible emotional crisis. I never discussed it with anyone, including my family who was going through the same thing.

It's like how you choose the Pope. They're in that room up there and when they finally make the decision, the smoke goes up. That's how you know everything is okay. I know close friends of mine sensed from my attitude that something was wrong and I know they could tell when it was okay again, but I never verbalized what was going on. Now that I think about it, it was kind of an insult that I didn't open up to them.

I went through a period where I intellectualized this intangible thing into a part of my life and now I've made it intangible again. I went through a heavy guilt period even before the abortion had taken place. I think I felt guilty just because of things I ignored. For a short while we didn't practice birth control. We were lazy for a while and then it happens and you end a potential life, kill something.

It taught me a lot of lessons. How you have to be smart. Like the old "it couldn't happen to me" thing is a lot of crap. Not just in terms of sex, but how you deal with your life.

It's so easy when you watch the news on TV. It's so unreal and also removed from your life. This situation occurs and you realize you're part of the world. It made me feel part of a much larger body of people, those who had experienced abortions.

It's hard to imagine people allowing themselves to go through an abortion repetition. I know men who have and I can't see how they do it. It certainly made me stop and think. Maybe men are conditioned to not even care about it. It's even weirder that a lot of women don't either. I find that more appalling. But, you find you can prevent it and we do now by the pill.

The clinic was very bizarre. Here I was in this packed waiting room, standing room only by the time we left, the combination of people . . . groups of women supporting one woman friend. I saw a young 14-year-old whose father was with her. Despite the situation, I respected him. It must have been tough.

I saw several couples. Every man in there had the same look on his face—wanting desperately to be someplace else.

I really wanted to support my girlfriend, but I didn't know what was happening. I'd read pamphlets and she'd told me about it. But, I hadn't thought about *not being with her*. I got up automatically and went to the door and the attendant stopped me. It really pissed me off. It's like my mother says—women's problems.

I waited and read every magazine I could find. I had bought a science magazine to read and in that issue they had a report with pictures on a special process—amniocentesis. I forced myself to look at it, but it was a real blow. I didn't say anything. We had already made the decision and I didn't want to rehash the argument there. I didn't need to see that, or maybe I did. Somebody could have hit me over the head with a sledgehammer.

How can you suggest changes, how can you make it easier? In the Soviet Union, they've made it an everyday thing. Like everyone has one. It wouldn't make it easier for me.

I took it solely as my fault that she was pregnant. I did it to her. I see now it's ridiculous. Why I felt that way, I'm not sure.

Fatherhood is a good thing; I want to be one.

The fetus, even to this day, took on a kind of other-world identity. I couldn't see it, I couldn't feel it. My girlfriend could. That's the biggest difference in that a woman experiences it in such a tangible way. A man's bonds are only emotional. A woman's bonds are both.

It's a wound you can't see or feel, but it exists. It heals, though. You go through the process of finding ways to deal with it. Guilt is pointless; it's like self-flagellation. You can pout about it or get over it. If it hadn't healed, I couldn't live with this woman now. It's finally something that happened in my life and I've had to keep going.

The hardest period was three or four days prior to the abortion. In a small way I felt relief the minute we stepped out of the clinic, although the guilt was there. Have you read Anne Sexton's poem about abortion? There's a line something like—"Someone who lived is gone." I read it and that's how I felt about it and still do. It's someone who didn't get a chance. . . This is good for me. I've thought about it a lot.

In the clinic no one came around to talk to us, like the brochure said. But I didn't seek out anybody either, so it's partially my fault. I probably wouldn't have said anything in the group discussions anyway, knowing me.

It would be a hard experience to go through watching it, not that I wanted to see it, but I wanted to be with her. They create a situation where she has to go through something alone. I did, too, but it was all a total head trip in the waiting room.

I went through a restless period in my life when I spent six months in a town and then just split. I was so used to living out of a couple of boxes, I could have run away from it. It was a test. I know a lot of men who have. I don't see the necessity for it. I'm better off for having faced it. I can intellectualize it now. I don't know if I could had I run away from it.

It brought our relationship down to earth from just romanticism and idealism. Before, we were just two people living together, off on different tangents. The abortion brought us into one, helped us grow together in more cooperation. We could go on ignoring whose turn it was to do the laundry, but the abortion forced us to define our relationship and roles.

Notes

1. In 1983 it was estimated that 1,600,000 legal abortions took place. Our 30 clinics believe 85% of their patients told the natural father of the pregnancy. Combining these figures, we believe about 1,360,000 men are involved annually in the abortion drama. As for the reliability of the 85% guesstimate, it is important to note that Bracken, Hachamovitch, and Grossman found 87% of 489 women had told their partners of their decision to seek an abortion (1974); Melamed's 1975 research on 188 abortion patients indicated 85% had told their partners of the pregnancy, and 83% of the decision for abortion. Michael Bracken, Moshe Hachamovitch, and Gerald Grossman, "The Decision to Abort and Psychological Sequelae," *Journal of Nervous and Mental Disease* 158 (1974): 157; L. Melamed, "Therapeutic Abortion in Midwestern City," *Psychological Reports* 37 (1975): 1144.

    Dr. Roger Rochat, director of the Centers for Disease Control (Atlanta) indicated in October 1983 that final figures for 1981 and 1982 had not yet been tabulated. After noting that not all abortions are reported to health authorities, he suggested that a final figure for any year would probably be 20% higher than any number listed (1980 = 1,3000,000). UPI, "Abortions Set Records, But Rate of Rise Slows." *The Patriot* (Harrisburg, Pennsylvania), October 10, 1983, p. A-2.

    Our 30 clinics also reported only 50% of their patients were accompanied by males, for a tally of over 600,000 waiting room men. The 85% and 50% figures are "guesstimates" from 30 clinics that may or may not be representative of the nation's 520 such institutions: Unfortunately, no national data could be found with which to compare our estimates. For conventional statistics on the clinics, see Stanley K. Henshaw, "Freestanding Abortion Clinics: Services, Structure, Fees," *Family Planning Perspectives* 14 (September/October 1982): 248–256. When we phoned the Alan Guttmacher Institute on July 13, 1983, and asked if the nation's leading source of abortion data had statistics on males, a very cooperative Communications Associate, Barbara Parks, indicated no such data existed (except with reference to family planning matters). When we phoned the National Abortion Federation with the same question, they sent a xerox copy of a 1981 *New York Times* feature column that focused on Art's research (Dova Sobel, "Man's Role in Abortion Decision," *New York Times*, November 9, 1982; p. B–12). While the Guttmacher Institute does have its own directory of clinics, we were told it will not share this address list for scholarly research.

2. Naturally, we sought a much larger sample of the nation's 520 clinics. We mailed a request for research cooperation to every clinic listed in the 1980–81 and 1982–83 *Directory* of the National Abortion Federation, a total of 243 clinics. Unfortunately, 199 never replied, 16 were not at the address given, and only 25 elected to cooperate with our research. It would appear that no source in the country at this time has a complete and publicly available directory of the nation's abortion providers, and *all* abortion statistics, therefore, remain estimates subject to unknown error.

3. In 1980, the last year for which national data are available, 79% of all abortion patients were unmarried (as were 82% of our respondents), 67% had no previous abortion (75% of our men), 70% were white (87% of our men), 34% have attended or graduated from college (45% of our men), and 30% were under 20 (35% of our men). While the matchup is generally close, it would seem that we oversample white males or that proportionately fewer black males accompany patients to the clinics: only future research will clear this up. For data on abortion patients, see Stanley K. Henshaw and Kevin O'Reilly, "Characteristics of Abortion Patients in the United States, 1979 and 1980," *Family Planning Perspectives* 15 (January/February 1983): 5–16. See also Howard Ory, *Making Choices* (New York: The Alan Guttmacher Institute, 1983).

4. We searched Social Science Citation Index and Sociological Abstracts on April 1, 1984. We found 239 citations on "women and abortion" and 40 on "men and abortion" for the years 1963–1984 in *Soc Abstracts*, and 271 and 29 in *SSCI*, with complete overlap.

5. Mark Randall Smith. "How Men Who Accompany Women to an Abortion Service Perceive the Impact of Abortion Upon their Relationship and Themselves." Iowa City, Iowa: The University of Iowa, 1979, p. 13.

6. In addition to the Smith Ph.D. thesis cited above, we used research by Arden Arbel Rothstein (1974), Robert Barry Lees (1975), Michael Finley (1978), Kristine Larae Rotter (1980), Karen Deborah Brosseau (1980), William Marsiglio (1983), and June Hill-Falkenthal (1983). See references in footnote #1 for Chapter 2 for the complete citation; space restrictions precluded having a Bibliography.

7. Linda Bird Francke. "Men and Abortion." *Esquire* (January 1981): 60. As recently as 1966 a reform activist characterized the entire subject as "...the dark secret of society. It has been relegated for so long to the darkest corners of fear and mythology that an unwritten compact virtually requires that it remain untouched and undiscussed."

Lawrence Lader. *Abortion*. Indianapolis: Bobbs-Merrill, 1966, p. 1.

8. The contributors are Roger Wade and Peter Zelles; the third author is Ann Baker. See elsewhere among the footnotes for the complete citations.

9. A wide variety of efforts were made to secure respondents; e.g., Art and Gary made radio talk show appearances in the phone-question format, and several more listeners later requested and completed questionnaires (WKVI, Seattle, WA; WXPN, Philadelphia, PA; etc.). An article by journalist Tim Harper in a Madison, Wisconsin, community newspaper (*Isthmus*) produced ten requests in February, 1983, for our questionnaire, and a note about the project that Art had inserted in a national men's movement newsletter (*Transitions*) attracted two questionnaire requests. Similarly, another such note inserted in the newsletter of the Pittsburgh men's collective secured cooperative requests from two readers.

10. Two clinics declined to attempt such guesstimates; a third withdrew its cooperation after providing a small number of completed waiting room surveys; and a fourth ignored repeated requests for completion of the survey form.

11. We drew here on the pioneering research of sociologist William Marsiglio of Ohio State University and remain very much in his debt. Only the second bloc of 500 men were asked to designate their choice of six possible clinic reforms, as this question came to our attention *after* we had gathered our initial 500 surveys.

12. Invaluable in this connection is a methodological critique prepared at our request by Dr. Joan Spade, which is offered in the book's appendix.

13. Reproductive Health and Counseling Clinic of the Crozer-Chester Medical Center, led at the time by Artis Ryder, gave the kind of sustained, sensitive, and unstinting support without which this research would not have been possible.

14. In an effort to reach clinics outside of the *NAF Directory* a search was made of abortion clinic ads in the telephone yellow pages of several cities (Atlanta, GA; Baltimore, MD; Los Angeles, CA; and others). Thirteen requests for research cooperation were mailed on February 24; 18 more on March 4, and six more on March 7. Unfortunately, nine of the clinics were no longer in operation (to judge from "order expired" stamps on the return mail), and 23 chose not to respond at all. We did, however, earn the cooperation of five clinics in this way.

Our 30 cooperating clinics contributed as few as two and as many as 101 surveys each, with only seven responsible for 5 to 12% of the total. Indeed, only two (Reproductive Health, PA, 12%, and Hillcrest Clinic, MD, 13%) actually made up more than 10% of the 1,000 cases. The spread, in short, was thin across a large number, making it unlikely that the characteristics of any one clinic's clientele biased our data in any particular way.

Part 1

The Abortion Experience

Guided by comparable research on the actual experience of women involved in an abortion, we focus in Chapters 2, 3, 4, and 5 on how men pass through the situation's various phases; that is, how they react to the news of an unexpected pregnancy; how they share in resolving the couple's dilemma; how they feel and behave before and during the actual abortion appointment.

Chapter 2 focuses on the social patterns that characterize the *pre*abortion process: What the men thought and did, with whom they talked, and how other people treated them from when they learned they were expectant fathers through to the day the pregnancy was terminated.

Chapter 3 concentrates on the clinic visit itself, and explores the reasons men have for coming along; their behavior during the three- to four-hour stay; whether they seek out and use professional counseling; and various other behavior patterns and experiences of personal significance.

In Chapter 4 we shift from discussing 1,000 respondents as a single bloc to looking more carefully at two specific types of males within the entire group: Some 20% were especially critical of abortion per se, and 25% were abortion repeaters. We isolate both types of respondents, and compare and contrast their abortion passage (or progression of events) with that of all other waiting room males—to better understand major variations in the abortion experience of American men.

Consistent with this line of subgroup analysis we focus in Chapter 5 on black males, a bloc equal to 10% of our 1,000 waiting room men. Comparing and contrasting their survey feedback with that secured from white males in the same 30 clinics, we explore the similarities and differences here between blacks and whites. As well, we discuss the behavior and attitudes of black males that seem to preoccupy them the most, to judge cautiously from our interviews with a very small number of these men.

Finally, in Chapter 6, we very cautiously venture beyond the crisis to explore its aftermath. What do men think about abortion months or even years later? What have they done to adjust to its impact? How has their relationship fared, and why? How would they do it any differently, should they soon find themselves among the one in four men in the waiting room who have been there before? Above all, how do they feel it has changed them, and how do they assess these changes? Women have a postabortion task of reducing its problematic aspects so they can establish a stable foundation from which to move on. So also do men seek a veiled and strategic adjustment, one for which few feel adequately prepared.

Taken in combination, these five chapters help make the point that the male experience is exceedingly malleable: Not knowing exactly how he is expected to feel or behave, and lacking a customarily rigid and unforgiving male role model, the typical man rushes to placate his partner, repress his emotions, and take his cues from an environment that others structure for him (e.g., the public, with its moral censure of abortion; the clinic staff, with their meager range of services for waiting room males; etc.). This is, at one and the same time, both a source of lingering discontent ("No one knew, or gave a damn about what *I* was going through!") and an aid in sheer personal survival ("I just rushed to do what anyone asked, and got through it all fine that way.").

From beginning to end, as these chapters try to help make clear, males struggle to restore self-confidence in their ability to manage unexpected events. They try to keep a suddenly strained love relationship from ending sooner and with less mutual caring than either partner ever envisioned. And they do what they can to make the best of it all. . . to define the situation in some fashion that promotes healing for *both* partners.

Chapter 2

Before the Abortion

I had to stop and look at my life, my goals. How much I'd like to do. We both decided we want to do a few more things before raising a family. There's certain things you'd like to do before having kids. We just weren't ready for that responsibility.

Single, 22, student

Men hear about abortion. They imagine culprits and callous lovers. No one ever talks about what the decent guys feel. Men remain ignorant, uncertain, and ashamed when they are part of an abortion.

Carole Dornblaser and Uta Landy, *The Abortion Guide*, New York: Playboy Paperbacks, 1982, p. 80.

We set up an appointment to get blood work and urine tests done, and we talked to a counselor about what our options would be if we were pregnant. I use 'we' because everything that happened to her affected me.

Single, 24, student

23

"We are all amateurs at this," a young man sheepishly explained to Gary during a long interview:

> We are picking among options, not all good, because there's nothing you can do to make it better. No way not to cause pain. It's just how much you cause. The whole idea of loving someone and having sex with them is supposed to be a joyful thing. And then, all of a sudden, you've got two people going crazy.

As the interview was ending over an hour later, he added thoughtfully, "I feel almost an obligation to speak to you to try to pay back something. It's such a serious situation, and yet we're all such amateurs at it."

As we listened to scores of such men, and spent hours studying their answers to our questionnaire, it seemed clear most had confronted five particular tasks: They had to satisfactorily explain, at least to themselves, how they had gotten into this predicament; they had to help decide who would share in knowledge of the conception; they had to help determine the fate of this particular pregnancy; they had to help reassure their lovers that an abortion was the "least worst" solution; and each felt he had to hide his own ambivalence or heartache.

The "Why me?" Reaction

On first learning of the pregnancy, many of the men recalled stepping back momentarily from the news and asking in bewilderment, "How is it possible? Where did we mess up? Why is this happening to me?"

While we did not gather statistics on the contraceptive history of our waiting room males, four earlier researchers explored this subject in clinic case studies. When they asked how many males had been part of couples *not* using any form of birth control, the answers were uniformly disheartening: 43% (1983, California); 57% (1980, Colorado); 53% (1979, Iowa); 55% (1978, Massachusetts).[1]

Even among those claiming to have "played it safe," as in the 1983 California sample of 106 waiting room men, none of the couples had relied on the IUD, only one percent on the pill, and 10% had trusted in such unreliable methods as douching or withdrawal. As many as 34% had depended on the rhythm method, while only

20% had employed the much more reliable condom/foam method of birth control[2]—little wonder a researcher in 1976 estimated over 50% of all abortions could be traced to user neglect or the choice of a poor method.[3]

Why is there this record of omission or reliance on high-risk (nonbarrier) contraceptors? For one thing, many men felt *none* of the available tools were especially user friendly. This discouraged them from placing any special reliance on these family planning aids, for example,

> One man felt it was unfair that most methods were for women only, all had undesirable side effects, and the man could not really participate in the decision because our warped social values have given women all the options, with none to the men. If I could take a pill, or have a reverse vasectomy, I would do it tomorrow.'[4]

Other men indicated they had been given misinformation by health professionals. One said, "She had been on the pill one week, and no one told us to use anything else for the first week." Another noted, "They told us to wait for her period before she could get an IUD, and not to worry in the meantime." An even larger number of men spoke about disagreements between them and their sex partners over the choice of the method; for example, the woman opposed the awkard use of condoms; the man raised questions about the safety of the pill. Lastly, a very few even admitted laziness, forgetfulness, or indifference.

Turning for further insight to our 1,000 men, we were certain their explanations would help illuminate the complexities of this social pattern:

> I *knew* there could be consequences when I had sex with this girl. But I felt I had to prove myself as a man with every girl I dated. At a young age, you are *so* horny, but now I look at it realistically, and want everyone to know the risks.

> She was aware she could get pregnant, and I urged her to go to a doctor because she seemed fairly naive. We went out five or six months before she got pregnant. She was paranoid about going to a gynecologist, having never been to one, and had parental pressure against anything related to her having sex...I felt I was playing Russian roulette—I *knew* something would happen.

When I was 17, I had been dating a girl I was totally in love with for almost a year. We were very sexually active and never used any type of birth control. I wasn't ignorant of contraceptive devices, but I hated the unnatural feeling of a rubber, and a diaphragm took away the spontaneity of the experience. We thought about going on the pill, but she was very scared her mother might come upon them. So, instead I used withdrawal as the only means of protection...I had a very strong suspicion she might have been pregnant because one time I didn't withdraw in time, and she was in her fertile time of her menstrual cycle. I remember the day of conception. She knew what I had done also, but as the male, I assured her I had total body control, and that I loved her too much to ever get her pregnant.

We both came from a wild life. She was layin' everybody and I was layin' everybody. It took us only two weeks to get pregnant. We went out to porno movies at the drive-in, and then to a hotel. She was on the pill, but she was also workin', and in school, and pretty run down...A lot of tears. I felt bad 'cause it happened. We both beat on ourselves for lettin' it happen.

Regrets were legion, with many men adding handwritten notes to our questionnaires that read, "To have prevented it would have been so much better"; "If we had only been more careful with birth control"; "Makes me see more in birth control"; and "Will be more careful about having sex." Not surprisingly, 91% of these men wanted adolescents to get information about birth control in school. And 93% said they now would be more careful about contraception.

Keeping the Secret

On learning of the ill-timed, unplanned, and unwanted pregnancy, many males in our study also learned they were expected to keep the news absolutely secret. Accordingly, when we asked 1,000 waiting room men whom they had turned to for help before the abortion decision had been reached, three out of four indicated their partner had been their *only* confidant.[5]

A small bloc (17%) had broken with the majority and reached out to close friends:

I talked it over with my married friend. She was expecting and I talked with her, and she told us to consider everything that's going on and to do what we needed to do.

That $165 was a considerable amount of money for a 17-year-old to raise on short notice...Luckily, I told a waiter at work who was like an older brother my problem, and that night he went to his bank machine and took out $190 for me. He gave me an extra $35 because he thought I might need it for related expenses. He told me not to worry about the money, and I could pay him $3 a week if that's all I could afford. I had the money in the bank, but my uncanny mother would have thought it was for either an abortion or something illegal if she saw a large withdrawal from my account, so I couldn't touch it.

While friends would do what they could, it was sometimes not enough:

I had discussed this with a close male friend at work, and guys there helped cover for me, because I was running around a lot trying to help her. I got support from them, but none raised the morality question, none raised what was really bothering me. Instead, they focused purely on the mechanics of it...not on feelings at all.

This 24-year-old store manager later added that he had thought about speaking with a priest, "but the church was not a comfortable place for me to be, and I didn't feel like being chastised."

Consistent with the difficult communications that characterize some parent-son relationships, only 8% confided in their mother, father, or both. Many of these very few men later regarded their trust well-placed and rewarded:

I discussed it with my mom. We never talked until I was 15, but once we started we could really break things open. You know moms, they can just make you feel better.... We both had to work it out between us, but we had one [friend]—my mother. She's a super-mom type, very understanding. She didn't push us either way; the decision was ours. If we'd kept the baby, she'd been behind us 100%. We made the problem and we're old enough to take care of the problem.

Other men took their brothers or sisters into their confidence, and some even spoke with other relatives, especially those known and valued as nonjudgmental and empathetic friends.

Overall, this sort of outreach to people other than one's partner was observed only in one in four men. The majority offered isolating sentiments such as, "It was a moral issue I had to resolve myself...involving my Catholic upbringing"; "Something you have to do for yourself"; "Not much to say about it"; "Trust in God, in your inner self"; and, "I would have liked to go to a counseling center/clinic, but I did not know of any that existed."

Intrigued by the decision of the majority to tell no one what they were going through, we pressed the matter in personal interviews. Some of our men, especially the younger ones, were still living at home. They feared their parents might somehow discover the secret if they told anyone else. Another individual, however, spoke for several when he explained, "My folks would have been supportive, but my girlfriend wanted no one but her girlfriends to know."

Others explained that no one seemed appropriate for this unique sort of intimate conversation. Some said simply that there was no one there:

> I really needed somebody to talk to at the time, but there wasn't anybody and I was so tired of dealing with the issue. I went to my father's empty house and sat there for two days and tried not to feel.

This remarkable absence of at least one very close friend, of a male with whom they could share secrets, is traced by counselor Roger Wade (in Chapter 8) to a fear of being betrayed, a fear some have that a trusted friend may turn against them and use confidences as verbal weapons.[6]

Beyond this, many of the men felt the subject so stigma-inducing and personal they barely knew how to begin. And, once begun, how they could profit from such a discussion. One man explained:

> It's not your garden-variety conversation—'Oh, let's talk about our abortion experiences....' It's not like you talk about your car, or

you talk about what the Giants are doing this year. It's not on any level, and I don't have a whole lot of intimate male friends. And, I would not talk about it with my female friends. . .it's not one of those things that's conducive to small talk.

Some of these men felt ashamed because they were in this predicament: They were reluctant to surrender their self-image as too worldly or careful to be "caught" in an unwanted pregnancy. Others felt guilty over the need to destroy the fetus, and wanted no one to know of their complicity in such an act.

Finally, as counselor Peter Zelles notes later in Chapter 8, many of the men who wait thought it was especially *her* secret. And, out of deep-reaching concern for their partners, they declined to discuss the pregnancy with anyone. Drawing a cloak of silence about the subject, they reduced any risk to the woman's reputation and, not coincidentally, honored a pledge of complete secrecy often urged on them by their anxious and insistent sex partners (see Table 2-1).

Table 2-1. Comparison of Clinic Male Confinement of Abortion Discussion to Sex Partner

	Percent Who Spoke Only to Female Sex Partner
Shostak and McLouth (1983)	75%
Zelles (1983)	63%
Rotter (1980)	65%
Smith (1979)	53%
Finley (1978)	83%

Sources: Zelles, Peter, "Feedback from 521 Waiting Room Males," this study (see Appendix); Rotter, Kristine Larae, "Men and the Abortion Experience: An Exploratory Study of Their Self-Reported Educational Interests" (Ph.D. dissertation, Southern Illinois University at Carbondale, 1980); Smith, Mark Randall, "How Men Who Accompany Women to an Abortion Service Perceive the Impact of Abortion upon Their Relationship and Themselves" (Ph.D. dissertation, University of Iowa, 1979); Finley, Michael C., "A Male Counseling Component for Aborting Fathers at Preterm" (Unpublished report, Preterm Clinic, Brookline, MA, 1978).

Resolving the Matter

In keeping with this sense of the pregnancy being especially difficult for their partners, many of the men relegated the decision—one of the most important they had known thus far in their lives—largely to their partners.

When they first learned of the pregnancy, many asked their partners what *they* felt must be done:

> It was basically her decision. I'm working and making enough to support a small family. It wasn't anything I couldn't deal with. But she was kinda young. She was happy she was pregnant, but sad that she didn't want to be. We looked at our situation, and decided it was too much of a burden at this time. . . . We waited a few weeks to see if our feelings would change. I worried about her health. I wanted her to be able to rear children when she wants to in the future. I was concerned about her future.

Other men echoed these sentiments. They recalled, often in vivid detail, the particular conversation they had in which their lovers essentially resolved the matter, emphatically, on behalf of terminating the pregnancy.

This is *not* to say the men were without *private* reactions of their own, although they were ones they keep guardedly to themselves. A researcher in 1979, for example, asked 91 males in an Iowa clinic waiting room how they recalled feeling about the pregnancy and the need to decide what to do about it:

- Some 45% had a *negative reaction,* and felt the pregnancy was coming at the wrong time in their lives or upset their family size and childspacing plans. A few felt trapped by the failure of their partner to tell them about changes she had made in her birth control techniques.

- The 44% who had had a *neutral reaction* dwelt on the fact that they had known the risks, and yet had taken no precautions ("Must pay the dues"; "Took our chances, must pay the piper.")

- The 10% who had a *positive reaction* reported the pregnancy brought them much unexpected "happiness" (75%) or pleasure in having their fertility established (25%).

While the reactions in the Iowa study varied widely, the researcher noted an "overall negative quality." He reported "...many interviewees expressed strong disappointment upon learning of the pregnancy, and adamantly spoke of the problems a child would bring to the relationship."[7]

When those opposed to abortion were pressed to be more explicit, eight responses were identified:

74%—mixed feelings about abortion and the fetus

55%—fear of medical complications for the woman

53%—fear of pain for the woman

26%—hard to get money

18%—other: morality of abortion; conflicting desires for a
　　　　child

10%—hard to find abortion clinic

10%—disagreed with partner

 8%—fear of doctors

Contrariwise, when those who favored abortion were asked their reasons, 11 different arguments were advanced:

45%—they could not afford to rear a child

39%—the female was not ready for parenthood

35%—the male was not ready for parenthood

33%—current relationship is not a good one

24%—current living conditions do not welcome a baby

19%—career goals (completing college)

17%—health of the mother

13%—too many children already

13%—did not want to give up child for adoption

12%—her parents did not want her to have child

11%—children too close together

8%—my parents did not want her to have a child

6%—feared fetus abnormality

Similar lists were obtained in both a 1978 sample of 192 Massachusetts men (where "interracial union" and "extramarital union" were also on the list) and a 1980 sample of 126 Midwestern men.[8]

Overall, all such lists, whether of reasons to oppose or support the abortion option, attest to the remarkable demands the situation makes on males. For example, 70% of the Iowa group judged it a "very" or "fairly" important event in their lives, while only 8% considered it an insignificant matter.[9]

Casting the Decisive Vote

While men have a variety of reasons to oppose or support the termination of a pregnancy, it is important to understand that the female typically makes the final decision.

Among the Iowa sample, for example, the idea of abortion was first raised by an outsider (doctor, counselor, relative) in only 12% of the cases, and by the male in another 20%. In over half of the couples, the female both initiated and strongly endorsed the idea of an abortion. In none of the 91 cases did any of the men feel they had ultimately made the decision...a finding that led the Iowa researcher to dismiss as "very questionable" the notion that many or most women are forced by their male partners to undergo abortions.[10]

Returning to our sample of 1,000 men at 30 clinics, it is interesting that 44% of our single men (and 44% of the divorced males, along with 58% of the "living together" types) indicated they had offered to marry their pregnant sex partners. And 28% of the unwed men (and 30% of the "living together" males) said they had considered the option of providing financial childrearing support if their partners chose to have the babies and rear them as single mothers. A total of 18% of these couples (21% of the unwed, versus 11% of the married couples) considered the adoption route, hardly evidence of male indifference to the fate of the fetus. This is especially interesting as many of the men told us of their strong private opposition to having someone else rear their children (see Table 2-2).

Some men, however, shared in the decision to abort the pregnancy by offering to alter the relationship to the female's desire, e.g., as an alternative to the abortion, 26% of the married men offered to marry their sex partner, a woman who may have been their fiancée or adulterous lover at that time. Others made their opinions known by dropping pro-abortion hints about their own priorities:

You know, I didn't like it really, but I couldn't deal with the kid right now, anyway. I gotta car that I can't even get out of the driveway because I ain't got no money for insurance. I couldn't deal with the kid right now. . . .

Table 2-2. Clinic Male Reactions to the Pregnancy

"When your female sex partner told you that she was pregnant, what was your reaction?"

1. Discuss it together until an agreement is reached	94%
2. Ask her what she wants to do about it	86
3. Go along with whatever she wants	66
4. Recommend she have an abortion	51
5. Offer to marry her and have the child [82% were single]	35
6. Offer to pay for the abortion, but no more than that	16
7. Urge her to have and keep the baby	11
8. Urge childbirth followed by adoption	9
9. Deny paternity	5
10. End the relationship	2

Note: This question was asked of only 505 of our 1,000 respondents. A comparison of this bloc with the remaining 495 suggests that an 8% greater representation of unwed males in the group that was not asked this question is the only significant difference.

Our minister, he told us she wouldn't want to walk up the aisle with her belly hanging out. We wanted a big wedding. When we talked about the wedding, he asked if she was pregnant, and she said, 'No.' After that night, we started talking about the abortion. I made the first move by calling a help line. . . . Both of our dads were having a lot of trouble. One was really depressed at the time, the other was having marital stress. So, we did it for them.

The decision to abort, while not totally explicit, did appear to be a joint decision. Only 4% of the 1,000 men felt they alone had favored the abortion. And only 5% characterized the decision as one forced on them by the female.[11] While 6% felt the abortion choice had neither partner's real support, an overwhelming 84% were convinced both parties had achieved a *joint* resolution of the matter.

An important corollary is the response of 58% that an unmarried man should have as much say in the abortion decision as his lover. Similarly, four out of five men felt a husband should have as much input as the wife. At the same time, however, 59% also felt a wife should go ahead and have an abortion even if her husband is against it. And, while 62% felt a female should be able to obtain a legal abortion for any reason of her own, only 18% endorsed the same idea where the reason was initiated or proposed by a male.[12]

Contrary to the suspicion of many arch feminists, the men asserted only an understandable desire to *share* in the decision making. They did *not* express a desire to control the decision, a demand for 51% of the "vote" or, in any other way, appear anxious to dictate terms to their lover.[13] Almost all seemed to endorse the notion that the female "owns" her body, and must have authority over its employ. In fact, a researcher who explored the matter with 192 clinic men in 1978 "expected that some men might have strong feelings about their political rights, as such, but only one expressed angry feelings. . . ."[14]

While women's power is diluted somewhat by the wish of the men to participate in the pregnancy's resolution, none of the men we interviewed seemed interested in a fight for power. Even when we pursued the matter in personal inerviews, they scoffed at such an idea and instead endorsed their own version of the female having the final say.[15]

Providing Reassurance

Once the couple had drawn their secrecy boundaries and had reached their decision, the males assumed a decidedly secondary and essentially supportive role. Their main function was to reassure their partners that it would all work out, it would all be okay in the end, they would see it through together. Some men even suggested they might come out stronger for this trial:

> I sort of felt a little in over my head from the start, although I immediately offered to spend as much time with her, to do this with her, to pay for it, since I was working and no one else was, and to keep our parents out of it. (*26-year-old white-collar worker*)

> Mentally, it definitely drained us. We were worried about something going wrong. She was scared, so was I, but I tried not to show it, so I could make it easier for her. (*24-year-old salesman*)

> I had tried to get her to talk about the options, and her feelings, including her strong anti-abortion feelings. But she was testing me about *my* feelings toward *her*, and, toward abortion. . .I felt I always had to play a supportive role, though I never got support back, and it turned into a conflict. I would go over to talk and walk, but it was *extremely* sensitive, and one of us would bolt away from each other, or cry a lot with each other. (*24-year-old store manager*)

Young men, especially those involved with high-school girls, had a special reassurance role. As one later explained, "I think a lot of girls in high school fear their lovers might bail out because they can't handle the pressure."

Anxious to demonstrate with acts as well as words their support for their lovers, 40% of the men accompanied their partners to any counseling sessions she attended prior to the actual abortion, often with unexpected gains for all:

> The middle-aged, female counselor asked me if I was the boyfriend. At that moment, I thought she was going to slap my hand or tell me how irresponsible I was for not using any birth control. I remember getting flushed; someone was going to directly hold me accountable for my stupidity. As bold as I am, I had trouble facing up to something I had done. It wasn't, 'Sorry mom, I left the milk out.' It was 'Yes, I'm the young man that got her pregnant.' Instead of being scolded, she gave me credit for being here with her.

> She told us that eight out of ten girls go the course alone or take a girlfriend, instead of the 'culprit.'

Other men recalled with appreciation a counselor reviewing the full range of options with the couple. However, the degrees of freedom were very few:

> He was trying to give us both support, and pretty much kept morality out of it. He asked us to call back with our decision, and reviewed places where we could either have the baby or get an abortion. She did not want the folks to know, so it was pretty clear-cut.

Overall, as counselor Andre Watson notes in Chapter 8, this sort of counseling served useful purposes. It helped provide guidelines for males new to this predicament (as were 75% of our men). Much like lighting a darkened room, preabortion counseling, in Watson's estimate, enabled certain men to prepare for the actual abortion appointment, as well as increase their ability to help their lovers through that very trying day.

In keeping with traditional notions of the male as the prime breadwinner, nearly three in four offered to pay all the costs entailed (between $175 and $200).[16] However, due to health plan coverage or to the earning power of employed females, only 57% actually paid the entire bill; 29% paid half. A total of 6% paid some of it, and 8% paid nothing toward the bill. For a few couples, financial aid was the last form of support left:

> It's such a serious, emotional situation that a minor change in emotion or atmosphere can precipitate a break by one or the other person. She said, 'Just give me the money!,' and I said 'Fine!'...I could afford to eliminate the evidence of my mistake. Other people can't.

For the largest number of men we interviewed, however, meeting the cost was a relatively minor concern. Paying for the abortion was another opportunity for them to say, "I'm here. I'm 100% behind this! I care!"

Why this intensified need to demonstrate support? Part of the explanation focuses on the fact that these were ongoing, steady love relationships of some length and emotional depth. A second factor involves the willful isolation of the couple from everyone except one another. This interdependency, a byproduct of their desire for secrecy, provided additional insight into the fact that only 3% of our men believed females involved in an abortion generally have an easy time of it.

Above all, however, the male role of unwavering support appears responsive to their notion of the (nonexistent) rules. The men seem to feel there is a prescription that defines the right thing to do, the manly way to respond:

> She did not have the money to deal with it, but that was secondary to the fact that I was involved, and she expected me to involve myself in this part of it now. That sat pretty properly with me. I felt the 'call to duty,' as it were.

Counselor Roger Wade links this search for rules to widespread confusion about how a man *should* act in this predicament, combined with a desire men have to succeed in all things. Intent on offering their partners as much help as possible (even though they often did not know how), the 1,000 men acted in terms of what they saw as their duty, as the only proper course open to men who care.

Hiding Stress

Beyond being responsible for keeping an extraordinary confidence, endorsing their lover's resolution, and bolstering her confidence in that choice, the men felt obliged to pretend they were someone else. That is, many men took full responsibility for their own doubts, hesitations, uncertainties, and even painful, opposing thoughts. They hid all of this from friends, coworkers, and especially from their partners. (Typical is a 1979 survey at a District of Columbia clinic that found 77% of the men convinced the best way they had to help their partners was by "controlling" their own feelings).[17]

In our interviews, many men recalled denying how they really felt, and putting on an act to keep up morale:

> I suppose I repressed a lot of feelings during the ten days between learning of the pregnancy and the abortion; I honestly don't know. All I remember is being scared...really scared.

Still other males added plaintive notes to our questionnaire that expressed their hesitation; for example, "I want the child, but she is too young to get married"; "It hurts more than I could ever write on paper"; and, "If I were to think about it a lot, it would cause much mental anguish." Little wonder that a concerned feminist journalist recently suggested such repression of emotions "must be dangerous both to their mental health and to the always precarious truce between the sexes."[18]

Some of the men who wait, of course, sense the toll exacted by their restricted communications and emotional disguise ("I only let on what I felt she could handle; I never let her know what I was really feeling."). A majority of the 91-man Iowa sample, for example, felt themselves poorly understood by their partner:

	Degree Man Understands Partner's Feelings	Degree Woman Understands Male's Feelings
Very well	51%	36%
Fairly well	35	51
Somewhat	7	6
Fairly little	3	6
Not at all	3	2
Missing	1	0

These were couples who claimed to have completely (56%) or almost completely (20%) shared their feelings about abortion (only 9% had avoided such an exchange). The men *still* felt less well-understood by their partners than they would have preferred, a likely source of discontent in the postabortion phase.[19]

Another major stressor, and possibly the single most costly one of all, was that many men discovered they somehow agreed with two *opposing* positions. While 39% believed the fetus was a human life, and 26% felt abortion was the killing of a child, 83% did *not* want abortion outlawed (see Table 2-3). Additionally, 75% did not expect lawmakers to make abortions illegal in the next five years.

Table 2-3. Clinic Male Views of Abortion, Based upon the Circumstances of the Abortion

"Under what circumstance, if any, do you feel that a woman should be able to obtain a legal abortion?"

91%	If the female's health is put at risk
82%	If the couple cannot support a child
81%	If the fetus has serious genetic defects
79%	If the pregnancy is the result of incest
79%	If the pregnancy may cause the female mental harm
69%	If the pregnancy is the result of a one-night stand
65%	If, for any reason, the couple wants the abortion
64%	If the female is physically handicapped
63%	If the female is a pregnant unmarried teenager
62%	If the female wants the abortion, for whatever reason
60%	If the couple already has as many children as they want
56%	If this pregnancy may cause a marital breakdown
48%	If the couple has just ended their relationship
37%	If the couple is on the verge of breaking up
31%	If the parents of this pregnant minor female want the abortion
18%	If, for any reason, the male wants this pregnancy terminated
13%	If tests reveal that the sex of the fetus is not what the prospective parents want at this time.

Thoughts about the child that would not be born occupied the minds of 52% of the men "occasionally," and "frequently" for another 29%. Only 20% claimed never to think about the fetus. Typical comments were:

How big is it? Or is it a baby? It has only been three and a half weeks.

I figure it's not a person yet, so it won't matter.

During an abortion, you're killing a fetus. If you have a child and can't bring it up well, you're killing the child indirectly. A lot of kids can't get out of their backgrounds.

He or she would not have everything a child should have.

I do not believe in fetus supremacy.

What set of circumstances have to exist to force one to commit murder?

We really want to have kids, *later*...the 'fetus' is a symbol of future possibilities.

Not surprisingly, of the 81% who admitted to thinking about the fetus, 35% characterized their thoughts as "curious," 25% as "troublesome," 21% as "sad," and 15% percent as "sad" and either "curious or troublesome." In interviews with Gary, many echoed the thoughts of a man who insisted—more to himself than to the interviewer—that "at this point in our relationship, this seems the right decision, and this outweighs whatever moral guilt I may feel."

A related major stressor involves the emotional demands the man felt incessantly from his partner, another anxious and needy human being. Counselor Stephen McCallister reminds us that men are not especially comfortable with their emotions. Shocked when an unexpected pregnancy occurs, they may suddenly confront, recoil from, and repress deep and unexpected feelings; for example,

> I realized it was partly my responsibility, and to that degree I wanted to be responsible about it. But what I also saw from the start was that she was not prepared to handle this even more than anyone else. That enabled me to put my own feelings aside. I did not afford myself the luxury of sitting around and determining how *I* felt about the abortion. The thing was to keep her alive and going through all of this.

Ironically, the silence of some such men can be misinterpreted by certain women as indicating the male has no feelings. Such suspicions are likely to estrange the sex partners in hard-to-heal ways. Counselor Susan Weinstein regards such silence as the most common response of couples, one that explains corrosive preabortion weeks of unsaid anger, guilt, and fear.

Underlying this emotional turmoil is a melange of feelings that include:

- *fear* of the health hazards his lover confronts;

- *guilt* over not having attended more carefully to their contraception responsibilities;

- *anxiety* over the possibility his lover may blame him inordinately for the mess they have gotten into;

- *self-doubt*, as in questioning his worth and ability to handle really tough situations;

- *self-pity*, as in a nagging uncertainty about whether he is victimizer, victim, or both at the same time;

- *sadness* over the loss of a potential child, over changes occurring in this love relationship, and over this unwelcomed event in its painful entirety.[20]

Counselor Roger Wade traces an inordinate amount of the problem to the exaggerated macho expectations males place on themselves:

> ...the man who believes that he should protect his partner from all harm may feel like a total failure because 'his woman' is pregnant and will have to run the risks of abortion. He may take all the blame for not using any birth control, or for having sex in the first place. He may think of himself as an ogre who manipulated this woman into bed.[21]

Later, in the same 1980 *Glamour* article, Wade advises the magazine's female readership that ''for most men, abortion is a very emotional issue; men have feelings people don't expect.''[22]

After considering the various items touched on above, two abortion counselors, Carole Dornblaser and Uta Landy, urge special attention to free-floating *anger*:

> Men are angry at themselves for not (somehow) having done more to prevent a pregnancy. They are angry at their partners who, upon learning of the pregnancy, may become withdrawn, irritable, or seem to shut them out. They are angry at their own helplessness and inability to fully share the burden of unwanted pregnancy. They are angry at the professionals who don't seem to recognize the degree of their own involvement and pain.[23]

It was not surprising, therefore, that 68% of the 1,000 men sampled disagreed with the statement that males involved in an abortion generally have an easy time of it. Another 11% were undecided—though often apprehensive, to judge from our interviews (see Table 2-4).

Keeping all this hidden from view, especially from one's own sex partner, proved a trying task for many of the men. These men tried to wear a reassuring mask and display an upbeat manner. Some men actually compounded their problems by overdoing attempts at humor, diversion, and other deliberately distracting gimmicks. Counselor Roger Wade observes that few stepped back far enough from their own self-deception to realize certain lovers privately shared their ambivalence and apprehension. Instead of daring to ventilate these feelings, the majority of men Wade counseled shied away from the opportunity. Possibly they had never learned how to make the most of an emotionally demanding exchange. Skillful at pretending one thing while feeling another, the men Wade knew avoided tough talks in hopes tougher feelings would go away.

Table 2-4. Clinic Male Views of Abortion as a Source of Stress

"How do you feel about these matters?"

	Strongly Agree	Agree	Neutral	Disagree	Strongly Disagree
1. Males involved in an abortion generally have an easy time of it.	5%	16%	11%	44%	24%
2. Females involved in an abortion generally have an easy time of it.	1	2	6	34	58
3. Males involved in an abortion have disturbing thoughts about it afterwards.	9	38	39	12	3

Summary

From the time an unwanted pregnancy is confirmed until it is surgically terminated, a male confronts several difficult role tasks. First, he must assume his share of the responsibility for the unwanted conception. Second, he must keep the couple's secret, while sharing in the decision making. Third, he must help keep up morale, and reassure his partner and himself of their commitment to one another. And finally, he must project confidence and conviction, even though he may privately harbor anxiety and doubt.

With all of this, men *can* emerge from the experience with a stronger sense of self, with finer insights into life and love. They can gain assurance that they have dealt with perhaps one of the most demanding challenges of their lives, a matter that "touches all of us at the level of our deepest concerns."[24]

Profile

Many of our men found the abortion experience happening at already distressing and chaotic periods in their lives. Herb, nearing forty, weathering a marital separation, and attempting to change his basic self-image, had a lot to say about how the abortion influenced his thinking.

His sense of isolation was palpable, yet he was neither desperate nor distraught. Herb did, however, want to change into a more sensitive and open person, and the sense of reaching out to do that was something in him that we felt in other men, too.

Whether their talks with us are evidence of their protracted growth or not remains to be established. We interpret Herb's quest as an example of a broadly based, albeit quiet movement among certain American men to work free of their isolation and to move toward each other.

Herb:

It was such a difficult time in my life. I had started therapy. There was so much pain over the divorce. I recall most—it happened three or four months after my marital breakup—I was fearful about being trapped, although I felt morally responsible and I thought if this woman had the child, I would declare paternity and support the child. I have two children; it would have been burdensome. I thought I might have a chance to get my head together, and now I might not be *free*. It was a *real* fear. Then there was a certain amount of anger attached. It was a threat. I wasn't very communicative about the depths of my feelings with the woman.

I only told my sister. She gave me moral support through the separation and abortion. I don't have shame or guilt, but I feel very private about guarding the woman's privacy and our mutual friendship. You have to maintain a certain amount of privacy to keep a deeper relationship.

I've discussed it with my therapist. He doesn't express his emotions or opinions, naturally. His approach is Freudian. I wish he'd give me a hug, but he'd rather I get pissed off—work on my anger—that sort of thing.

I wanted my freedom. I didn't want to be forced into anything. The ball was in her court and I was passive in dealing with it. She said she wanted an abortion and I agreed gladly. Another fact that scared the shit out of me was that she wanted to raise a child—anyone's. She didn't care. She'd had abortions before, but it wasn't the right time for her. I would have felt this sense of responsibility. It would be a pain in the ass. There was enough going on in my life without that!

I was discussing abortion in general with a friend. His attitude was, 'tough shit' for her; he wouldn't care what she did. I had wished I could be like that. I have avoided the topic. I have a sense of anonymity discussing it with you.

Her mother died during that period and she mentioned that the abortion added to the difficulty of the time. It also came up with my kids in front of her—how they would feel if I had other kids. She said later that it had been very painful for her.

I don't think about the fetus, but a fetus is not quite a person, but I don't doubt that life begins at conception, so if you abort the day after, it's the same as aborting months after. But there's no guilt tied up with that. If it were a live human being (out of the womb), it would be different. You have to look at where in the spectrum of life things are.

In the emotional-mental life then, I was so much more confused than I am today. The other issues just steamrolled over this thing. That's the biggest thing, separation, the family breakup and facing in therapy the painful things in the other parts of my life. They were dominant.

Today, I would definitely get in touch more firmly with how I felt about what I wanted out of the relationship. I would be more assertive. I probably would have made the same decision, but I'd assert my feelings, my opinions: 'This is what *I* want!' In my life, I have done what others have wanted me to do and I was very unhappy for a long time.

Advice? Find out what you want to do. Kids are one hell of a lot of work. It's wonderful, but it's a lot of expense. I would recommend that people investigate the realities of child rearing.

I have a feeling that nobody gets pregnant accidentally. On a subconscious level you want to get pregnant. My wife had gotten pregnant on birth control pills. The relationship wasn't so good in the beginning. She may have had a kid to put something in the relationship, or between it. There's enough information for people to avoid pregnancy. Some people desire kids for something to put love into their lives.

Maybe high-school kids ought to be taken to a scared straight type of situation, only involving unwed mothers. There's a lot of fantasy involved, and some hard reality encounter is necessary. Have kids carry an egg around all day as if it were a kid.

I'm sad today. I'm moving. I'm going to be forty in October. I'm finishing therapy. There's a lot of sadness as I look back and I have a sense of sadness about this abortion. I'm looking for happiness in my life and this *not* a happy thing. I don't regret I went through it, just sad. . . . There's also a sense of relief. The kid would be a year-and-a-half old and I don't know where I'd be now.

I have colluded in my relationships. My present gal isn't giving me what I want. It's the first time in my life I'm saying, "FUCK, I want what I want." And, if she's not going to give it to me, and she can't, I'm going to find someone who will. So, if I'd had that aborted kid, I might very well hate it in some way and that's not good.

My marriage was a neurotic hope that maybe tomorrow, when she finishes her Ph.D., things will get back to normal. She's writing a book now and it would have been the same thing.

I used to let women have their way. My whole family was like that. So, I colluded in this a lot. And that was because of a fear of her anger and hope for her affection. I could have wound up with what I didn't want. I was just lucky she didn't want the child at the time. I didn't have the ability at the time to get in touch with what I wanted. It was clouded by fears of rejection. Psychically, I was still a child dealing with this relationship with this woman. There was part of me still looking for Mom's love. I'm letting go of that need now.

I avoided talking about birth control because I was having trouble with impotence at the time. So I was worried about getting it up. There was so much anxiety connected with not feeling good about myself. . . today, I'm much more comfortable and I would ask. I would tell the woman, "You take care of it."

How do we learn to love, to communicate? That's what it comes down to. Most people learn from their families, and a lot of them are fucked up.

Men have to get in touch with each other. They're afraid of each other, have no frame of reference. They should get together; they have to get together and talk.

Notes

1. June Hill-Falkenthal. "Counseling Needs of Men About Abortion." Sacramento, Calif.: California State University, 1983, p. 23. Unpublished paper. Karen Deborah Brosseau. "Utilizing Male Partners of

Adolescent Abortion Patients as Change Agents." Boulder, Colo.: University of Colorado at Boulder, 1980; p. 51. Unpublished doctoral dissertation. Mark Randall Smith. "How Men Who Accompany Women to an Abortion Service Perceive the Impact of Abortion Upon Their Relationship and Themselves." Iowa City: The University of Iowa, 1979; p. 90. Unpublished doctoral dissertation. Michael C. Finley. "A Male Counseling Component for Aborting Fathers at Preterm." Brookline, Mass.: Preterm Clinic, 1978; p. 3. Unpublished paper. Finley adds that "among the 55% who were using no method, it is difficult to generalize about attitudes toward birth control with one exception: the men were not indifferent about birth control...there was strong indication that the issue had been seriously discussed between the partners...One recurring theme was a serious dislike of all birth control methods." (pp. 3–4).

2. Hill-Falkenthal, op. cit., p. 23. Kristine Laral Rotter. "Men and the Abortion Experience." Carbondale, Ill.: Southern Illinois University at Carbondale, 1980; p. 122. Unpublished doctoral dissertation. Rotter's study of 126 midwest males in 1980 found 26% had relied on the pill; 22% on condoms; 16% on withdrawal; 14% on rhythm; 14% on foam; 8% on diaphragms; and 2% on the IUD.

3. Lisa R. Shusterman. "The Psycho-Social Factors of the Abortion Experience: A Critical Review." *Psychology of Women Quarterly* 1 (1976): 106. A 1983 report indicates that a woman using no method of contraception from age 17–44 could theoretically expect to have 14.3 births or 31.2 abortions (rhythm, 2.5 or 2.9; diaphragm, 1.9 or 2.2; the Pill, 0.2 or 0.3). Howard W. Ory. *Making Choices*, p. 37. New York: The Alan Guttmacher Institute, 1983.

4. Finley, op.cit., p. 4. See in this connection, Carol Atwater. "New Ways to Block Pregnancy." *USA Today*, October 7, 1983, p. 6–D. On the strategic importance of the male partner, see Zimmerman, Mary K., "It Takes Two: An Examination of Contraceptive Risk-Taking and the Role of the Male Partner" (Unpublished paper read at the 1984 meeting of the Midwest Sociological Society.)

5. 65% of Rotter's 82 men discussed the decision with no one other than their partner; 13%, with his mother; 8%, with his father; 24% with a male friend(s); 10% with a female friend(s). A much larger bloc, or 83% of Finley's 193 men, had been in relationships where the couple made the decision alone. Contrariwise, only 53% of Smith's 91 men had consulted with no one other than the female: 74% of those who reached outside contacted friends; 23%, doctors; 21%, parents; 19%, other relatives; 7%, "others" (counselor, teacher,

foreman, etc.); 1%, clergy. See in this connection, Rotter, op. cit.; Finley, op.cit.; Smith, op. cit.

6. See the Wade essay in Chapter 8 of this book and also Burt Avedon, *Ah, Men.* (New York: A&W Publishers, 1980); Eric Skjei and Richard Rabkin, *The Male Ordeal: Role Crisis in a Changing World* (New York: G.P. Putnam's Sons, 1981).

7. Smith, op. cit., p. 102.

8. Finley, op. cit.; Rotter, op. cit., p. 119. Some 42% of Rotter's 126 males cited not ready to become a parent; 37%, interfere with career/school; 36%, unable to support a child; 34%, unmarried; 14%, parental disapproval. No other reason earned as much as 10% citation.

9. Smith, op. cit., p. 167.

10. Ibid., p. 104. Only 4% of our 1,000 respondents felt they alone had favored the abortion decision.

11. Hill-Falkenthal asked 106 men at two California clinics in 1983 who should have the final say in the abortion decision if there is a conflict of interest between both partners. Contrary to the pro-female answer we secured from 1,000 men in several states, her West Coast sample preferred a shared decision (64%) to the woman alone (35%) and the man alone (-1%). Had the respondents been forced to choose an answer other than both man and woman together, however, the results might have shown still more pro-female sentiment. Finley's 1978 study of 192 clinic males found 63% who felt a woman should make the final decision if there were any disagreement between a couple. While 32% were unsure or cited someone outside the relationship (parents, mediator, arbitrator), only 5% felt the man should make the final decision. See, in this connection, Hill-Falkenthal, op. cit., pp. 26–27; Finley, op. cit., p. 2.

12. Some 85% of the men told of the pregnancy by Melamed's 1975 sample of 188 abortion patients approved of the female's later abortion decision. It should be noted, however, that only 85% of all the women in the sample told their partner of their pregnancy and their ensuing decision for abortion. When Smith asked 91 Iowa men about this in 1979, only 8% reported disagreement with the decision, and 79% "very much" or "somewhat" agreed with it (50/29). Another 13% were neutral in the matter (p. 141). L. Melamed. "Therapeutic Abortion in Midwestern City," op. cit., p. 1145; Smith, op. cit., p. 227.

13. In Rotter's 1980 sample of 126 males, 65% said both made the deci-

sion; 25% felt the female was most influential; and 10%, themselves. Overall, 81% felt the couple had mutually agreed to end the pregnancy, though another 12% felt the female was more in favor of the abortion than the male, and for 6%, the reverse. Smith's 1979 findings for 91 Iowa men had 54% reporting having jointly decided; 36% thought the female alone, and 6%, the male alone, had made the decision (p. 106). Rotter, op. cit., p. 56; Smith, op. cit., p. 222.

14. Finley, op. cit., p. 3.

15. We repeat here a question originally constructed by Patricia C. Dunn (Associate Professor, Health Education, East Carolina University) and Ione J. Ryan (Professor and Counselor, East Carolina University, Greenville, N.C.). We were in close touch with these pioneering researchers, exchanged data with them, and appreciate their cooperation and support. See their 1981 paper, "Male and Female College Students' Attitudes Toward Shared Responsibility in Abortion Decision-Making: Implications for Counseling." (Unpublished paper, East Carolina University, Greenville, N.C.)

16. Bogen's 1974 research had only 58% of the males paying for all or part of the costs. Smith's 1979 study of 91 Iowa males had 28% paying for all, and 40% sharing the cost with the female. In only 9% of the cases did the female pay all, and in 21%, medical insurance covered the expenses. Bogen, I. "Attitudes of Women Who Have Had Abortions." *Journal of Sex Research* (1974): p. 99; Smith, op. cit., p. 223.

17. Judith Patterson, "Whose Freedom of Choice?" *The Progressive*, April 1982, p. 44. Most of these men, Patterson noted, said they had made the decision jointly: "...they felt that discussing the decision had strengthened the relationship."

18. Ibid, p. 44. Patterson quotes Washington psychologist Arnold Medvene who warns that abortion is "undeniably a death experience, a loss experience, and a separation experience with immense reverberations for everybody. If all of that gets blocked and is not resolved, it is bound to have a dramatic and destructive impact on the relationship."

19. Smith, op. cit., p. 108.

20. We draw here on a much longer list of six items (of which we use three concepts and alter the remaining items) that first appeared in Carole Dornblaser and Uta Landy, *The Abortion Guide: A Handbook for Women and Men*, pp. 80–81. New York: Playboy Paperbacks, 1982.

21. As quoted in James C. Lincoln, "Abortion: How Men Feel About One of the Biggest Issues in a Woman's Life." *Glamour*, February 1980, p. 243.

22. Ibid. See also Peter N. Stearns, *Be A Man: Males in a Modern Society*. New York: Holmes and Meier, 1979.

23. Dornblaser and Landy, op. cit., pp. 80–81.

24. Patterson, op. cit., p. 43. See also Warren Quinn, "Abortion: Identity and Loss," *Philosophy and Public Affairs*, 13 (Winter, 1984), pp. 24–54.

Chapter 3

Clinic Day

Abortion is a far greater dilemma for men than researchers, counselors—and women—have even begun to realize. Men of all ethnic backgrounds, ages, and socioeconomic levels have trouble dealing with abortion—and sometimes more trouble than women have. Unable to bear children themselves and powerless to prevent their partners from terminating a pregnancy, men who care are the silent sufferers, bewildered and frustrated by their emotional responses...Nowhere are the differences between men and women more clearly defined. A fertile woman can decide to have a baby almost anytime she wants. A man cannot.

Linda Bird Francke, "Abortion and Men"
(*Esquire*, January 1981, p. 60)

I remember being at work later that day as a waiter, dropping glasses, feeling guilty, blaming myself. I went into the bathroom, looked in the mirror, and started to cry. My buddy, the waiter who had lent me the money, comforted me by saying I did the mature thing by sticking it out with her and taking responsibility for my actions. She came in later that night to visit me at work, and it was as if the world had been lifted off her shoulders.

Single, 17, student

What was the actual clinic experience like for 1,000 men who were willing to answer our questions about it?

Most were keenly aware of all that was happening. They could vividly recall the scene long after the event, for example:

> I remember everything about the day it happened. Even the minute details are still clear. I remember asking the doctor how the procedure was done. I wanted to know everything that was going to happen. I remember when the operation was on, I was sick several times. I remember after the procedure was over the weight lifted off my chest when the doctor said everything was fine. That was my biggest fear, what if something happened. I remember going into her recovery area and sitting by her bed. I began to cry, thinking about what she was thinking, feeling, and how this would affect her.

While almost all were barred by clinic rules from the recovery room, many would share tales of their own experiences elsewhere in the clinic. Anxiety, anguish, fear, concern, and relief overlapped, and filled in a crowded space of three to four extraordinary vigil hours.

To some observers, such as the clinic public relations specialist and two writers quoted below, the waiting room scene appears everywhere the same:

> *New York City* (1975): One sees "men staring into space, gulping coffee, snoozing, fiddling with shoelaces, gabbing, reading, twisting friendship or wedding rings...."[1]

> *Nationwide* (1981): "You see them in the waiting rooms of all the clinics. Nervous and apprehensive, they leaf through tattered copies of old magazines, leaving the stories unread. For the most part, they avoid eye contact with one another, and when the fight to concentrate on the magazines is lost, their eyes remain fixed on the floor. An abortion takes a long time...the men are sometimes left hanging for three hours or even more."[2]

> *Boston* (1983): "They're in abortion clinic waiting rooms everywhere. They leaf through old magazines, never reading the words. Some simply gaze at the floor and tap their feet. Rarely do they look at one another. Rarely do they talk to one another."[3]

Our research suggests this surface reading of the scene masks six underlying tasks: The men first had to decide to come along. Then they had to handle a clinic-required separation as best as possible. At that point, they have three to four hours of waiting to fill. Many have to decide whether or not to ask for counseling at the clinic. A very few have to decide whether or not to go along during the surgery, if their partner asked that of them and the clinic offered that option. And, above all, they have to mentally prepare for the postabortion phase ahead of them.

"Why bother?" Reaction

Given the estimate of our 30 clinics that at least half of their patients had a man accompanying them, the first task a man had was deciding whether he would be in that half or the other (see Chapter 7, "Men Who Wait Elsewhere").[4]

  We did not use our questionnaire to ask about the decision to go to the abortion clinic, although we did explore this topic in our interviews. Another researcher, Kristine Larae Rotter, gathered both relevant comments and statistical data in her 1980 study of 126 males in two Midwest clinics:[5]

> So we can complete what she is here for. We're together.

> I figured I was half to contribute to the pregnancy, and I should be here at least for moral support.

> To offer support and share the experience that was partly my fault.

> Since I'm the one who got her pregnant I felt I should be here, because we're in love and it's my duty to be here.

> I feel that this is a moral as well as psychological situation, that must be shared by the male as well as the female. My partner should not have to bear the total burden of this situation without my support.

More recently, researcher June Hill-Falkenthal also asked the same question of 106 males in two California clinics. The Midwest/California data produced similar rankings:

California*		Midwest†	
80%	1. To provide moral support and company	62%	1. To provide support
		19%	2. From love and concern
31%	2. Express belief in the decision	15%	3. Mutual involvement

| 28% | 3. Being there if partner becomes ill | 11% | 4. Do not know; along at partner's request; providing only transportation |
| 13% | 4. Do not know how helpful I would be | | |

Sources: Hill-Falkenthal, June, "Counseling Needs of Men about Abortion" (Unpublished paper, California State University, Sacramento, CA, 1983); Rotter, Kristine L., "Men and Their Abortion Experience" (Ph.D. dissertation, Southern Illinois University at Carbondale, 1980).
*June Hill-Falkenthal, "Counseling Needs of Men about Abortion," op. cit., p. 32.
†Kristine Laral Rotter, "Men and the Abortion Experience," op. cit., p. 113.

The vast majority of waiting room men appear to have had a clear, compelling, and very caring set of reasons for having come along to the abortion appointment. Californians, for example, told Hill-Falkenthal that "things will go easier with support you're used to." Additionally, the presence of these men will, hopefully, reduce guilt associated with the procedure.[6]

Without doubt, a few of the men came along against their wishes and others were lukewarm at best. The 1980 study of a 91-man Iowa clinic sample found 9% in the former category, and only 15% in the latter; an overwhelming 73%, however, recalled wanting "very much" to make the trip together. When asked if they thought their coming along seemed to have actually helped their lovers, 2% thought not and 2% were uncertain. On the other hand, 22% felt it had helped "somewhat," and an overwhelming 74% thought it had "very much" made the difference the man desired.[7] Why go along, in short? Because it felt right, seemed right, and appeared to make a loving difference!

The Shock of Separation

Many men recalled in interviews being emotionally unprepared for the forced separation of the couple. This sometimes came only minutes after their nervous and awkward arrival together in the clinic reception area.

A very small number found this especially hard to take:

I really wanted to support my girlfriend, but I didn't know what was happening. I'd read pamphlets and she'd told me about it. But,

I hadn't thought about *not being with her.* I got up automatically and went to the door, and the attendant stopped me. It really pissed me off. It's like my mother says...'women's problems!'

Others tried to accent the positive:

We went together. They were very nice; they made us feel at home, very comfortable. The whole time I was there they came out and told me what was happening. I wanted to go through the whole thing with her, but they wouldn't let me. I felt it was as much my responsibility as it was hers.

One man spoke for many with his angry insistence that "I saw my first baby born and I should be here, too!" Another put his separation anguish particularly well:

Clinics should allow more involvement for the male. I don't like letting her go through this *alone!* Up until walking through this door this has been a shared problem...suddenly it becomes entirely hers to deal with. Somehow, I think my support would be better than that of a counselor.

Especially moving was the insistence of still a third man who felt he had had a grip on things until his lover had been ushered alone through the swinging doors, and an "utterly bewildering mystery began for me."

A total of 88% of the clinics that cooperated with our research barred men from both the procedure and the recovery room. Many men made much of the jolting and unwelcomed nature of this involuntary separation. Abortion counselor Susan Weinstein traces much of their discomfort to "being in a medical facility that keeps them separate from their partner for almost four hours, that offers them counseling on a catch-as-catch-can basis, unless, as it so often happens, we are short staffed, and then not at all. While abortions go on in back, the clinic waiting room is smoke-filled, magazine-strewn, and tense."

Filling the Time

Obliged to fall back on their own resources, the men who wait invent revealing ways to help pass the time; for example,

In the waiting room, I paced back and forth. Think of that!

I didn't talk to anyone. The other guys, like myself, were all there because they cared. They were all equally as nervous. Consequently, everyone was in their own troubled world of guilt, relief, and the hardest fact to swallow, giving up a child that was part of yourself.

I could have sat around the waiting room and read magazines, but I preferred not to. So, I just went out, walked around, bought some things, and I got back there around 11:30. I was really nervous. I thought, 'holy shit,' you know, what if something happened? I'd heard stories, like they'd suck their guts out, and things like that. I was really nervous about that.

Sitting in the waiting room was really mind-boggling, because it's totally out of your control. All you can do is hope. It was hard for me to sit there and know we were both in it, but she was the only one who could get us out of it.

I sat there the whole time, read, watched TV, drank coffee. All they did was keep me posted. It was like they let you sit in your soup.

Especially common was the "Jack-in-the-box" behavior of men who would spring up to ask how things were going: "Was everything okay? Was there any news? Would she be coming out soon? Was there anything he could do?" One chap even rushed from a clinic to a nearby florist, brought a bouquet of roses, and asked a very surprised and admiring nurse to take them to his lover in the recovery room.

A very small number of our 1,000 men, or those who dealt with 15% of our 30 clinics, could see an orientation slide show, video tape, or short film designed to help them understand what was happening, and what lay ahead:

I was impressed with the clinic. They showed husbands and boyfriends a little film which helped us...They took the feeling about taboo out of abortion, and made us feel more comfortable. They offered counseling; a nurse explained the procedure; other nurses put on a slide show. I hadn't known how they did it. The more aware the public became of the procedure, the less it would be looked down on.

Far more available (62% of our 30 clinics) were offers of pamphlets on "men and abortion" (some of which were authored by contributors to Chapter 8).

To Counsel or Not to Counsel

Filling the time would seem to have been a bit easier for the men in the 38% of our 30 clinics that offered group counseling sessions to males, 62% that offered contraception education sessions, and 100% that offered pamphlets about contraception. What is even more, 96% of these clinics informed the females their male partners *could* see a clinic counselor at their request.

However, given that 48% of the men felt they did *not* know all they needed concerning the medical risks involved, and 54% felt the same about relevant local laws, we can assume many did not take advantage of clinic counseling options. Indeed, there was considerable male resistance to anything labeled "counseling," and it was difficult for clinic staffers to overcome macho role obstacles to male involvement. Only 20% of our 1,000 men finally asked to talk with a clinic counselor, either alone or with their partners present. And only about 28% participated in group counseling or contraceptive education sessions (see Table 3-1).

The small minority that elected to use the counseling option were offered basic medical information, along with correctives to the propaganda of the anti-abortionists, and help with sensitive male-female issues. A 1983 study of 106 California clinic males, for example, found 86% of their concerns focused on the safety of the procedure. Some 60% asked about the degree of pain and discomfort the patient experienced. Aftercare services interested 50% of the men, and 59% wanted to know more about aftereffects on conception and childbearing.[8]

Each counselor, of course, focused on a topic their hundreds of hours with these men highlighted as deserving special attention. Counselor Sylvia Hampton, for example, explored threats to relationships:

> The biggest message I try to get across to men is that pregnancy affects a woman emotionally. I tell them that they might have noticed their women friends behaving differently, acting moody, and that this is normal; it's part of the biological reaction to pregnancy. I also explain that when a woman undergoes an abortion, she's going from a pregnant to a nonpregnant state in about 15 minutes. Her body has to go into reverse, and the biological changeback may take two or three weeks.[9]

Table 3-1. Counseling Options Used By Males in Abortion Clinics, as Estimated by the Clinics

"As best as you can estimate, what percent of each of four types of males found in your waiting room have the following characteristics?"	Teen-Age Males $\left(\begin{array}{c}14-19 \\ \text{years}\end{array}\right)$	Single Adults $\left(\begin{array}{c}20^+ \\ \text{years}\end{array}\right)$	Husbands	Platonic Friends
1. Participates in any group counseling or educational sessions?	27%	28%	23%	22%
2. Asks for counseling?	11	18	20	4
Percent of all waiting room males	25	44	28	10

Note: The data are from 26 of our 30 cooperating clinics, and are averaged from guesstimates.

Hampton urged the men to give the woman time and space, a type of patient and sensitive support made plausible by the (rare) understanding the men gained of female realities.

Another common focus was on releasing pent-up emotions in characteristically tight-lipped males. As counselor Bruce Rappaport explains:

> Everyone involved in an abortion is pretty upset, either for moral or religious reasons or because they're not sure what effect it will have on their lives. We give a man 'permission' to be freaked out himself—and most men usually are.[10]

As far too many waiting room males, according to counselor Andre Watson, feel they "should always be in control—rational, cool, aloof, self-contained and restrained,"[11] teaching men how to face and release their feelings remains a primary thrust of much clinic counseling—especially when conducted by males for males.

A third and final point of emphasis, resisted however by most counselors, had certain waiting room men intent on learning the "game rules." Eager to do their duty, but unsure of its details in this unique and morally ambiguous situation, they want to be told what to say, feel, and do—only to have most counselors offer instead to facilitate the assumption of one's own responsibility in the matter.

Overall, counseling got high grades from its small minority of users. Typical was this recollection from an individual who opted for counseling together with his partner:

> The clinic provided a lot of information and counseling. Good solid info. They had us discuss why we were there, contraception, the works. They treated us like they cared, and yet they were very professional about it. Under the circumstances it was one of the most enjoyable health centers or medical places I've ever been. They looked at you as a person and a human being, and not as a dollar bill or a client. I really enjoyed that.

Later in the interview, the gentleman added that "they treated us like we were human beings instead of someone who had committed a crime."

Another young man especially appreciated the nonjudgmental air of the experience:

> The clinic was scary at first. The first place we had called was ornery. The second was okay. Getting through that door was damned hard. All those people in there...they talked to both of us. They didn't make you feel like you was killing a baby. The counselor talked to me; he was a nice guy. He explained what was happening, was very warm. You can't ask for more than that....

The clinic staff let the chap "know what was happening all along the line. They didn't make us feel guilty or let us sit there and wonder."

Still another individual emphasized the learning dimension:

> Everyone at the clinic was real friendly. They made us feel comfortable. Abortion is a real negative thing to do, but it's not as bad when people are compassionate. Basically, it was nice to have someone to talk to. It really brings the man into the experience. It makes him aware that he is part of the reproductive process.

"It's good," the 28-year-old single store clerk concluded, "even if all it does is plant some seeds in the man's mind about his participation and responsibility."

As for the effectiveness of the birth control educational component offered by 62% of our 30 clinics—all of which offered the waiting room males pamphlets on family planning—rare feedback below from 521 users of a Minneapolis clinic suggests this was a particularly vital use of a man's vigil time:

Type of Birth Control

	Preabortion		Postabortion (chosen on Clinic Day)
25%	Condom	4%	Condom
21	None	15	Don't know
21	Rhythm	1	Natural family planning
20	Pill	56	Pill
17	Withdrawal	—	
13	Diaphragm	14	Diaphragm
8	Condom and Foam	5	Condom and Foam
7	Foam	1	Foam
2	IUD	6	IUD
6%	No Answer	49%	No Answer
		7%	Vasectomy

The dramatic switch away from high-risk techniques (#2, 3, 5, 8) to low-risk methods (#4, 9) would seem to attest to both the undesirability of repeating *and* the effectiveness of clinic contraceptive education.[12]

Going Through It All

Given the fact that only 12% of our 30 clinics permitted males to stay with their partners in the abortion procedure room, and only 12% allowed males to sit with their partners afterward in the clinic recovery room, these two options were a decidedly minority experience.

When, on rare occasion, one of our interviewees told us of the meaning either or both of these forms of participation had for that individual, we wondered anew about the 88% of the prohibiting clinics; for example,

> She went in, and about 40 minutes later they come out and told me I could go in and see her in the recovery room. I went in, and there were four beds there, each occupied with a woman who had just had an abortion. One of them was obviously married to a Protestant clergyman, and he was sitting next to her, holding her hand. They were talking, and it was actually a nice little scene between them. Another woman was sobbing uncontrollably behind them. My lady friend, after having expressed total fear going in, was so shot up with valium that she greeted me with the words—I felt like a percolater—and gave a little laugh afterwards. So, I felt that maybe the worst was over, and her smiling after this so soon was good. . . .

When we asked how many men would have preferred to accompany their lovers through the procedure or, into the recovery room, a resounding 69% and 91% answered in the affirmative—although hardly any had had the option when they "voted" in our survey.

Preparing for Postabortion Realities

The sixth, and last of the tasks, concerns the need to promote both a healing process and a renewal of love in the weeks ahead. (Typical was the belief of 89% of a 1983 Minneapolis single-clinic sample of 521 men that their relationship would continue long after this particular abortion.)[13]

Many told us in interviews of remarkable introspection and resolution making. Some, especially among the 3% convinced the abortion was helping to end their relationships, and others among the 47% who could not be sure of its impact, dwelt morosely on the erosion of love. (Counselor Katherine B. Oettinger notes that "opting for abortion often involves a ruthless shattering of romantic fantasies, the intrusions of the grimmest kind of reality into an uninformed view of life.")[14]

Others, especially those 31% assured the abortion was helping to bring the couple closer together, dwelt on the possibilities of strengthened love. Characteristically part of relationships strong in trust, intimacy, and communications, these men had worked

out preabortion difficulties together with their lover. Many therefore hoped to jointly eliminate as much residual guilt, regret, and
anger as possible. Ironically, however, a rare study of the stress
levels of such men, versus the stress of others far less loving, suggests the former actually experience far more abortion-related
stress: The lovers had much to process and get in hand before they
could feel equal to a postabortion relationship with their
partner.[15]

Typical of the agitation and mental exertion the more empathetic and caring men experience is this 24-year-old's account:

> Although in my body I had no strain, I paced about. . . and I never
> had a chance to get knocked out. I just kept thinking about it. I had
> to hold it all in, and be very supportive of this girl, and I could have
> used someone to dump it all on. . . I prayed that everything would
> turn out okay; that this girl and I would be happy; that it wouldn't
> haunt us every day of our lives, not to forget that we had started
> a life. . . .

Another man recalled worrying all over the place, as he struggled
to contain his various fears:

> . . . all of the guys waiting were in the same boat. . . I felt I had let
> myself down as well as my woman, and had violated life itself. Be-
> cause of my irresponsibility, I had taken a life. Not just a life, but
> a part of my life. What about if, for some reasons or another, I
> couldn't have children later in life? What about the statistics chart
> of complications they showed us? What if something happened to
> my girlfriend? Incomplete abortion, damage to her ovaries, or worse
> yet, 1 out of 1,000,000 die, and I would be directly responsible.

Later in the interview, this 17-year-old male recalled that when he
and his friend finally left the clinic, they were "very melancholy,
but relieved."

With all of this cogitation (and agitation), a difficult time for
many waiting room men involved their reunion with their partners. Counselors recall many strained meetings of reunited couples. On learning their lover has entered the recovery room and
will rejoin them in about an hour, such males often ply counselors

with anxious questions about what to say, ask, or do at reunion time.

Overall, how do the men themselves sum it up? When we asked our 1,000 men for a terse summary thought, they wrote:

> My feelings are not important. I just hope my partner doesn't have a bad experience.

> I do not want to see her suffer or have derogatory feelings toward herself.

> Wish the two of us had been more verbal in what we were feeling, instead of me feeling sorry/sad for her.

> Want to better understand the emotions and thought patterns of the female.

> Enable my wife and I to share our feelings and grow from this.

> I really wanted my child, but if she is okay after the surgery, and able to have kids after this, then I will be happy.

> Want to be as responsive as possible to my girlfriend's needs and feelings.

> Brought me closer to my very best friend. Now we need to learn control, and start being more careful.

> Hopefully, it will bring us closer together with ourselves and our children.

> If I still had an active relationship with her, I could have a shoulder to lean on after we leave this place.

Especially striking was a man's wish that his partner realize "that an abortion happens as much to a man as a woman."

When the 91 users of an Iowa clinic were asked in 1979 to sum up their clinic day and related experiences, some 81% agreed they had definitely been changed by it all. Only 15% thought they had been changed in a negative direction, while the majority (53%) claimed instead *positive* gains—as in the increased intensity of their relationships and in their sense of "growing up." Looking beyond the day itself, 44% thought the best was still ahead (another 36% expected no further changes, while 21% were uncertain). Pressed to explain how positive changes might unfold, the 44% bloc with optimistic expectations talked about increasing maturity in relationship responsibilities (e.g., doing more about sharing responsibility for birth control).[16]

When we put the matter to our 30-clinic, 18-state bloc of 1,000 men, a similarly cautious set of expectations emerged:

- 47% felt that males involved in an abortion generally had disturbing thoughts about it afterward. Another 39% were uncertain, and only 14% rejected this grim possibility.

- 18% felt more uncertain now than before the abortion about wanting the experience of fatherhood (24% were more eager than ever for that experience).

Overall, as the largest number knew two or more males with an abortion in their background, their guarded, even anxious behavior was understandable.

Summary

The problem on clinic day is not sudden outbursts of explosive violence from males who lose control—almost all of the men who wait, according to our 30 clinics, never cause any sort of disturbance at all. The problem, instead, is what does not meet the eye.

Males on clinic day, from naive boys of 16 to young students of 22, husbands of 30, and divorced "lady killers" in their forties, wrestle with the same six role tasks: Do they come along or wait elsewhere? How do they handle the clinic-required separation? What can they do to usefully fill their four-hour wait? Should they try the counseling offered by the clinic? Should they ask to accompany their friend throughout her entire experience? And, how can they mentally and emotionally prepare for the trip home, and for life and love after an abortion?

Few teens, young adults, family men, or other types of American males find themselves well-prepared for these six tasks—or, especially well-helped by the people best-positioned to compensate for their initial inadequacies, the professional staff of the nation's 520 abortion clinics. Little wonder that many of our 1,000 men referred to their vigil as the longest, hardest half day of their lives...an encounter, never forgotten, with "that dark involvement with blood and birth and death."[17]

PROFILE

Regardless of other variables in the circumstances of our 1,000 men, their one common experience was that of the clinic on abortion day. The impact and impression made on them depended upon the particular clinic, of course, and especially on the clinic personnel in charge at the time.

For Jim, a midwestern businessman in his mid-twenties, the clinic became the focal point of his anger and frustration. Although he did not impress us as a generally bull-headed or vindictive person, his constant references to what went wrong at the clinic illustrated how a bad clinic experience could exacerbate the emotional trauma of abortion.

Jim also exemplifies how much many of our men cared for their pregnant sex partner. His overriding concern was for his girlfriend, whom he struggled to vindicate (though she did not need it) throughout our interview.

Jim:

The relationship went through a lot of remorse. The getting used to her not being pregnant, a lot of fighting, not talking . . . It took a lot of time for us to do something about how one another felt.

Now, it's coming along very well. I think we'll probably be married in a year or so. We've redefined our roles. She was taught to be career oriented and I was to look for a career woman, and we found out she wants to take care of a family, and me. That's totally against what we'd been brought up with. I'm young, busy, and working hard to grab the brass ring and support both of us.

She and I both enjoy our new roles and our parents think we're both nuts. But it's really stabilized our lives as to having to make an abortion decision again.

I was very upset with the clinic. They put up a facade, but it was cruel, brutal, inhumane. She got the feeling she was being punished and ridiculed. I've thought of suing them. If they want to do abortions, they should stay out of moral judgment. They weren't equipped.

Group therapy sessions were a bunch of shit. They hurt me more than they helped. She saw the other women come out crying and upset.

I was separated the whole time, but it looked like an abortion mill. Screams could be heard. Women were herded around like cattle for slaughter. She tried to get up right after the injection, and they held her down saying it was too late, and did the procedure.

This was my second abortion experience. The first was with a different woman and done on a one-to-one counseling basis. I was in the room for the procedure; it worked out very well.

You try to pick up the pieces after a nightmare like that. By the time she came out to me, she ran to the elevator, pushed me away and cried, "Why did you do this to me?" Strangely enough, it was her decision to do it. I told her I would have had the child, and that's because of the experience. It hurts her more because she's dealing on a more personal/physical level.

I try to empathize as much as I can, but you can't match going through the physical experience, especially a brutal one.

My anger is blatant anger toward the clinic. It will never go away. I'd like to close the door of that place. If I didn't want to keep our business personal, I'd initiate a class action suit, but that would prolong the whole problem, so I just don't want to deal with it.

Thoughts and feelings about a child are more significant for her. I don't know for sure what my feelings are about it. I look forward to having children though. The anger over the clinic is harder than any guilt.

I have no doubt that abortion was the right thing to do at the time. She *just* graduated from college, *just* started work, and now we're getting a better handle on what our roles are. It would have been *very* difficult. It's a little bit confused, still, but the combination of kids, house, and work will probably still attract her.

Cost is insignificant. Pick your doctor. Make sure your woman is under a doctor's care as soon as you know she's pregnant. Everybody should have that kind of close contact with a physician. It's much more important than having group approaches. Stay out of the mill setup.

She had medical complications, which in any case may have required the abortion. I would pay $1,000 to get a good job done. She's scared to get pregnant again. The thought traumatizes her. It's very sour right now, and it could have been prevented.

The clinic had it down to shifts and schedules, meticulously organized, just like a butcher shop. Twenty young girls and men in the morning, and I could see the shift changing for the afternoon, no individualization.

I guess if I had to work there day after day, I'd be a little cuckoo, too. That's why I think a family physician should be involved, the one who can react warmly, knowledgeably, professionally.

She saw the fetus. That terrified her. She has a very vivid memory. It was a pile of mush and blood, two inches long and one inch wide. She asked, "What is it, what is it?" They said nothing, and hurried out. It's taken two months for this to come out for us to deal with it.

The whole time I was completely snowed (in the clinic). The only time I got worried was five minutes before she came out, when two girls ran out crying. I asked what was going on. The staff said, "Don't worry," but I always worry—I love her very much. I was kept isolated from the whole thing.

Most of them are done without anesthesia. You can't get your wisdom teeth pulled without it. But for some reason they didn't make it comfortable for her, she said it was like they didn't want to see her.

It's had a profound influence on my thinking about human life...how fragile people are and how fragile they are in dealing with it. It's a major change to carry a baby to term too. Changes in moods are like a complete 180 (degrees).

It just boiled down that I love her very much and I wouldn't hurt her for the world, or let anyone else hurt her either. She's very carefree and sheltered. It was a shock to her that those people were like that.

I assumed that because several years ago that I'd had a good experience that this would be the same. I was naive enough to assume that. A person that walks in for an abortion deserves the same professional treatment that they'd get for any other medical procedure. I doubt if those people were doctors, because doctors are humanitarian and wouldn't treat anyone like that, and if they were doctors, I'd haul them up before a medical board of review.

Just because it's an abortion doesn't mean its the same for everybody in the group. There's a great need for privacy for the woman, her partner, and their doctor. No one should go through it alone, but each person and couple deserves privacy.

It helps to blow off steam. I've kept a lot inside that I haven't been able to share with anyone, family, friends. Neither of our families was involved, had no part, no knowledge of the decision. Hers are strong Catholics, and mine are strong Protestants. It's really a feeling of ours that it's none of their damn business. It would cause great strain.

We separated for two weeks. It came close to being broken. It took awhile apart to put it back together.

She has no tolerance for pain. They didn't consider that. I had a broken finger for two days before I got it looked at. I feel a little guilty that I led her to believe it would be professionally and sensitively done.

You can call me back in a month or the month after that to see how things are going. It's had a big impact, and things are always changing.

PROFILE

George is one of the 31% of our men who claimed the abortion was bringing his relationship closer together. Our interview several weeks after the abortion sketched a picture of a growing intimate relationship, thanks to joint decision making, good communication, and damn hard work by both partners.

Even though George did not rail against the clinic he considered it the "worst part" of the entire experience. In his case, and in the cases of many other such men, their separation (some would call it quarantine) from their women was emotionally jarring and very painful. It deprived them of their tangible role they had—supporter—and recast them instead as lonely, helpless worriers.

Fortunately, George was not severely rattled by his half-day wait (the clinic was an especially clean and well-managed place). And, thanks to the maturity of his relationship, the abortion did not have permanent negative consequences.

From our viewpoint, the difference between what the clinic judged as an acceptable experience and what George considered beneficial is particularly instructive where the case for abortion clinic reform is concerned.

George:

It's gotten much closer. We were at the stage of our relationship where we relied on each other. It was too bad it happened, but we got through it, so it hasn't hindered our relationship. We both really came to the same conclusion on our own. Then, we thought about it and discussed it.

I talked to two friends, but not in any depth. I tried to keep it to a minimum number. She did the same, so between us, only four people know. I'm glad we didn't talk about it because people would have a negative attitude toward her, and I was worried what they'd think.

For people who haven't experienced abortion, they look down on it. When you think about it, like I did before it happened, you think people don't take care or are stupid. Then it happened to us and we were careful. Planned Parenthood recommended condoms. I bought them and they ripped.

It's human nature. People are influenced and have viewpoints that are molded by right-to-life or pro-choice groups.

I really appreciate the fact that we got through it and that we are close and not blaming each other. We just worked it out together. We'd been going out four or five months. Our relationship was built on strong ties quickly, good communication.

The clinic was the worst part of the whole deal. They tried to be very helpful, but after it was performed, you should be able to go in with her. They tell you to go for a walk after three and a half hours that seem like days, and all you can think of is being with her.

Before at Planned Parenthood, I waited while she got tests and counseling, and then a brief visit for lists of clinic options. She was counseled by herself at the clinic, but I should have been involved. I felt like I was in left field.

They had a slide show to get waiting room people acquainted and to clear up confusion. It was a help, but not satisfying. It was a nice office, well furnished, clean, music softened atmosphere, well decorated. People were nice and willing. But, I had a lot of feelings and I wanted to be with her during the procedure, and especially in recovery. That's the part that wasn't satisfying.

Before, during and after, if you play your cards right, and you're close, it shouldn't ruin your relationship. It can strengthen it. Getting by obstacles with each other—you become each other.

The word 'abortion' shouldn't turn you off. You have to give your girl a lot of support. It's her going through it physically and you mentally. It was tough, especially beforehand. She cried a few times. I tried to comfort her and learn about it, but first hand experience is challenging.

I was in Sweden for a year and over there a high percentage of females are on birth control. They don't conceal it like women do here. Here, people *tend* to get a negative reaction if they don't know the girl well. They may think she's a slut and not just seeing one guy, so they're further ahead of us in that respect. In fashion, too.

Both of us are mature, but not enough to have kids. We want to enjoy life and are not ready for the responsibility of kids now.

During an abortion, you're killing a fetus. If you have a child and can't bring it up well, you're killing the child indirectly. A lot of kids can't get out of their backgrounds. Unhappy marriages or child abuse is possible.

We've concluded we just want each other now. We love each other very much.

I like sharing this with you. It's different talking with someone who's gone through it.

Notes

1. Eileen Milling. "World's Largest Abortion Clinic." *Pageant,* July 1973, p. 4.

2. Linda Bird Francke. "Abortion and Men." *Esquire,* January 1981, p. 59.

3. James McBride. "Men and the Pain of Abortion." *Boston Globe,* January 25, 1983, p. 37.

4. We use the guesstimate of the 30 clinic representatives to reach our 600,000 estimate of the annual number of clinic waiting room males: If the nation had 1,600,000 abortions in 1983, and 85% of the women involved informed their sex partner before the procedure (or so the 30 clinic spokespeople estimate), and if half of these 1,350,000 men so informed came along on the appointment day, and if perhaps 10% went to the office of a private physician or a hospital for the procedure, about 600,000 or more males waited in one of America's freestanding abortion clinics.

5. Kristine Laral Rotter, "Men and the Abortion Experience," op. cit., pp. 132–133.

6. Hill-Falkenthal, op. cit., p. 32.

7. Mark Randall Smith, "How Men Who Accompany Women to an Abortion Service Perceive the Impact of Abortion Upon their Rela-

tionship and Themselves," op. cit., pp. 166–167. "These data show clearly nearly 90 percent of the men who accompany women to the ETP Unit do so because they want to, and over 90 percent of the men think they help their partners. Conversely, less than one man in ten did not want to accompany the woman. Even fewer men think they are not helping the woman. It might be of interest to determine in future studies the degree of help experienced by the women who have partners with them."

8. Hill-Falkenthal, op. cit., p. 30.

9. As quoted in Carol Lynn Mithers, "Abortion: Are Men There When Women Need Them Most?" *Mademoiselle,* April 1981, p. 253.

10. Ibid., p. 263. "We found that in all the area clinics performing abortions, there was no help for men, and it was assumed that they didn't want any...When we checked it out, though, we realized that that wasn't true."

11. Watson, Chapter 8 of this book, "Men Who Counsel."

12. See the item added to the Appendix, "Feedback from 521 Client-Partners," by Peter Zelles.

13. Ibid. Similarly, 66% of Smith's 91-man Iowa sample did not think the abortions had put a special strain upon the relationship, a figure comparable to the 66% of our 1,000 men who felt it made no difference (19%) or they could not tell what difference it was making at the time (47%). Finley reports that 78% felt the abortion would either make no difference in their relationship, or would bring them closer together. Smith, op. cit., p. 224; Michael C. Finley, "A Male Counseling Component for Aborting Fathers at Preterm: A Needs Assessment," op. cit., p. 3.

14. Katherine B. Oettinger. *"Not My Daughter": Facing Up to Adolescent Pregnancy,* p. 18. Englewood Cliffs, N.J.: Prentice-Hall, 1979.

15. Robert Barry Lees. "Men and the Abortion Experience: Anxiety and Social Supports," pp. 57–60. Ann Arbor: the University of Michigan, 1975. Unpublished doctoral dissertation. Note that Lees remains open-minded about the full significance and long-term impact of his findings: "...the men's increased anxiety may represent a potential reduction of the crisis nature of the experience for the social system...It would be interesting in future studies to follow up on couples who seek abortion to determine whether in fact high anxiety in the males reflects a high degree of empathy and thus leads to a strengthening of the relationship." (pp. 59–60).

16. Smith, op. cit., p. 158. "...it seems the effect of abortion upon men is mixed, and the need for longitudinal studies which accurately assess the changes foreshadowed is apparent." (p. 162). Finley reports that 94% of his men noted behavioral changes which they associated with the abortion experience: "Among the more significant behavior changes were desire to spend more time with the woman but less interest in sex, enjoying work or school less, socializing less, sleeping less, and drinking more." (Finley, op. cit., p. 5.)

17. Joan Didion, "The Woman's Movement." *New York Times Book Review*, July 30, 1972, p. 14.

Chapter 4

Naysayers and Repeaters

This might seem kind of corny, but sometimes I'll be thinking, was it a boy or a girl? Hell, if it was a boy I could have taught him a whole lot of stuff...shoot, I can think about a trash compacter somewhere, and there's my little baby getting all smashed up....

> 22-year-old, unmarried, blue-collar worker

Abortion is a moral conflict in which there is no single clear resolution of the competing claims, and where the possibilities for violating the rights of others and/or the self are real, and, in some instances, unavoidable.

> Belenky, M. F. (Qualifying paper, Harvard University, Department of Social Relations, January, 1977, p. 7.)

It makes the boys proud," says a black counselor for Planned Parenthood. "Many of the single black women coming in here for abortions haven't told their boyfriends they were pregnant because they know the guys would encourage them to have the baby. It's a macho thing.

> Francke, Linda Bird, *The Ambivalence of Abortion*, New York: Dell, 1979, p. 70.

Over and again, a sustained discussion of this topic comes around to focus on two sub-groups of particular interest, or those who wait in a personal hell (the abortion detractors in the clinic waiting room), and those who have waited before (the repeaters). We have gathered some new data on each, though far less than if our primary focus had not been broader than subtypes. Our material therefore raises fully as many vital questions as it answers. In the regrettable absence, however, of any other recent field data on these two types, we share it to better illustrate the specific costs of the unattended needs of certain men who wait.

Abortion Naysayers

The overwhelming majority of men we met in clinic waiting rooms were neutral about the morality and politics of abortion. They recognized, as researcher Judith Smetana has explained, that abortion can be considered a moral issue of life, a social-conventional issue of sex roles or sexual mores, or a personal issue of autonomy and individuality.[1] Most of our 1,000 respondents preferred to dwell on their partner's right to "protect" herself (her reputation, her relations with her folks, her schooling, career, etc.). They also made much of their related responsibility to help her secure these "rights." Very few felt negative about the moral dimension of the subject: They did not believe abortion is immoral (83%) and they believed the fetus became a human being at birth, or with the ability to survive outside the womb (36%, with another 25% "uncertain," one way or the other; see Table 4-1).

At the same time, however, 10% "strongly agreed" and 16% "agreed" with the antiabortion argument—"Abortion is the killing of a child."—and 20% felt a fetus became a human being at conception. As 17% felt abortion is "morally wrong," it was not surprising that 19% expected it to be made illegal within the next five years.

Who were these men? And why were they, however reluctantly, complicitors in an act about which they had severe reservations?

To judge cautiously from a rare question asked in a 1979 case of 91 Iowa clinic users, many naysayers came to their abortion "trial" with strongly negative attitudes: 34% of the Iowa sample were "somewhat" or "very much" opposed to the entire idea

Table 4-1. Scale of Moral Attitudes of Clinic Males

Which of the following are *morally* wrong?

1. Homosexuality	63%
2. Use of hard drugs	61
3. Sex before age 16	32
4. Pornographic movies	24
5. Smoking marijuana	21
6. Abortion	17
7. Living with someone of the opposite sex	8
8. Sex between 2 single persons	7

Percent of clinic males who judged Item morally wrong (except "abortion"):

All 7 items	17%
6 of 7	24
5 of 7	23
4 of 7	17
3 of 7	11
2 of 7	4
1 of 7	2
None of the 7	3

Abortion was not included in the scale so that the morality index could be correlated with abortion. The alpha reliability coefficient for the morality index is 0.68. The internal validity of the morality index is supported by its relationship with whether a respondent checked abortion as morally wrong (gamma = 0.63), attitudes toward abortion ($R = 0.14$), and whether abortion is considered the killing of a child ($R = 0.21$).

prior to this pregnancy. (Another 40% lent it immediate support, while 26% recalled being indifferent.[2]) Similarly, 21% of a 1978 sample had not agreed with the decision initially, though only 5% were left on clinic day willing to admit they still opposed the termination (as were 11% of our 1,000 men, and 13% of 521 Minneapolis men).[3]

Focusing only on our respondents, we can share impressions gathered from interviews with many, and from our discussions about them with concerned counselors. As compared to other waiting room men, naysayers seemed a bit older, less well-schooled, and disproportionately concentrated in the ranks of the unwed males (as many as 91% were single). Stereotypes not with-standing, only a proportionate number had been reared as Roman Catholics. Whatever their religious affiliation, naysayers regarded themselves as very religious (see Table 4-2), and leaned toward fundamentalist theologies. While four in five were white, the black men who waited were significantly over-represented in this cate-gory (more on this racial distribution appears in the following chapter).

Table 4-2. Characteristics of Naysayers versus Supporters:
Demographic Data

	Naysayers	Supporters
	(N = 110)	(N = 890)
Age (N = 960)		
21 or younger	34%	35%
22–30	41	49
31 or older	25	16
Education (N = 892)		
No H.S. diploma	17%	9%
H.S. graduate	39	45
Some college	28	27
College graduate	15	18
Marital Status (N = 954)		
Married	9%	19%
Living together	20	11
Divorced, widowed	15	10
Single	56	61
Religion (N = 889)		
Protestant	48%	45%
Catholic	28	34
Jewish	4	2
Other	5	5
None	15	15

Religiosity (*N* = 936)

Very significant	30%	19%
Somewhat significant	41	48
Not very significant	16	19
Not at all	12	14

Race (*N* = 910)

White	81%	90%
Black	19	10

Occupational Status (*N* = 825)

Student	26%	29%
Blue collar	33	35
White collar	21	19
Professional	9	5
Unemployed	6	3
Other	6	9

Naysayers are those responders who felt abortion was the killing of a child, believed the fetus became a human being at conception, and felt abortion was morally wrong. Because this survey was not a random sample, probabilities are not reported, although all statistics are significant at .05 or lower.

Given this rough, tentative, and only impressionistic profile of ours, some clues to the abortion opposition of these men are already apparent:

• Their *youthfulness* makes it likely that this pregnancy was their first affirmation of virility, their first opportunity at parenthood, and their first demonstration of "macho" prowess, all dimensions of an emerging manhood difficult for some males to surrender.

• Their *unwed status*, albeit in the context of long-term committed relationships, makes it likely that some regarded the unexpected pregnancy as a spur to marriage and childrearing, only to learn their female partners had other needs and plans.

• Their *religiosity*, especially in its fundamentalism, makes it likely that many shuddered at the thought of killing a "child," at participating in the annihilation of an innocent human being.

• Where the *black males* were concerned, their participation in a pronatalist black culture, one with historic tolerance of

egitimacy, an association of conception with macho pride, and
ligious condemnation of "baby genocide," makes more and
ore understandable their disproportionate presence among the
naysayers.

Other explanations, of course, especially those concerning estrangement over the female's insistence that this *particular* pregnancy end now, were common—though distress over complicity
in the "destruction of the baby" seemed to outdistance all others.

Policy preferences that appeared to set black men apart from
the whites included:

- a decided preference for males' having less say in the abortion
  decision than the female;

- a smaller-than-average endorsement of birth control education
  through the schools;

- an inclination *not* to accompany a female to an abortion appointment ever again. . .should circumstances raise the possibility any
  other time.

Above all, when we reviewed our list of 17 possible circumstances
under which they might feel a woman should be able to obtain a
legal abortion, their level of acceptance was remarkably low on every count, including the commonly accepted "hard" reasons (incest, rape, health hazard to the mother).

Along with this hostility toward abortion-on-request, we found
a disproportionate number of these men convinced—resentfully—
that the 1973 Supreme Court decriminalization decision had actually encouraged people to have more abortions. Opposed to this
example of state interference, they nevertheless lent support to
other possible directives from the authorities, such as a proposed
requirement that clinics inform a husband before performing an
abortion on his wife. Again, more so than others, they favored this
prenotification requirement even where the couple was not married. As many as one in four expected abortion to be made illegal in the next five years (versus nearly one in five of the entire
1,000-man group).

Perhaps as vexing as any impression made on us by these men
was their dread of the negative aftermath of abortion, their expec-

tation of the spiritual and psychological punishment waiting un-
avoidably for them. A close runner-up was the deep-reaching
sense of personal loss many felt: "I mean, that's part of me that
just got snatched out, you know, thrown in the garbage." Some
insisted they had had an alternative plan all worked out: "I
couldn't deal with the kid right now, but my mother said she'd
watch it or take it over to my aunt's or something like that." Overall, the naysayers brought to mind Terkel's image of "the walking wounded among the great many of us," a small, anguished
collection of self-maimed casualties, there because they cared, because honor demanded their presence, because she insisted—but
there under protest.[4]

Repeaters

Few categories of men involved in abortions stir as strong emotional reaction from the public—and from clinic staffers—as does
this one: "Lynch the bastards!" is a relatively mild response from
certain parties, especially strident feminists and "worn-thin" clinic
counselors. Others, similarly outraged, mutter about compulsory
vasectomies or mandatory birth control education (much as required of drivers convicted of reckless or drunken driving). Only
a small minority react with neutral curiosity, and even fewer respond with the sort of compassion that makes authentic understanding attainable in matters as complex and ambiguous as this
one.

How many are repeaters? Why? How do they compare with
the first-timers along with them in the nation's waiting rooms?

One in four of our 1,000 men (and 25% of the 1978 sample of
192; 32% of a 1983 sample of 106) had been through the abortion
experience before.[5] Focusing only on our sample, 18% had one
previous experience; 4%, two; and 3%, three or more abortions
in their backgrounds.

It is no surprise that the older the waiting room male, the
greater the likelihood of his being a repeater: 13% of all those 21
or younger, but 36% of those 31 or older were repeaters. Race,
however, made only a slight difference (23% of the white and 36%
of the blacks were repeaters). Similarly, religion distinguished only
weakly among this type of man (26% of Catholics and 22% of Protestants, but 36% of the "nonbelievers" were repeaters). Other

standard variables—marital status and educational attainment—
showed only the association with age that would be expected (see
Table 4-3).

What *did* stand out were certain attitudinal characteristics of
our 250 multiabortion types. Contrary to their harshest critics,
many claimed to have suffered emotional distress in some or all
of their abortion experiences: 68%, versus 38% of the first-timers,
put themselves in this category. Similarly, as many of the former
as the latter thought abortion was morally wrong (17% repeaters
versus 16% first-timers). Accordingly, hardly any seemed at all cav-
alier about contraception "next time": Fully 91% of the repeaters
(and 96% of the first-timers) indicated their intention to be "more
careful about risking pregnancy after this abortion."

Taking them at their word, why, then, were they repeaters?

For one thing, they appeared somewhat more permissive
about abortion: Whereas only 45% of the first-timers felt a woman
should be able to obtain a legal abortion if the couple has just
ended their relationship, the figure rose to 59% of the repeaters.
Similarly, where only 34% of the novices agreed in cases where
the couple was on the verge of breaking up, the multiabortion men
"voted" 48% approval. Consistent with this, 63% of the repeaters,

**Table 4-3. Characteristics of Repeaters versus Nonrepeaters:
Demographic Data**

	Repeaters (250)	Nonrepeaters (750)
Age (N = 913)		
21 or younger	18%	40%
22–30	57	45
31 or older	25	15
Race (N = 866)		
White	23%	77%
Black	36	64
Religion (N = 846)		
Protestant	39%	48%
Catholic	34	33
Jewish	1	3
Other	5	5
None	21	13

but only 48% of the first-timers, agreed that government funds should be provided to help poor women pay the cost of an abortion.

Along with this seeming permissiveness, some of the repeaters evidenced hard-boiled fatalism about contraceptive failure—and knew a lot about the many shortcomings of currently available paraphernalia. Typical was a 30-year-old unmarried pharmacist profiled in 1982 by a San Francisco journalist. After admitting to ten abortion experiences, he insisted the women "knew all about birth control, all of them used it...But, it just happens; sometimes you buy a bad rubber...if you're with someone for a long time, you're going to try a few times [with no protection]." Pressed about his ten experiences, he recalled telling his various partners, "You know, you didn't go through this whole thing alone...I think both women and men go through a hell of a lot during abortions." Never once in his ten clinic visits, he later added, had he chosen to join a counseling session, with or without his partner: "No, I don't need any counseling. Anyway, just the word 'counselor' bothers me."[6]

Another type of repeater held his partner responsible rather than the reliability of any contraceptive method. Typical was a college student profiled in 1982 by a Minneapolis journalist: The student complained that he would have trouble financing the coming semester because this was the second time in six months that his girlfriend needed a $250 abortion:

We've been dating for a year and a half, and she wasn't taking the pill. It was a mistake.

The second time occurred after she began to feel ill, blamed the pill, and secretly went off of it. After explaining to the reporter his strong opposition to the adoption route, *and* his moral queasiness about both pregnancy terminations, he indicated they would not be back again soon as they were going to practice abstention.[7]

Still another type of repeater rationalized his own track record by attributing comparable insensitivity and abortion-prone ways to his entire sex:

...it's the kind of event that makes people more reluctant to learn about their sexuality, instead of more interested. It produces guilt, emotional deadness. It's an awful kind of thing, and it gets to the point where abortion ought to become a kind of very rare thing. But it won't, because in the short term, it's the easy way out. In the long term, it's not.

Do you think there are a million guys running around the country who are upset or care about it? My guess is that it's a small percentage. It's just 'Hey, it's one of those things, man!'

Fearful of the prospects of having to have a third abortion with his lover (a woman herself deeply opposed to "still another"), this 35-year-old married man finally agreed to end the relationship and return exclusively to his (estranged) marriage.

Finally, a very, very small number of repeaters insisted they simply had no choice. Typical was this tale told by a 24-year-old unmarried garage owner, a "veteran," as he put it, of three abortions that he knew about:

I work in a garage and women approach me, so what can I do? I'm always at the garage, and they figure I'm making a lot of money...I've given money to three that I can remember. Their husbands were big men, really big, and the abortions were just in time.

Later in the interview, this "serial aborter" commented, "The only thing I can say is that I just won't go through it no more. It hurts really bad...If I have to go through it again, I think I'd rather shoot myself first...I want to have something carry my name, not to throw into some garbage somewhere."

First-timers who heard the stories volunteered by "old-timers" confided their lack of sympathy and even disgust:

Some people were talking about having had them before. It hurt to hear it...What got me was listening to some of the lower-class people talk in the lobby like this was nothing.

Morally, I *still* have questions about it. If I had the choice between risking another abortion and making love with a woman without protection...even if horny...I'd jerk off first.

Convinced no comparably hapless fate would soon overtake them, the 750 first-timers swore up and down they'd never be back—

perhaps as much as had an unknown number of the 250 repeaters before them.

Summary

Those who wait in their own personal hell, and those who have been there before, are all in need of a custom-tailored response. Both types pose separate and distinct challenges to professionals intent on relieving clinic day stressors and improving postabortion prospects, as well as to the women down the hall in the procedure or recovery rooms who love them. Until we secure substantially more understanding of these men, our best intentions—whether as family planning educators, clinic counselors, sex educators, couples counselors, family life educators, or the like—may miss critical refinements necessary to really "reach" them where they are, and in ways that make a difference valued by *them*.

PROFILE

The following poem (and explanatory essay) were mailed to us by Jonathon, a graduate student from the midwest. The poem arrived first without explanation, in a plain envelope. After a long phone conversation with the young man, he sent us the accompanying essay containing the story behind the poem.

We think the background not only gives necessary context to Jonathon's verse, but also exposes the vast gulf between a priori philosophy and post-experience emotions. Jonathon will never forget the woman he had loved and, in a way, he is fortunate to have in his poetry a therapeutic outlet. Many others are left at a loss to express their hurt and disillusionment.

Take It Like a Man

I'm to be a father or murderer.

But who screamed overpopulation and
Indians fuck too much? That
people are garbage in festered mass.

The big 'A' is a mercy killing.
I conceived,
now my child will have to die
before life kills it.

"That's a feeble justification
which gives you no right. . ."
Up yours, Saviour!
Tell it to shriveled humans
pickled in third-world jars.

I want my son
and love his mother.
Abortion makes sense of death
It sucks life.

It was I who screamed (of) overpopulation and (that) Indians fuck too
much, in deference to one of the many Chicago Board of Education's con-
trived filmstrips depicting the swollen-bellied children of India begging for
gruel amidst sacred herds of healthy brahmin cattle and precious pet rats. I
didn't understand the subsequent reprimand of my otherwise atypically jovial
seventh-grade science teacher. He scolded not my use of the word, "fuck"—
which I said—but the fat American ignorance of my premise. Excluding the
socioeconomic, cultural, and religious factors, how was I to comprehend the
implicit evils involved with the indoctrination of something like abortion? I
still do not.

It was 1973. Homosexuals were coming out of the closet and abortion
out of the alleys. Along with the only chicken kiev to be found in Uptown,
my family passed Watergate, ERA, and abortion around the dinner table. As
the hot lemon butter spewed out of the rolled up breast on my plate so, too,
did words of frustrated sarcasm spill from my mouth. Like mom's dishwasher,
abortion was a modern convenience that could clean up the dirty mess of
people. Overweight and full of logic, I thought all those who condemned
abortion were asinine—a favorite word of mine at the time.

Fuck you, Saviour,
Tell it to shriveled humans
pickled in third-world jars.

My mother appreciated my frankness, and looked at me with the wonder of a woman who gave birth at 19. She told me I would soon enough learn
not the answer, but the why of the problem.

Abortion makes sense of death
It sucks life

I suppose as with the vocabulary of a foreign language one cannot help
but associate, indeed, implicate gender within both the denotative and con-
notative context of abortion. . .the female being the first-person subjective,

and the male, a mere passive tense. Obviously the woman is the ultimate benefactor of all the physical unpleasantries involved with such a procedure. It is the affecting repercussions; i.e., guilt, remorse, etc. . .which I hold to exist between both the individuals—providing they care in the first place.

When Marianne aborted our child she completely divorced me from the problem. I was in college, younger than her, naive (she had two previous children), and therefore in no position to even discuss alternatives. The questionable reality of our relationship, although founded on true love, overwhelmed her with grief as only a mother can experience. I could give her no support and our tumultuous situation was consummated by a phone call: 200 miles away in a dark corner of my room I screamed into a dead receiver about a love which I have yet to abandon.

When Marianne terminated the life inside her she severed the umbilical cord of our relationship, casting me into the farthest recesses of her mind. This fact is what did, and still does, hurt the most. She will never understand . . . my point of view.

> I want my son
> and love his mother.
> Abortion makes sense of death
> It sucks life.

PROFILE

A total of 25% of our men have been involved in more than one abortion. One might suspect a variety of responses to their repeat performances, but calloused, devil-may-care words were rarely heard from the men themselves.

Phil, a 32-year-old musician, discovered that each one of his own abortion experiences reinforced the characteristics of the relationship, but during and after each of them he was compelled to process his own largely unexpressed feelings and concern.

Phil now battles his own cynicism with hope and hard work. Trying to set meaningful priorities, he starts with his job and strives to organize his future by resolving his career status. His example helps sharpen the question of how men deal with their feelings in terms of their careers. He leads us to wonder whether men like Phil ever truly "resolve" career status quandaries, and if that is what they are really after.

Phil:

I was 26 and she was 22, the first time it happened. It had been a rough relationship for 8 or 9 months. But the pregnancy happened at the best and tranquil time in the relationship.

For her it was the second time. She was 16 the previous time, and the guy had blamed her and was cruel about it. Having to go through it again traumatized her. I didn't know what to do. It numbed me out. My feelings for her and about her were pretty twisted. It's difficult to categorize it, but it was another wall that went up between us over the next 1½ years.

She broke up eventually with me in a cut-and-dried, cold fashion, which I think was a result of the abortion. I was just starting out in show business, and I had no money, and didn't want to have a child with her anyway. I had some anger about the predicament.

The second time is very different—with my present girlfriend since early '82. She knows I had been through it before. She hasn't. We don't have wedding plans nor are we living together.

I felt a lot of compassion for her and me. It happened out of more significant feelings. She was scared. I was very caring and close to her, especially at the clinic, I kept an eye on everything.

I tend to block this out, but I felt a real loss. I have two nieces: one 4½, one born right after this happened. I think a lot about what the child would have looked like, what it would have been.

She waited for 6 to 8 weeks and felt attached to the fetus, but knew she had to rationally get on with it, because of her beginning career and the prohibition of children.

To this day, I feel loss. I have a lack of understanding as to why it's so hard for me to accept how I feel, the pain or hurt or whatever it is. I want to derail it, but I think about it when I'm alone or when somebody brings it up. I don't really allow the feeling, even now, as I talk about it. I'm knotted in the stomach, up-tight.

The whole thought of the responsibility of a family—I'm 32, and I don't feel like a grown man and this happens, and it all comes out. . . .

I've lived alone with my feelings for so long, been involved with a selfish career so long, that I don't begin to get to personal needs and desires, and I won't until my career status is resolved. It puts questions like this further away, questions of family.

I feel guilty. Morally, in this day and age, it's not the end of the world. I don't see it as taking life away. I feel guilty in the sense that it's an unpleasant situation. You did start something, but I don't feel it's killing. If I did, I'd go nuts, I suppose. I don't relate to hunting, but I eat meat and I don't think of this as killing something, but I feel bad about it happening.

I thought we handled it well. She says I was compassionate, gentle, and attentive. But, I feel deep down that there's some latent resentment, but maybe that's my own cynicism. I feel there's something in a woman that changes from it, but we almost never talk about it. So, I don't know. It was such a better experience than the first one.

The clinic was uniform, regimented, didn't take long. They were as warm as they could be. It was as good as you might expect.

I went along, but as far as they were concerned, I might as well have

not been there. I waited with all the other guys. They're just practicing medicine; it's happening to the woman and you're an appendage. I didn't feel I
was a part of it. I don't know if they cared about her. She said they were decent, but she just kind of came out in shock and didn't say much. That was
that.

I think it's pretty lousy, but I don't know what else they can do. These
places are overloaded, so they aren't going to deal with the man. I don't think
anything is going to be changed. It might be nice if some part of the team
helped man and woman. That's probably too idealistic.

It's run all right, typical hospital procedure, but you carry these feelings
around for years and they never get out. I'd like to see it changed in the future. We don't have time or money for psychological damage. Having spent
most of my life in Los Angeles, I try not to see it like that, but there's too
many people and not enough time. The reality of 25 million in a 50-mile ra-
dius (sic).

Apparently these people have an inability to deal with the situation as
much as I do. Maybe it's like homosexuality was 20 years ago. Religion and
political doctrines prevail, and bring a standstill.

Talking about feelings is not a popular subject in this country; it's not
good for business. If you're not watching your p's and q's, you're scaring people off, and that's not healthy. But, in order to get by, that's what you have
to do. And, abortion is right at the crux of that. When it is talked about, it
is religious or political, but I haven't seen people get into their feelings on
TV or in public.

This is America to me. I'm not real happy about it, and hopefully, by the
time I'm forty, I'll be able to live closer to feeling what I am and coping with
things the way they are. This issue brings up everything. I can't help it. We
are not conditioned to have our feelings freely.

I'm in therapy, which has helped me deal in a more mature fashion during this second time. But I'm too scared to deal with having a child to even
think about it. It's easy to pretend with my nieces for two or three hours.

I did not want to have the child either time. Whether that means in those
situations or ever, I don't know, but I did not want it either time. Both times
it was carelessness: mine in the first relationship, hers in the second one. I
never talked with anyone else, maybe a friend or two, but not over the decision.

Maybe my guilt comes from having to admit that I didn't want the kid.
And, you're supposed to want them. I think of myself as a child sometimes.
Maybe the guilt comes from my small-town type background and my inability to accept my feelings that I don't want children. We had a Donna Reed
kind of family.

Maybe when my career solidifies, the rest, children, will fall into place.
I love children too much to involve them in this.

Notes

1. Judith G. Smetana. *Concepts of Self and Morality: Women's Reasoning about Abortion*, p. 9. New York: Praeger, 1982. "...thinking about abortion is structured by conceptions of self, society, and morality, and reasoning and decision-making about abortion should be considered in terms of an individual's understanding of these issues."

2. Mark Randall Smith, "How Men Who Accompany Women to an Abortion Service Perceive the Impact of Abortion Upon Their Relationship and Themselves," op. cit., p. 146.

3. Michael C. Finley, op. cit., p. 2; see Chapter 8 of this book, "Feedback from 521 Client-Partners," by Peter Zelles.

4. Studs Terkel. *Working*, Chapter XI. New York: Pantheon, 1974.

5. Finley, *op. cit.*, p. 4; June Hill-Falkenthal, "Counseling Needs of Men About Abortion," op. cit., p. 21.

6. Eleanor Smith. "Counseling Men About Abortion." *California Living Magazine*, January 17, 1982, pp. 8–11.

7. Gordon Slovut. "Abortion: The Rationale and Ramifications Involve Men, Too." *Minneapolis Star and Tribune*, May 16, 1982, pp. 1-F, 4-F.

Chapter 5

Black Men Who Wait

I find myself suddenly in the world and I recognize that I have one right alone: that of demanding human behavior from the other.

Fanon, Frantz, and Charles L. Markmann, *Black Skin, White Masks* (New York: Grove, 1967, p. 7.)

The men who do stick around are sometimes suspended between helpless rage at the destruction of part of themselves and fumbling attempts to be supportive. And since abortion is supposedly a 'solution,' many men and women seem doubly mystified by the depth of their emotions.

Lindsy Van Gelder, "Shades of Gray" (*The Nation*, April 15, 1978, p. 440).

As sparse, uneven, and dated as is the literature on Caucasians caught in the abortion drama, it is even less adequate where America's nonwhite minorities are concerned. Native Americans, Hispanics, and Asian Americans are hardly represented at all, though a steadily growing (small) body of literature focuses on black women and black teenagers (commonly the female).

National opinion surveys over the years have documented less support for abortion from black than from white respondents.[1] At the same time black women, who make up 12% of all American women, account for 34% of all abortions (a rate twice that of whites).[2] Some commentators, therefore, argue actions here speak far more realistically than do opinion poll data; that is,

> ...by enabling blacks to avert what must have been a substantial number of unwanted births, and thereby to reproduce at a rate more compatible...with the well-being of the family unit, abortion may rank as one of the great social equalizers of our times.[3]

Others, of course, strongly disagree. Diatribes against abortion from the most religious, least educated, and most rural sectors keep the topic fiercely controversial within the black community.[4]

Our small contribution to the subject takes the form of questionnaire data from 100 black males who completed our survey in 30 clinics across 18 states. The number, of course, is too small for elaborate, multicell analysis, and, as nothing is known of the universe of all such men, *no* claim of representativeness is made or should be inferred. Instead, as before in the case of both abortion detractors and serial aborters, we offer our material for its intrinsic interest *and* to possibly whet the appetite of some future researcher.

In terms of the standard demographic variables, our 100 black respondents tended to be older (27% were 31 or over, versus 17% of the whites) and, consistent with this, were more often presently or previously married (53% versus 39%). While far more were Protestant than were Catholic (65%/12% versus 43%/35% for whites), this seemed to reflect a prevailing religious distribution among all black Americans, rather than any distinction of our men. Quite striking, however, was the considerable religiosity of the black men: 78% thought themselves "very" or "somewhat" religious, as opposed to only 57% of the white males (see Table 5-1).

**Table 5-1. Characteristics of Black versus White Clinic Males:
Demographic Data**

	Black Males (N = 100)	White Males*
Age (N = 944)		
21 or younger	26%	36%
22–30	48	47
31 or older	27	17
Marital Status (N = 935)		
Single	47%	61%
Married or living together	37	29
Previously married	16	10
Religion (N = 877)		
Protestant	65%	43%
Catholic	12	35
Jewish	1	2
Other	8	4
None	14	15
Religiosity (N = 918)		
Very	41%	18%
Somewhat	37	48
Not very	12	20
Not at all	11	14
Education (N = 874)		
No H.S. diploma	11%	10%
H.S. graduate	52	44
Some college	24	27
College graduate	13	19
Social Class (N = 741; self-reported)		
Upper	4%	0%
Upper middle	14	3
Middle	73	80
Lower middle	8	12
Lower	2	5

Note: N = ca. 900; varies by item.

It was in the realm of attitudes that religiosity became seem-ingly more relevant. Considerable misgivings about the develop-ment of the fetus set the two racial groups apart: Whereas only 18% of the white males believed the fetus was a human being at conception, 37% of the black males concurred. And, while 16% of the whites thought childbirth alone conferred personhood, only 9% of the black men agreed. Not surprisingly, therefore, while only 25% of the whites thought abortion was the killing of a child, the figure rose to 48% of the black respondents, who nevertheless had a higher incidence of repeat involvement with abortion (36% were repeaters as compared to 23% of the white men).

Related here was survey evidence of considerable pro-family conservatism on the part of the black men:

- Whereas only 7% of the white males thought living together was immoral, 16% of the blacks labeled it so.

- Whereas only 24% of the white males thought a female under 18 years of age should have to notify her parents before she could have an abortion, 40% of the blacks concurred.

- Whereas 50% of the white males felt a man should be required to pay child support if a woman had refused his request that she have an abortion, 66% of blacks concurred.

This conservatism did not extend to financial aid questions, at least not where accepting government support was concerned:

- Some 66% of the black males, but only 50% of the whites, be-lieved government funds should be provided to help poor women pay the cost of an abortion.

As well, moral conservatism here was apparently compatible with urging single parenthood (as did 42% of the blacks and 23% of the whites), and not contributing to the cost of the abortion (as was true of 13% of the blacks but only 8% of the whites).

Especially striking were black male misgivings about abortion-warranting circumstances, as presented in Table 5-3.

In only two cases did black men show more support than the white men, the case of approving a legal abortion when the par-ents of a pregnant minor female want the termination (40% vs.

Table 5-2. Moral Attitudes of Clinic Males; by Race

Which of the following are *morally* wrong?	Black Males ($N = 100$)	White Males ($N = 900$)
Homosexuality	69%	62%
Use of hard drugs	66	59
Sex before age 16	35	31
Pornographic movies	24	24
Smoking marijuana	27	21
Abortion	24	16
Living with someone of the opposite sex	16	7
Sex between two single persons	10	6

30%), and the case involving preference for the gender of a fetus (15% to 13%), for an average of 12% lower support in 15 of 17 cases.

Given this across-the-board hesitation about the grounds for a "respectable" abortion, it follows that slightly more blacks than whites (24% vs. 16%) thought the entire matter "morally wrong." Only 30% recalled recommending an abortion as the "least-worst" response to this particular unwanted pregnancy, while 46% of the white males had such a recollection. When asked if abortion was the killing of a child, some 48% concurred, in contrast to only 23% of the white group. Therefore, when asked their stand on a proposed law to declare that human life begins at conception, a law that would make abortion a crime of murder, the two racial groups moved quite apart:

	Black	White
Favor	20%	8%
Oppose	62	86
No Opinion	17	6

Table 5-3. Clinic Male Views of Abortion Criteria; by Race

"Under what circumstances, if any, do you feel that a woman should be able to obtain a legal abortion?"	Black Males ($N = 100$)	White Males ($N = 900$
1. If the female's health is put at risk	87%	92%
2. If the couple cannot support a child	81	83
3. If the pregnancy may cause the female mental harm	76	80
4. If the fetus has serious generate defects	65	83
5. If the pregnancy is the result of incest	64	82
6. If, for any reason, the couple wants the abortion	56	66
7. If the female wants the abortion	55	62
8. If the couple already has as many children as they want	55	61
9. If the pregnancy is the result of a "one night stand"	54	71

10. If the female is physically handi-capped	53	66
11. If this pregnancy may cause a mar-ital breakdown	46	58
12. If the female is a pregnant unmar-ried teenager	42	65
13. If the parents of this pregnant mi-nor female want the abortion	40	30
14. If the couple has just ended their relationship	24	51
15. If the couple is on the verge of breaking up	24	39
16. If, for any rea-son, the male wants the abortion	15	19
17. If tests reveal that the sex of the fe-tus is not what the prospective parents want at this time	15	13

A revealing hint of ambivalence and distress was evidenced by the fact that 23% of the white males, compared to 36% of the black males, had been involved in one or more previous abortions. At the same time, only 23% of the whites, but 42% of the black men, recalled trying to persuade their lovers to have the baby as a single mother (with full assurance of his financial support for the child's rearing).[5]

A black respondent of ours shed additional light with these embittered words:

...this one girl I met a year ago popped up pregnant, and I didn't mind. But she was going to school. She got an abortion in March. I'm still messing around with her, but I really didn't like the idea of the abortion. Because to me that's a little baby that never had a chance to do nothing.

I know a lot of people who are against it, but that's the way it went...Her mother didn't like the idea. I didn't like the idea. I tried to find a way to stop her from doing it, you know. I'm not married to her, so she just did what she wanted to do....

A couple of my friends told me their girls were talking about getting abortions, but they changed their minds real quick. The guys said, "That's part of me, and if you think you're going to rip out part of me and throw it in the garbage, you might as well jump in there with it! If you didn't want to get pregnant, you should never have gone to bed in the beginning!" Now, one guy has got a baby, and the other has one on the way. The girls are on welfare, and the guys are living with them.

As for himself, the young man was incredulous about certain female behavior after the procedure:

The girls think it ain't nothing, like changing a pair of socks. Go away, come back three hours later, "Hey, party time!" The only thing—they may bleed for a couple of weeks. After that, so what? Still go out there and party. Well, it's no party, and it shouldn't be thought of like that. It's supposed to be a serious matter. That's one little life that's not gonna see nothing....As far as I'm concerned, they can take abortion and make it a capital offense, because I think they take it too lightly.

Should any of his lovers ever again tell him of a pregnancy of hers that she wants to terminate, he will repeat his previous insistence on raising the child alone by himself, if necessary. Or, possibly, do worse: "Sometimes, when I'm with Trudy now, I feel like punching the hell out of her. That's what I feel like doing."

Alongside the three leading interracial differences in attitudes—moral conservatism, abortion misgivings, and the questioning of certain female attitudes—there was *much* the men shared in common. Both agreed, for example, about the considerable say husbands and unwed men should have in the abortion decision. They agreed that men should be offered counseling, and should

be taught more about birth control. They even had a matching record as abortion cost supporters (53% of the black males and 56%
of the whites paid all costs). They agreed that men did not have
an easy time of it and, generally, had disturbing thoughts about
the abortion afterwards. They agreed about the impact on their
fatherhood notions and their thoughts about the fetus. As might
therefore be expected, over 90% of both races declared their intention to be better contraceptors in the future (91% of the blacks,
96% of the whites).

Summary

All things considered, the 100 black waiting room men who
cooperated with our research sketched a picture of themselves as
more moralistic, traditional, abortion-leery, fetus-concerned,
pronatalist, and solemn than the whites sitting alongside of them.
Given the high use of abortion being made by black females, the
picture suggests a one-sided "cultural lag" on the male's part:
Many appear to resent the "take charge" assertiveness of "modern" females increasingly reluctant to bear and rear more children
than makes sense to them.[6] While much more research is required before this hunch can be validated, the black men who wait
seem to bring more ambivalence and regret to their vigil than appears wise, healthy, or desirable for anyone.

PROFILE

Darryl, a 28-year-old black man, has a B.S. from a southern black college
of national reputation. He is single, and claims strong personal religious feelings. Employed as a publicity and public relations/media agent in Washington, D.C., he is an abortion repeater, a fact that has changed his attitude toward abortion and his involvement in any future abortions.

Darryl:

The first abortion was with Ravina. It was a steady relationship in college. We were exclusively going out with each other. I was a junior in 1976.
We had a good relationship. We sort of played around with rhythm, rubbers,
and a diaphragm. You know, it was something like . . . "It's okay," or "I think
it's okay," and on extreme occasions, "I *hope* it's okay." We had a steady
sex life; looking back on it, I think about how good it was.

She said, "I think I might be pregnant." We looked at the calendar, and
I could remember when it was and that we blew it. I'm a partner kind of guy,

but I guess I feel that the woman is a more responsible person. If it were my body, I'd be damned sure about what happened to it. So, she got pregnant.

I had known her feelings about abortion—that she would have an abortion if she got pregnant, that she would not have a child with me. That's been important in my subsequent relationships. My sexual activity is profoundly influenced by the woman's feelings about abortion and, more specifically, having *my* babies.

Some women are pro- or antiabortion, but when pregnancy happens, they change their minds. If I met a woman and she was willing to have my kid, and there were no contraceptive devices, I'd say forget it. Because slip-ups like this have happened to me—a lot.

In the beginning I trusted women a lot for knowing their bodies—when they would or could get pregnant. I just fully trusted them. But there were two abortions with Ravina within one year and they really profoundly changed that.

Then I picked up a woman in a Bermuda club. She was really obnoxious, but I pursued her and during sex I asked her if she were protected . . . and she said, "No." Everything was great, but when she said "No," I just stopped. Later I learned that she was ready and willing to have my child if something happened. She was 34, married, and she told me I looked enough like her husband to get away with the kid. I started suspecting that some women didn't think like I did.

Another woman, mother of three, assured me she'd had her tubes tied. But . . . SURPRISE, I was the one in 64,000 chances that made it through. She was happy and wanted me to be happy about it, but I want to consciously choose the mother of my child, and she was one of the last I'd choose for that.

With Ravina I was involved, supportive. It's theoretically half my fault. As a man I don't feel it's right for me to say it's more than half her fault, but if I were a woman—got it—a woman, I'd *feel* more than half responsible because it would be my body going through the changes.

She went away for the first abortion. She didn't seem to go through many changes. There were no complications. It seemed pretty routine from my viewpoint. We talked about what the kid would look like, but it wasn't a heavily emotional scene.

The second one was juicier. I was in the clinic while it was happening. It was more painful for her emotionally and physically. It was emotionally painful for me, but I didn't know until later. And, I was embarrassed that her mother knew about both times. I was uneasy about seeing her. I felt some guilt and shame. I didn't hide, I didn't feel like we were killing, but we blew it . . . an unwanted pregnancy.

We were in a New York hotel. I was upset that she had had pain, that she'd gotten pregnant, that we couldn't have sex, that we'd gone through another abortion. I wanted my healthy partner, not her painfully doubled over and crying, and I was mad at myself for feeling like that. I was ranting and raving around the room. I threw some things. The frustration was too much. I didn't blame her, I was just pissed off at the situation.

I didn't want to become a father. I thought about it abstractly, but any of that fatherhood thing was about the future, not right then. Those normal thoughts every man has about fatherhood were brought to focus, but not directed to RIGHT NOW. Was I ready to be a father? No, so let's have an abortion.

More recently, I was involved with a very steady partner, lots of sex, good relationship, but relatively new and exclusive. Diaphragm a lot; she didn't care for prophylactics. She's older than me, five years. She decided when she was young that she never wanted children and had mentioned it to me. I knew her feelings on abortion, which were that if she got pregnant, she'd have one.

"Darling, I'm pregnant." What a pain in the ass. I visited her in the hospital because she was also having a tubal. I was supportive. Things were fine. We waited the five weeks to resume sex. There was a decided lack of interest on her part after the first time, and it got worse. So, that's how the abortion/tubal affected her, but I contend that it's regret over the tubal which was really brought about by my getting her pregnant and causing the abortion. It has led to a separation of sorts, even though we're still "in love."

It took months, but I'm now feeling guilty about the tubal, for which she now blames me. Maybe she really wanted kids. I began to think about abortion. I feel stupid, irresponsible. Moral things are beginning to come into play.

I think if I'd had the first kid, it would be ten years old, running and playing. I'm not losing sleep, but I definitely think about those things. This last one made me think about abortion on a moral level. I feel responsible about being part of a woman not being able to have kids, and that has led me to consider abortion as a more moral issue.

It started out as a convenience. No pain for me. But as it went on I thought about what could have been—a baby—a child. I've changed in some other ways. When does life begin? I used to think that when you scraped that stuff out, it wasn't life and it may have been some occult belief [I had] that it didn't begin until the cord was cut. I believed the soul hadn't entered that body. To some extent I feel the same, but I think about the possibilities . . . if no abortion. There *will be* a human being, a person.

My main view, maybe a way of not dealing with the issue, and my new feelings, is to just *not* get a woman pregnant. It's a cautious viewpoint. Now, I don't want to go through an abortion again.

Contraception stops life from beginning, so does abstention, so does abortion. There are two extremes, neither acceptable to me. Abstention and abortion. That means I have to practice contraception, including abstention at particularly fertile periods.

I've concluded I have potent sperm, since it's happened with birth control. I guess I've begun to feel my seed was important and I didn't want to waste it on just anyone. I feel equally responsible in any case.

Being a parent is a very responsible deal. In the old days, you saw a woman you were attracted to and courted her, trying to get away with what you could. My folks were young when they married. They made love, and the first pregnancy was the first kid. That didn't mean they were ready. I think most babies are mistakes, even though they are wanted.

It's an incredible responsibility—beyond basic food and shelter support. The stuff that's really hard is listening to the kid, talking with the kid, making personal sacrifices. The whole abortion experience has made this more important to me. It's made me think about kids, and parenthood, about effort and time.

Notes

1. See, for example, Dennis S. Meleti and Larry D. Barnett, "Nine Demographic Factors and Their Relationship to Attitudes toward Abortion Legalization." *Social Biology* 19 (1972): 43–50; Lucky M. Tedrow and E. R. Mahoney, "Trends in Attitudes toward Abortion: 1972–1976." *Public Opinion Quarterly* (1979): 181–189; Helen R. Ebaugh and C. Allen Haney, "Shifts in Abortion Attitudes: 1972–1978." *Journal of Marriage and the Family* (August 1980): 491–499.

2. "The nonwhite abortion rate is more than twice the white rate because nonwhites have more unintended pregnancies. When faced with an unintended pregnancy, however, nonwhites choose abortion only slightly more often than whites. In spite of their higher abortion rate, nonwhites have a fertility rate 37 percent higher than that of whites." Stanley K. Henshaw and Kevin O'Reilly. "Characteristics of Abortion Patients in the United States, 1979 and 1980." *Family Planning Perspectives*, 15 (1, January/February 1983): 5.

3. M. J. Kramer. "Legal Abortion Among New York City Residents: An Analysis According to Socioeconomic and Demographic Characteristics." *Family Planning Perspectives*, 7 (1975): 135. See also James M. Robbins, "Out-of-Wedlock Abortion and Delivery: The Importance of the Male Partner," *Social Problems*, 31 (February 1984): 334–350.

4. Michael W. Coombs and Susan Welch. "Blacks, Whites, and Attitudes Toward Abortion." *Public Opinion Quarterly* 46 (4, 1982): 510–520.

5. Striking in this connection was the fact that 77% of the white males, but only 57% of the blacks, felt they presently knew all they needed to about the costs of the abortion.

6. For a current account of differing viewpoints on abortion among lower middle-class black teenagers, see Daniel B. Frank, *Deep Blue Funk and Other Stories: Portrait of Teenage Parents*. Chicago: University of Chicago Press, 1983. See also Michael B. Bracken, Lorraine V. Klerman, and Maryann Bracken, "Abortion, Adoption, of Motherhood: An Empirical Study of Decision-Making during Pregnancy." *American Journal of Obstetrics and Gynecology* 130 (3, February 1, 1978): 251–262; Eugene Vadies and Darryl Hale, "Attitudes of Adolescent Males toward Abortion, Contraception, and Sexuality." *Social Work in Health Care*, 3(2, Winter 1977): 169–173; Raye H. Rosen and Lois J. Martindale, "Sex Role Perceptions and the Abortion Decision," *Journal of Sex Research* 14 (November 1978): 231–245.

Chapter 6

Abortion Aftermath

The day we had it done, we went 150 miles. So no one would know. On the way home it became a relief. The stress and arguments stopped, and things have just been getting better since.... There were some hard feelings right afterwards. For two weeks we didn't say much, pretended it didn't happen. We've gotten married, and are now trying to have a baby.

> 24-year-old, married, factory worker

Now, I saw her once for dinner, and she seemed to have resolved it all, made her peace with it. But she never asked nothing about *my* feelings! It was selfish on her part, as she never considered *me* now....

The abortion was *such* a stressful matter that it just brought us to leaving each other when it was over. There just wasn't anything left....

> 24-year-old, single, college student

As we have seen, the time leading up to and including the day of the abortion is fraught with challenge. But what happens later? How does the abortion affect the men and the relationship of the couples? How many of the men revert to a macho, unsupportive role? How many continue to think about the fetus? About their lost opportunity for fatherhood? Or, other clinic day stressors? How do men process and live with this unique experience? How do they seem changed by it? Does abortion maim, and how do men attempt to mend its wounds? Above all, what does their example suggest about helping other men better cope with it?

Fortunately, over the course of the 2 years that we researched material for this book, 75 men outside of our 1,000 waiting room group learned about our project and volunteered to tell us (via our questionnaire) about their abortion experience of months, and often years earlier. Gary McLouth was able to interview a small number, and excerpts from these sessions lend much helpful detail to the discussion below. Thanks also to the cooperation we have had throughout from counselor Peter Zelles (a contributor to Chapter 8), we have information from his 50 follow-up phone interviews with former waiting room men (Midwest Women's Clinic, Minneapolis, Minnesota).

Even with our 75 surveys and Peter's 50 phone interviews, the total is still far too small to sustain any claim of generalizability. Moreover, our 75 men are *not* a random sample of the 1,000 respondents. We therefore strongly urge readers *not* to leap to conclusions on the basis of our sketchy material. We share it for its intrinsic interest and its value to future researchers.

Abortion Veterans

As our 75 volunteers were reflecting back on abortion experiences that had occurred months or even years earlier, they were older, on the average than our clinic day men: 39% were 36 years of age or older, as compared to only 8% of the larger sample. In keeping with this age difference, the veterans had much more schooling (43% had a college degree or better, as compared to only 18% of the larger group). Finally, while matched fairly evenly in race and religious distribution, the older, better-educated veterans judged their religious beliefs less important than did their clinic day counterparts: Only 46% of the former indicated "very" or "somewhat important," versus 67% of the men filling out a questionnaire at the abortion clinic.

Given these demographic variables, how did the 75 veterans sum up their abortion experiences?

Abortion Impact: Relationship

On clinic day, 47% of our 1,000 men could not tell how the situation was changing their relationship. By the time we caught up with 75 *different* men long after their own clinic day, much of the mystery had cleared up—and only 27% of these men were still uncertain. All the shift, however, seems to have been in a negative direction. While 30% felt the abortion had helped bring the relationship closer together (see Table 6-1), and 18% felt it had made no difference, 25% blamed it for contributing to the end of the relationship (as did 20% of Zelles' 50-man group, of whom only 10% claimed any improvement traceable to the abortion encounter).[1]

Unexpected guilt and remorse sometimes became too much to endure: the abandoning of the relationship may have brought relief from tension, or escape from a partner who reminded one of things better forgotten. For example, the isolation felt by a male

Table 6-1. Comparison of Expectation of, and Actual Experience of Abortion Impact

"How is having the abortion influencing this relationship?"	Clinic Day Men (1,000)	Postabortion Men (75)
Do not know at this time	47%	27%
Helping to bring us closer together	31	30
Makes no difference	19	18
Contributing to our breakup	3	25

unable to really communicate his feelings, though still acting supportive, was too much for a single, 24-year-old male:

> The abortion was *such* a stressful matter that it just brought us to
> leaving each other when it was over. There wasn't anything left. . . .
> I felt very guilty about it, and angry that I wasn't supported by the
> girl, and she did not know how *I* felt, that she would not carry out
> any decision of mine. You can't win if the odds are totally against
> you, and the rules are constantly changing.

This relationship did not suffer from a lack of sensitivity and emotion, but from the man's inability to express himself and from his
unmet need for guidance and attention. We heard variations on
this theme repeatedly—from comparably frustrated males.

A black 29-year-old industrial designer, whose relationship
eventually broke up, believed the feelings he and his girlfriend
withheld from each other contributed to their separation:

> If the two of us had been more verbal in what we were feeling in-
> stead of me feeling sorry and sad for her, it would have been bet-
> ter for both of us, then and later.

When such couples went through bench-mark experiences in self-
willed isolation, there was little likelihood of the mutual growth
which could have helped them continue their relationship.

A young New Jersey college junior we interviewed, for example, vowed to keep the abortion a secret. The couple had dated
since high school and had developed a close relationship in which
joint decision making played a major role:

> For weeks after, she got all of my attention! I felt I owed it to her
> to be caring in any way I could. Nevertheless, after another year,
> we broke up, only to keep the vow of not telling anybody about it.

> After a few months, I began feeling very guilty about what hap-
> pened. I needed to talk, but I couldn't. I needed to let out steam,
> but the fear of letting someone in on the secret stopped me.

> My ex-girlfriend didn't want to talk about it, let alone talk to me.
> I taunted myself on why I paid money to kill something that was
> part of me.

> I guess the old adage "time heals all wounds" works along with
> helping to understand. My own research on others helped me com-

prehend my/our decision making. It doesn't help get back the dignity and pride I felt, or the girl I shared this with.

This kind of soul searching was typical, especially by the young men whose relationships ended.

Another source of bitterness concerned the problems posed for males by the female's new fear of sex. A director of services at a White Plains, New York clinic observed that when she speaks with patients about birth control, "they often regret it, insisting 'I'll never have sex again.'" Easily intimidated by, and quick to accommodate such misgivings, many of the men we interviewed remembered long periods of celibacy and considerable difficulty reclaiming the "joy of sex," they associated with the preabortion phase of the relationship.[2]

Abortion Impact: Fatherhood Lost

Far more complex was unraveling how these abortion veterans now felt about the child that had not been born, and about their lost opportunity at fatherhood, as sketched in this interview excerpt:

Guess that's my lasting impression...here's this kid of mine that didn't have a chance because the mother thought, "I'll get money from the father, my parents won't change my life any. Quick and easy way to do it."...My main thought on the whole issue is that the women I know—there's an attitude that it's an accident and you repair accidents.... My kid never had a chance.

This 27-year-old carpenter's two-year relationship broke up, even though he had assumed they were headed toward marriage. He felt he had agreed to the abortion because it was "her body," and there wasn't anything he could really do about it. Afterward, he could not maintain his love for her, though he hadn't replaced her despite three years of separation. It was the unborn "kid" that remained the focus of his reflections, and he could not totally separate his feelings of fatherhood lost from his girlfriend's decision to abort.

A lingering malaise concerning fatherhood's end was mentioned in our interviews by a very small number of men, though only future, deep-reaching research will take the full measure of this. Certain psychiatrists argue that the image an expectant father gains of himself as "father" never leaves that person, even if a medical act like an abortion ends the new life in utero:

> Whether or not the creator-father continues as parent, indeed, his part in the creation of a new life signifies an elemental reality which no legal, social, or medical act (such as abortion) can truly alter.... It is the biological act which sets in motion the forces that will in time alter consciousness, self-perception, and even attitudes toward the outside world.[3]

While more is steadily being learned about the "pregnant male," his opposite brother, the suddenly "unpregnant male," remains much of a mystery, although strong feelings that have been stirred up in an expectant father may not shut down with an abrupt end to the actual pregnancy.

Some support for this notion was found in the remarkable persistence of certain (though not all) mental ties to what might have been, as shown in Table 6-2. While the intensity of fetus imagery seems to fade over time, related attitudes do not, and the frequency of "occasional" thoughts about the fetus remain unchanged.

Men who volunteered comments here seemed more moved by the topic than the cold statistics above begin to suggest:

> Sometimes I regret it. I have friends who have young or infant children, and when I go there, I kind of regret it. Maybe you love kids when they're someone else's....

> I personally really love kids, so it was kind of rough for me.... So, I kind of always wonder what kind of kid would this have been.

> Now, often, I wonder what the baby might have been like. And for awhile after I thought about asking her if she wanted to try it all over again. We broke up about six months after it....

Other researchers have found similar memories:

> Yeah, I still think about it. Not often, but sometimes.... My brother and his wife are having a baby in the next few months, and that brings it to mind—they're having a kid, I'm not.

> I didn't think about what was happening in concrete terms like 'This is my son,' and I knew abortion was the only possible solu-

Table 6-2. Comparison of Fetus Imagery, During and After an Abortion Experience

	Clinic Day Men (1,000)	Postabortion Men (75)
1. Have occasional thoughts about fetus	52%	60%
2. A fetus becomes a human being at conception	20	18
—at birth	15	13
—cannot be determined	25	28
3. Agree that abortion is the killing of child:	26	23
disagree with this—	42	61
4. Feel the abortion has not especially influenced my ideas about fatherhood	58	56
5. Have no thoughts about the fetus	19	31
6. Have frequent thoughts about the fetus	29	9
7. Were these thoughts generally—		
sad	21	21
curious	35	31
troublesome	25	10
8. Believe that abortion is morally wrong	17	18

tion. But I still thought, What a shame! This is the combination of her and me.... It could be such a beautiful child....[4]

We heard, over and again, of day and night dreams of the child that wasn't born, and about fantasies of their adequacy as new fathers—though all emphasized the effort they made to consciously control these mental maladventures.

Abortion Impact: Male-Female Ties

Unfortunately, in several cases, persistent, and even growing anger focused on the collaborator in the abortion, a woman some men were now seeing in a very different light:

> I'm angry toward her for manipulating us around the issue. Her main focus was anger toward me, and not the fetus. (25, single, artist)

> Our relationship has deteriorated a little. It's different.... Maybe we grew together as people, but grew apart as lovers. We never had problems communicating. But, we now don't see as much of each other, and our physical relationship has totally stopped until we see how things work out for awhile. We just had to stop and reevaluate where we were in our lives, and see what we wanted for the future. (31, divorced, businessman)

> We didn't discuss it except for one argument over the expense of the abortion.... I felt like a chunk of me was going at the time.... I would have been happy with the kid, but she had the final say.... We were still arguing over the clinic this week, how much it bothered me. It might have been the only thing to slow me down from drugs, having the baby. She's under the impression that it didn't bother me, but it did, more than her, I think. (24, single, musician)

Other veterans spoke with barely controlled anger or grief about the source of conception ("She was trying to trap me into marriage."), the power ratio in decision making ("She was strong-willed; I had no say at all."), and the post-mortem ever since ("She now claims I forced the whole matter; she cries a lot and insists I made her do it.").

Some, of course, rued the loss of love and deeply missed their partner:

> I have regrets about everything. Not the abortion itself, but what

it did to our relationship. We'd never had to deal with any realities prior to it—we were students; our biggest problem was where
to go for dinner. Afterward, there was a loss of freedom. We were
more—I guess the word is—sober. After the abortion, there was no
way that relationship was going to work. That's what makes me
so sad, because I think in many ways it was the nicest one I'll ever
have.[5]

These were men especially set back by the entire experience, and
many dwelled on their multiple losses (the affair, the woman, the
unborn child, the sense of being able to manage their lives).

Even with a considerable amount of questioning of the part
their sex partner played, the veterans gave even *less* support to
male parity than had clinic day men (see Table 6-3). Abortion veterans appeared far less intrigued than did men who wait with
claiming an equal share in decision-making responsibility. This is
a curious finding that suggests time operates to dilute a clinic-day
preoccupation with matters of parity and powerlessness. Abortion
veterans, in short, deferred more than before to the female's he-
gemony over the couple's behavior, preoccupied as they seemed
to be with licking other wounds.

Abortion Impact: Contraception Plans

Given the many stressors noted to this point, it was not surprising to find that veterans were intent on avoiding any repeat experiences; e.g.,

> I'm not going to let it happen twice. If pregnancy happens again,
> we'll keep it. I don't want to go through another one, because I
> don't like the idea of abortion.

> If I had to do it all over again, I wouldn't be such a stupid, clumsy
> lover. Damn, but we were innocent.

> If I was to get there again, it would depend on who it was, and the
> quality of love between us. I would not let her have an abortion,
> as I definitely want to have a child, and I would care for it...if she
> would not marry me. As long as it was someone I loved, I would
> oppose another abortion. If it was a playmate, I would probably go
> along, as the fetus is not the issue. If we just enjoyed each other
> in bed, the abortion would not be a problem.

As many as 83% of the veterans (versus 67% of the clinic day men)
felt those who wait should be offered counseling and/or education

Table 6-3. Comparison of Views on Power Allocation
and Prenotification, During and After an Abortion Experience

	Clinic Day Men (1,000)	Postabortion Men (75)
Husband should have as much say as his wife	80%	53%
Unwed male should have as much say as lover in abortion decision	58	38
Wife should go ahead and have abortion even if husband opposes	59	64
Clinics should be required to notify a husband before performing an abortion on his wife	56	36
Men should be consulted under the law before a woman decides to have an abortion	66	50

about abortion and contraception. Some 88% of the followup men
(and 93% of the clinic day men) insisted they would be or were
now more careful about risking pregnancy than ever before.

A few actually went for irreversible birth control, as did three
of Zelles' 50 men who had vasectomies, the choice of 42% of
11,600,000 couples who now rely on sterilization (this technique
has only recently pushed the pill out of first place as America's
leading birth control method).[6] Typical of explanations for taking

this emphatic step was one offered by a middle-aged gynecologist, a father of three, whose wife had a diaphragm "failure":

> I had always said I was pro-choice in principle, but that I was ambivalent personally about abortion. When we learned she was pregnant, it took both of us 28 seconds to become unambivalent. She had the abortion. No regrets. I went to a urologist the next day and had a vasectomy. Let me tell you, it is a lot better than a diaphragm.[7]

Other men with whom Gary McLouth spoke also expressed some interest in this possibility, though most hesitated in deference to its awesome finality.

Abortion Impact: Political Preference

Vital in this connection is the fact that, regardless of their personal problems as a troubled individual and/or member of a troubled relationship, the postabortion men remained as *pro-choice* as our clinic day bloc had ever been (see Table 6-4). Only 18% of the postabortion men (and 17% of the clinic-day men) finally judged abortion an immoral act—a constancy in ethical reflection *and* political partisanship that suggests postabortion males can be counted on by the pro-choice forces. Having been there, and knowing of what they speak, they told us they supported the availability of legal, safe, and affordable pregnancy termination procedures. This by no means minimizes the "dues" many felt they had personally paid for their share in an abortion experience (see Table 6-5). Little wonder, then, that a 27-year-old investment banker explained to Gary, "There's a sense of sadness about the whole thing. This woman I love is going to carry a scar deep inside for who knows how long. A sense of relief or satisfaction doesn't even apply to me."

Abortion Aftermath Analysis

Given the absence of *any* social science literature here, we appreciate the insights available from the steadily growing reflective literature on men and their maturation challenges. Poet Robert Bly, for example, offers insights into the relevant confusion of many young men he has been meeting:

Table 6-4. Comparison of Views on Pro- and Anti-Choice Policy
Options, During and After an Abortion Experience

	Clinic Day Men (1,000)	Postabortion Men (75)
Oppose a law to make abortion a crime of murder	83%	88%
Expect abortion to be made illegal in next five years	19	11
Support abortion if the female wants it, for whatever reason	62	61
Support abortion if the couple wants it, for whatever reason	65	67

Part of their grief was a remoteness from their fathers, which they felt keenly, but in part, too, came from trouble in their marriages or relationships. They had learned to be receptive, and it wasn't enough to carry their marriages. In every relationship, something fierce is needed once in awhile; both the men and the women need to have it.

At the point when it was needed, often the young men didn't have it. He was nurturing, but something else was required—for the relationship, for his life. The male was able to say, "I can feel your pain, and I consider your life as important as mine, and I will take care of you and comfort you." But he could not say what *he* wanted, and stick by it; that was a different matter.[8]

Throughout the demands of the abortion experience, the inability of these men to express their viewpoints and feelings was accentuated by the necessity to play a totally supportive role for the women they loved. Yet, they were disappointed in ways neither sex fully understood at the time.

Bly suggests men don't have to hurt someone else in showing their anger, but by repressing their anger, men can seriously

Table 6-5. Comparison of Views on Abortion Impact on Males and Females During and After an Abortion Experience

	Clinic Day Men (1,000)	Postabortion Men (75)
Disagree that males involved in an abortion generally have an easy time of it	68%	75%
Disagree that females involved in an abortion generally have an easy time of it	92	87
Agree that males involved in an abortion generally have disturbing thoughts about it afterwards	47	63

hurt themselves.[9] Ironically, attempts to be supportive in this anger-sublimating way are often ineffective.

Fortunately, not all of the postabortion men took a repressive approach to their feelings and reactions. There were philosophical perspectives and well-resolved male experiences. A 21-year-old college student we interviewed recalled:

> Afterward, naturally, we were much closer than ever before. It was as if we had weathered a crisis, a psychological crisis, together.

> Sometimes, after that, we would talk about what it would have been like to have had the kid. Never the bad sorts of things, only the pleasant, fun sorts of thing, like showing him off. We did not know how we would handle the social stigma, or stuff like that, so we never talked about that.

> She was really worried about the next guy, like maybe her husband, and whether he would mind that she was not a virgin, and

whether she would tell him that she had had an abortion. I tried
to calm her down, and urged her to do what she felt was right in
the circumstance.

A 28-year-old teacher had a particularly sober view of the past two
years:

> ...it certainly made me feel more worldly. And I look back on it,
> just in terms of the raw experimental quality of it; I'm glad it hap-
> pened. It's another thing to experience. That's kind of a cold way
> of looking at it, but I can do that with a lot of my life; I can look
> at it that way.

Similarly, a 33-year-old white-collar worker put it all very starkly:

> I don't find myself scarred from it. It's been reduced to another of
> life's problems. It is now resolved. I have been to Nam, and I know
> the sense of power you get from looking down the barrel and
> deciding on a life. The abortion of a fetus is lower on the scale of
> phenomena. But I no longer use absolutes—"all" or "never." I
> think the controversy over abortion is based on poorly defined ab-
> solutes.

A 30-year-old manager counseled patience:

> The hardest thing is time. It seemed like a day was 58 hours be-
> forehand. The only thing that helps afterward is time. You have to
> do what you think is best at the time, and let time take its course.

A 34-year-old regretted a failure to share:

> Our relationship was never the same. We'd lost something, and
> part of the problem was that we never did get to talk about what
> was happening. Everything was so hush-hush. It was all such a big
> secret that whenever any feelings came up, we didn't have the time
> or the freedom to talk about them.[10]

A 19-year-old construction worker recalled more personal investment, and possibly more personal growth:

> We've often wondered what it would be like right now to be par-
> ents, for me to be a father. I was feeling guilty for awhile.... I'd

done away with something that had been mine. We both felt the same way, but we learned to live with it. If anything, it's brought us that much closer. It was a learning experience. It made us think we should take special precaution.

Every such tale we heard of hard-won intimacy and cooperation (the claim of 30% of the veterans) was a welcomed respite from more common accounts of postabortion estrangement and divisiveness.

Writer Ellen Goodman traces much discontent to opposing sex roles in situations of extreme loss:

> Women mourn, men replace. A gross generalization, generally true, is that men tried to tough it out, while women tried to work it out. Men tended to close the doors behind them, to reject, regret, to try to take a shortcut through grief. Women tended to...mourn.[11]

Such grief, it should be carefully noted, is natural and even healthy, a notion foreign to far too many "uptight" emotion-denying postabortion men. As sociologist James M. Robbins notes, "...mild, time-limited feelings of unhappiness, ambivalence, or regret common to many women after abortion should *not* be mistaken for serious emotional distress."[12]

Bringing it all together as well as any comment we came across was this thought from a 34-year-old man: "I wasn't broken up by the experience. I was saddened, though. Even if you have no set moral or philosophical problems with abortion, it's still taking something away from both of you."[13]

Summary

What difference did the passage of time seem to make? Some things changed very little, if at all:

- Hardly any of the men seemed to alter their attitudes: the vast majority remained pro-choice and eager to see males get birth control schooling. Many, however, also remained troubled by thoughts about the fetus and fatherhood.

- All remained intent on avoiding another abortion.

Other variables changed a great deal:

- Fewer men remained uncertain about the impact of the abortion experience on their relationship.

- More relationships broke up than men had suspected they would when asked on clinic day.

- Fewer men seemed as interested in male parity as they had on clinic day.

- Sex relations and contraception questions caused new stress immediately after the abortion.

Perhaps as cogent a summary statistic as any was the 16% increase in the number of men who felt males generally have disturbing thoughts about it afterwards—a vote from abortion veterans who should know.

As for the critical matter of the impact of an abortion on relationships, our limited data and interview material leads us to believe that outcomes are generally foreshadowed on clinic day by the preabortion quality of the relationship. Professor Michael Bracken of the Yale University School of Medicine, for example, contends that "having an abortion is not going to send a marriage onto the rocks unless that's the course it's already sailing."[14] And counselor Andre Watson adds, "For better or for worse, an abortion brings out the stark, naked truth of a relationship."[15]

All the more vital, therefore, is the provision of sensitive counseling for couples before and during the day of the abortion—if the couples are to steer the course they *really* desire thereafter.

She talked about it so much. I tried to listen, made an effort to be as sympathetic as I could, but eventually I said, "Hey, I'm getting real tired of hearing about this...." I thought I knew all about abortion and I thought it was a real routine procedure—you made the decision, it was done, and everybody went back about their business. Well, maybe that's true medically, but it didn't hit me till afterward that it's also very emotionally distressful. It's real hard on a woman, something that's going to be on her mind for a long time. I'm more sympathetic about that now. Maybe I would have been before if I'd known what to expect.

As quoted in "Abortion: Are Men There When
Women Need Them Most?" Carol Lynn Mithers,
(*Mademoiselle*, April 1981, p. 231).

PROFILE

Pregnancy/abortion decision making forces one to face the future quickly. A relationship can be propelled through what might be characterized as a time warp. One day a couple is tentatively exploring the forms of their fragile togetherness; the next, they are asking themselves questions of posterity, seeking to envision each other as husband and wife, father and mother, from a perspective they barely had clear as boyfriend and girlfriend.

As with other critical life events, an unexpected pregnancy makes extraordinary demands on us, regardless of our readiness or preparedness for its consequences. It can be a highly focused experience. Subconscious thoughts of marriage and parenthood surface, and we take a close look at ourselves and our partners. We feel the pressure of testing, the crucible of change, the pain of growth.

Billy and Shawn discovered common realities facing them in their individual situations, and contrasting results. Billy, only 17, seemed to see his situation as more problematic than had Shawn. The decision of Billy and his girlfriend to have the abortion more accurately reflected their circumstances than did Shawn's. His desperate heartache typifies the remorse and regret of men who have lost relationships, and have also realized abortion was not as easy a solution to their problems as they had hoped.

Billy:
Everything's going fine. We don't talk about it. I think about it once a day. I read about it in the paper and stuff, but it didn't ruin our relationship.

At first, we did it behind our parents' backs. Then we broke down and told her mother and my dad. Luckily, my dad took it all right. My girl had problems telling her mom, but she broke down and did. She had gotten sick because she didn't have her medicine, tetracycline; I think. I'm glad she did tell, because I don't feel as bad. I had a 15-year-old sister who got pregnant, and my folks would have flipped.

Right now, she's on birth control pills, and we don't know after that. I'm going in the service and she's going to college, but it's 50/50 on what will happen. That's two years off.

I thought to myself we'd have to be preparing to have the baby now, but it'd be too early. She's in the eleventh grade. I just graduated. I doubt if we could have handled it. Maybe if she'd graduated with me, we would have. It's not that I would mind doing it—being a father and getting married. In my junior year a lady came in health class and told about pregnancy and options, and a friend went through it, so I knew what was available.

I was scared at the clinic. I didn't talk to anybody. They talked to her. I sat down and waited. I called to set up a date for pregnancy testing and after that, they told me I had to stay out of it.

We discussed what would happen if she got pregnant and so, when it happened, there wasn't any argument or anything. . . . If somebody had come out and talked to me, it would have been better.

I would have gone in if I could have. I wanted to, but they didn't allow it, and she didn't want me to. I figured she would feel more comfortable, but she didn't want me there. I didn't ask why, maybe it was because of clinic policy.

Since then things are better. At the time there was nothing but worry. Our sexual relationship is better now with her on the pill. We were really nice to each other around that time. I took her out a lot. It went a lot better than I thought it would.

I knew what was going on. My sister, who had a baby at 16, was really helpful. She wanted me to have it until I explained everything.

I'm glad that place is there. Grown-ups think that's a horrible thing to do, but it's one person's decision. I'm glad it's there, I don't think it's so bad. I don't know what we would do without it . . . . I'll tell you what; I'll never forget sitting in that clinic for 5 hours. I really learned a lesson.

She's definitely a lot happier on birth control pills. Her cycle is more regular, and generally, things are in A-1 shape, right now. I'm glad you called. It's good to shoot the shit about this.

Shawn:
Horrible. . . . We broke up. Like, after it happened there was nothing between us. She lost her love for me. I don't know why. If it was going to happen or not, I don't know, but things really went down the drain.

Now, I feel we shouldn't have done it. We could have had it even and not gotten married. I didn't have a good job, so we didn't have it. My family is good, upper class. We only talked to her mother and she said, have the abortion. My parents wouldn't have let it happen.

At the time we thought it should be done, but it could have been prevented. I *could* have supported it, but she has a side too. She wanted to finish college. If we would have had the kid, we would have managed, because we come from upper middle class families. My Italian parents would have done well by us, they are against abortion. Hers are divorced, Jewish, and I guess her mother didn't want her daughter to get stuck.

I'm still hurt about it. I know she is, but she doesn't show it that much; but I saw her and she said she'd be three or four months pregnant now. I don't know, I can't figure it out. Before it happened we were in love. Afterwards, it died. I think if I really wanted to, I could have convinced her to have it. Looking back, I wish I had, but who knows? It bums me that it happened.

I haven't talked to anybody about my feelings before this. I want to talk to my mother, but I don't want her to know; she'd flip out. She'd go by her beliefs. I would explain why I did it and everything, but it's over and done with now.

My girl asked what sex it was; they told her, a girl, which hurt even more. I think she's going to have some problems with this too.

Fatherhood? I think about what I'd be doing. It would have changed my life. You know, I could have handled being a father, I could have been strong, but. . . . When this happened, I figured I'd be a man and take it, but afterward it was a different story.

We went through marriage, money, where were we going to live, and everything, and abortion seemed the right thing to do. But now, in my mind, I say, why did I let it happen?

I think she wants to be away from me so I don't remind her of what happened. When she sees me, she gets upset. We were engaged, then we got unengaged, a couple of months later we had the abortion, and now . . . . She took the ring off, but we were still the same. I still think we'll get back.

I'm trying to go out with other women to get some relief. It makes it worse. She's going out with one other guy. There's girls waiting in line to go out with me, but what are they going to get me but sex. I'm still in love with her. We'd been through everything in three years. I'd been addicted to drugs, we'd traveled together, lived together.

We'd done coke and grass and drank at the time she got pregnant, and we were afraid something might be wrong with the fetus, a minor reason not to have the kid (more in her eyes). There are tests to find out and we could have taken them.

It's hard for me to talk, but I've got to do it. I'm an emotional guy. There are friends that don't give a shit. It's programmed in them to think like that, but I don't think they love the women they've gotten pregnant.

If I were to get a woman pregnant on a one-night stand, abortion would be right. With my girlfriend, I loved her, I loved what was inside her.

It still bugs me; it's always going to bug me. I had plans to someday marry this girl and have a family. I'm just trying to cope with it. It's hard, really hard. I'll never forget about it, never. Sometimes I feel like a killer, a killer. . . and I could have changed it.

When you go to the clinic, they should talk to you about what and how you are feeling. A psychologist should talk to the guy to find out if he is making the right decision, to see if he can survive it, like in my case.

I waited for five hours. They didn't talk to me, or counsel **both of us** together. They only asked if we wanted to do this. No discussion. I sensed she wasn't sure either, but we said, yes. It's haunting me now.

I'm even willing to go on TV, that's how involved I am. I think other guys should know what's going on. Put my name anywhere you want. There's other guys doing this and they don't know what they've done. They think they have to.

I didn't like the decision I made. Other guys should look more closely at things. The subject was—was that was our baby and one way or another, I would have worked it out, if I had been counseled the right way, everything would have been brought out in front of her and me.

Men seem to think one way, but deep down inside there's a whole different story. Just take my case. It's such a touchy subject, I'm just trying to live with it.

PROFILE

Doug's anguish reminds us how few young people are prepared for sex relations, let alone for an abortion. His choked-up and subdued voice recalled many confused and lonely stories we heard of boys suddenly plunging into manhood, and into man-sized trouble.

Doug:
The relationship is over. I went to Ohio for a couple of weeks and when I got back she didn't want to see me any more. I want to get back with her, but she doesn't want to take any more chances. . . . I miss her a lot.

I haven't talked to anyone. . . thought about it last night. It had something to do with a TV show. There was a girl going through an abortion and it hurt me.

It hurt me wicked, when she told me she didn't want to see me. I wished I had used protection *all* the time. She's fifteen. . . and I'm seventeen. I'm not ready for fatherhood and I know it. She said if she was pregnant again, she'd keep it.

We got serious pretty quick—before a month. It's all we ever did. She got sick of it being so serious. She didn't want to think she was pregnant all the time. I'd go out with her in a minute.

I'm glad you called; I really needed to talk to somebody. I talked to my 23-year-old cousin about it. Her two abortions were tough, and I talked to my best friend, but he doesn't know what to say. He hasn't done anything with a girl.

She treated me bad so I'd drop her, but I couldn't. Today, I saw her walking and asked her if I could talk with her and we did at her house for two hours, but then, she kicked me out.

Notes

1. ''We've done no official study, but places where we work estimate half the people they see have had their relationships broken up over abortion: men don't know how to handle the situation, so they back

off; the women rightly feel deserted and end the relationship. But if a man is supportive, it reassures the woman that she's not going to be losing the possible baby *and* her boyfriend or husband. They'll see it through together." Former abortion counselor Bruce Rappaport, as quoted in Carol Lynn Mithers, "Abortion: Are Men There When Women Need Them Most?" op. cit., p. 253.

2. As quoted in John Tido, "Men and Abortion." *Hustler*, January 1983, p. 126.

3. Arthur and Libby Colman, *Earth Father, Sky Father: The Changing Concept of Fathering*, pp. 13–14. Englewood Cliffs, N.J.: Prentice-Hall, 1981. "The father's creative act is at the deepest, most unconscious level, impelled by (an) impulse toward immortality...with the possible exception of a commitment to a romantic love relationship, there is no other adult act that will compromise individual identity, change personal goals, transform self-image, shape ongoing experience, and influence future directions so profoundly as becoming a father."

4. As quoted in Mithers, op. cit., p. 231.

5. Ibid., p. 250. "...even a well-established, committed couple can be inadequately prepared for abortion, and the strain may prove too great for an existing bond."

6. Market Facts, "What U.S. Women Think and Do About Contraception." *Family Planning Perspectives*, September 1983, p. 12.

7. As quoted in Gordon Slovut, "Abortion: The Rationale and Ramifications Involve Men, Too," op. cit., p. 4-F.

8. As quoted by Keith Thompson in "What Men Really Want: A *New Age* Interview with Robert Bly." *New Age*, May 1982, p. 33.

9. Ibid., p. 51: "...the ability of a male to shout and to be fierce is *not* the same as treating people like objects...Getting in touch with the wildman means religious life for a man in the broadest sense of the phrase."

10. As quoted in Mithers, op. cit., p. 250.

11. Ellen Goodman, *Close to Home*, p. 127. New York: Fawcett Crest, 1980.

12. James M. Robbins. "Objective versus Subjective Responses to Abortion." *Journal of Consulting and Clinical Psychology*, 16 (1979): 995.

13. As quoted in Mithers, op. cit., p. 231. As far back as 1973 a staffer at the world's largest (legal) clinic estimated that about 70% of the

relationships broke up within a month after the abortion: "This happens either because the relationship is not strong enough to have weathered the storm, or because the reality of the pregnancy and the fear of it happening again acts as an incentive for them to scrutinize the relationship and decide if it is really what they both wanted." Eileen Milling, "World's Largest Abortion Clinic." *Pageant,* July 1973, p. 5.

14. As quoted in Judith Patterson, "Whose Freedom of Choice?," op. cit., p. 43. "Watson thinks conflict over abortion often affects a relationship—and sometimes destroys it." See in this connection, Ellen W. Freeman, "Abortion: Subjective Attitudes and Feelings." *Family Planning Perspectives* 10 (3, May/June 1978): 150–155. Note, however, that Rotter's 1980 study of 126 men in two Midwest clinics found a low percent (nine) blaming the experience for a breakdown of the relationship, while 51% thought the experience was having a positive impact. Kristine Laral Rotter, "Men and the Abortion Experience: An Exploration Study of Their Self-Reported Educational Interests." op. cit., p. 118. Robbins advises that "contrary to myths surrounding abortion, there is no evidence that the relationship of aborters deteriorates more than those of deliverers when the strength of ties to the partner before the procedures are taken into account." James M. Robbins, "Out-of-Wedlock Abortion and Delivery," op. cit., p. 341.

15. Personal conversation with Mr. Watson, November, 1983. See also his contribution to Chapter 8, "Men Who Counsel."

Part II

Others Who Count

Having now vicariously gone the distance as readers—from the unwelcomed news of an ill-timed pregnancy through to the postabortion scene months, or even years later—we are ready to discuss
three special types of actors in this drama: those who are absent
from the clinic, those who counsel in the clinics, and those who
seek to dramatically change the entire clinic scene.

In Chapter 7, we focus on examples of over 600,000 men (some
50% of those annually involved in the abortion drama), men who
wait elsewhere rather than in a clinic. Exceedingly, difficult to identify, locate, and interview, these nonclinic attenders do not share
a waiting room experience with our 1,000 respondents. They have
no access to male or couples' counseling. None of them have the
close affinity with their partner's actual abortion experience known
by waiting room males. Instead, theirs is a particularly stressful
episode, marked and marred by more-than-usual emotional turmoil, as they experience the abortion from afar, in more ways than
one.

In Chapter 8, we turn to men who could not be any more present if they tried: Employed as full-time abortion counselors, our
four contributors—Peter Zelles, Stephen McCallister, Roger Wade,
and Andre Watson—have helped over 10,000 waiting room males
in recent years. At our invitation, each prepared a short essay exploring insights drawn from their own field experience, reflections
on male needs, and suggestions for overdue reforms (some of
which we use later in Chapter 14).

Finally, in Chapter 9, we share the ideas and emotions of two outstanding and diametrically opposed abortion change-agents. The first, William Baird, a long-time leader among the pro-choice forces, could not be more controversial—with his pro-choice compatriots as well as with his anti-choice detractors! Prime among the latter is our second luminary, Joseph Scheidler, a high-ranking anti-abortionist who claims considerable recent success both in forcing the closedown of clinics and winning uncertain males over to his viewpoint. Baird and Scheidler agree that the status quo is unsatisfactory, though each would alter it in radically different ways. Their ideas merit the thoughtful assessment of everyone seriously interested in this subject, pro- and anti-choice alike.

Chapter 7

Men Who Wait Elsewhere

I don't even remember discussing the pregnancy with my husband. I just told him I was going to get an abortion, which was legal then. I was going to do it all alone, drive myself there, check in, and come home all alone. It was part of my shtik not to need him then.

Francke, Linda Bird, *The Ambivalence of Abortion*, (New York: Dell, 1979, p. 147.)

In most instances, the male partners who accompanied the women were perceived as sharing in the emotionality of the abortion experience. It is interesting that these same observations were made less frequently for the other types of accompanying persons. The women tended not to perceive the same level of concern and involvement in parents or friends. If the women's perceptions were accurate, then it is possible that the males' biological role in pregnancy led them to become more deeply involved than other persons. It must be pointed out, however, that over half the male partners were not present.

Zimmermann, Mary K. *Passage Through Abortion: The Personal and Social Reality of Women's Experiences*, (New York: Praeger, 1977, p. 157.)

What can we share with you about the 50% to 60% of male partners of abortion patients who are absent from clinic waiting rooms?

Very little. Our research focused on attendees, not absentees.
As word of our research spread, however, we received a small
number of offers to complete our questionnaire from "absentee"
men who heard us on radio or TV, or read about our work in the
local press. In all, 18 men volunteered data, and we managed to
interview a few in person. Naturally, we make *no* claim, nor mean
to imply any generalizability for this sketchy, uneven, and tiny
sample. We share our material only for its intrinsic interest, and
in recognition of the near-total absence of *any* writing about this
50% of all sex partners of the nation's 1,600,000 female abortion
clinic users.

Nonattendees: A Profile

When we compare the 18 men with the 1,000 men in our study
there were differences, not surprisingly, in four areas:

- Nonattendees appeared *far less involved emotionally* with the abortion patient: Only one, for example, went along to any counseling sessions with their partner, as compared to 40% of the
  1,000 men. Six were "very casual" or "frequent" dates, as compared to only 10% of the attendees, and only one was married,
  as compared to 17% of the attendees.

- Nonattendees appeared *far less supportive of the abortion resolution:*
  As many as four of 18 felt only the female had favored having
  the abortion, as compared to only five percent of the attendees.
  Similarly, five of 18 were paying none of the costs, versus only
  eight percent of the 1,000-man group.

- Nonattendees appeared *somewhat more opposed to abortion per se:*
  While 64% of the attendees rejected the notion that abortion was
  the killing of a child, only eight of 18 of the absentees went along
  with them, and six were neutral (as were only 11% of the larger
  group). Similarly, while 71% of the attendees rejected anti-
  abortion views of the fetus and personhood, only eight of 18 absentees concurred.

- Nonattendees appeared *far less likely to have their relationships persist after the abortion:* Whereas only three percent of our 1,000

men, and 25% of a 75-man sample of follow-up cases (see Chapter 6) reported the abortion contributed to a breakup, the tally was seven in 18 for the absentees.

Despite this abortion-related stress, and related, perhaps, to the estrangement evident in these relationships, the 18 absentees reported a much higher incidence of "serial abortion" than the attendees (10 in 18 versus only 25% of the 1,000 men).

Brosseau, the only other researcher we found who paid even speculative attention to the existence of these nonattendees, helps with her contention that "personality characteristics" may significantly differentiate the men:

> Presumably, [attendees] had less difficulty overcoming the obstacles to absence from school or work. They were also apparently willing to sit for a large portion of two consecutive days in a clinic where the staff and clientele are predominantly women, again presumably feeling their presence to be an appropriate expression of their commitment toward the woman involved and their relationship with her.[1]

Our subjective impression was consistent with these insights, and Gary McLouth's interviews with several absentees has him go even farther to argue their situation reflected symptoms of instability *unrelated* to the abortion.

A total of 26 of our 30 cooperating clinics guessed—at our urging—that nonattendance had the sources outlined in Table 7-1. Whatever the background reason, the nonattendees remain a phantom type. They are little studied, hardly understood by any concerned parties, and are conspicuously absent from the *one* location where their emotional, spiritual, and family planning needs *might* receive overdue attention.

Each of our nonclinic interviewees told Gary McLouth that talking with him was an overdue, emotional, and welcomed experience, a source of purging and perspective the nonattender had sorely missed and needed. Five of these interviews, and a brief anecdotal experience a cabdriver shared recently with Art Shostak, follow below. Together with the highly qualified discussion above, this skimpy and anecdotal material begins to hint at the discomfort and distress that seems characteristic of many nonattender situations.

Table 7-1. Explanations Offered by Female Patients for Absence of a Male Partner during an Abortion*

''As best as your staff has learned from your clients, why do larger numbers of men not accompany the female to the abortion appointment?''

1. **27%** The man is working, and cannot/will not take the time off.

2. **16%** The woman prefers female company (girlfriend, sister, mother, etc.).

3. **14%** The woman does not want the man along (and *has* told him of the abortion).

4. **14%** The woman does not want the man along (and *has not* told him of the abortion).

5. **6%** The man is opposed to the abortion, and declines to come along.

6. **4%** The man has indicated that he is too upset to come along to the abortion.

7. **19%** Other.

Note: The data above are averaged from 26 of our 30 cooperating clinics; four did not share these guesstimates with us.
*As recalled by clinic staffers.

PROFILE

Noel, an apparently casual 34-year-old sex partner, was surprised that his lover had had an abortion, and was miffed that she had not even told him about it until it was over. He probably would have agreed with her decision, so why, we wondered, was he so upset? And why weren't they continuing their sexual relationship?

Some men, we learned, expect the simple courtesy of being told about the pregnancy and the woman's decision to abort *before* the event. But some women feel if that is all their sex partner needs, he can get along without knowledge of the pregnancy and any news of the abortion whatsoever.

Aloof, and communicating poorly (if at all), unclear about and doubting the motives of each other, these couples tend to drift sharply apart—the abortion drama serving only as a catalyst for divisiveness in the relationship.

Noel:
The first I knew about it was when she told me she was pregnant and she had decided to get rid of it. I thought she was takin' care of the birth con-

trol, since she already has *seven* kids, and jeez, you'd think she'd know what she was doin' by then.

She's in her early thirties, but has the body of an 18-year-old, small and neat, and I thought she was protectin' herself. She said she had made arrangements with a place in New York, and asked me to see her off on the train. That's all she ever asked, not even for money. She likes to be independent, and in the two years since her old man and she split up, she's done it all for herself.

I never thought about marriage or anything, so I had no right to tell her anything. But, it still hurt not to be asked nuthin', not to have my opinion considered. I would have liked her to at least ask me what I thought. I would probably have said 'Go ahead and do it, but at least I would have counted for something.'

You know, I'm really against abortion. Deep down I don't feel right about it, what with all these people hungerin' for a baby to adopt. But I wouldn't have told her that, as it has to be *her* decision.

She's got seven, I've got two by my 'ex'—we certainly didn't need another.

Now, since the abortion, we see each other, maybe twice a day, at the place she waitresses at, and we're real close friends. Not lovers anymore, however, not since the abortion.... I really wished she'd let me have some say in it.... I wasn't really sure it was really true, until she come back and showed me the papers, and bill, and medical stuff from the New York place...and then I knew she had done it.

PROFILE

Ron read about our research in an upstate New York newspaper and decided that he wanted to satisfy his curiosity and to make contact with another man who had experienced an abortion. His two-hour interview was the fullest attention Ron had paid the subject in over ten years. As we talked, we could sense very intimate pieces of his life falling into place.

Ron:
Well, it was late '71 when I first met this woman who I ended up being married to later on. And it was my second Great Love kind of thing. And we played around trying to avoid falling in love with each other, 'cause we'd each fallen off of bad experiences, but it was inevitable...we fell madly and passionately in love, and we were both 18, and it was wonderful and we ended up declaring our love and flopping through the fields, and we ended up making love, on Halloween.

And, of course, there was no thought about it. Just we were going to make love, and that was it. Afterwards, she decided, well, her period was late, and she got concerned about it. And, so she went to a physician, a gynecologist, who indicated that she wasn't pregnant, and so she had an IUD put in. So, then she was having a lot of problems with her IUD, so she went to another physician, and he said that the first physician was incompetent because she was pregnant.

So, we decided that we couldn't afford it, emotionally, financially or otherwise, so she would get an abortion. So, I went down with her to New York.

It was pre-'73, but it was legal in New York, and so I went down with her and a friend of ours. And they're going to perform the abortion, and the physician says there's nothing here to abort! So, so, this is weird, so in the interim, well first of all, she had the IUD, and then subsequently when she thought she was pregnant, she had the IUD taken out, so of course we kept having sex. So she . . . subsequent to that, she really *did* get pregnant.

And then, by then it was '72, around Easter time, and I was away, and she was living alone. So she went to the abortion clinic again, but I didn't go with her the second time, when it actually happened.

I felt really badly that I didn't go. It would have been very difficult to have to explain to my parents that I had to stay at college during Easter Recess my first year off, to go to my girlfriend's abortion. And, actually, I didn't know exactly when she was going to do it, she just did it. She told her mother, and she and her mother went down. I knew she was going to do it, but I . . . .

It was just weird, it did affect us eventually. This was spring of '72 when she had the abortion. And, ultimately, we got married. Ten years ago.

And you know, I felt in a very weird position. What ended the relationship was partially monetary. She didn't have any money, and I had even less then she did. Partially, her change over to a new religious faith, and I suppose, on some level, the abortion, all had something to do with it. Because she realized that she had done something that was against this religious creed that she believed in.

I've taken the fairly classic liberal position. Which is, that I don't know what it means. I don't know when the soul begins, and I don't know . . . I'm not sure . . . The whole thing is that I thought the ideal of having legislation for abortion was, is a good thing, because it's better than having back-room coat-hanger butchers. And the fact that the woman has to bear the child has always led me to feel that it ultimately has to be the woman's decision: whether or not she's going to have an abortion. And it's not that I wouldn't want to take the responsibility, or don't care at all. But I don't have to bear the child. I don't have biological responsibility. I may have a moral responsibility, and an economic responsibility.

I hadn't talked about it, except to one of my friends, who's a mutual friend of my ex-wife's, and after that point it never came up. It's not your garden variety conversation: "Oh, let's talk about our abortion experiences. . . ." It's not like you talk about your car . . . or you talk about what the Giants are doing this year. It's not...on any level...and I don't have a whole lot of intimate male friends. And, I would not talk about it with my female friends, who are far more numerous. I mean many of them know as a fact, but it's not one of those things that's conducive to small talk.

Put in the same situation again, I would have to see what the circumstances were, but my feelings about it might actually be different. If I ever got in that situation where I got somebody pregnant again, which I can't forsee, you know, I would imagine, you know, that I would find out what the dynamics of the situation, of the relationship were, and what options were. My financial options now are a heck of a lot better than they were then. I had no job then, you know. It's just all sorts of little things like that. So, it's hard to say.

PROFILE

Perry, 35-years-old, is divorced, and works as a college administrator in Massachusetts. In our interview we could not help but think that it wasn't love that hurt so much as no love that can hurt even more.

An abortion experience had sharply broken the spell of love for Perry. But his rather passive acceptance of the relationship's end did not help him vent his anger or frustration. His reflections since about the experience and its connection to how he was now leading his life (and his new relationships) seemed to serve as a catalyst for personal change. Perry felt he was no longer wasting opportunities for love, and like many of our more mature abortion veterans, he sought to be much more sensitive to mutuality in his intimate relationships.

Perry:

The experience was like a wedge—it opened up a view of myself.

Up until the abortion, up until the whole part of my life, it was full and rich, but very routine. In some ways uneventful in a negative way. Probably the most traumatic thing in my life till then was falling out of a tree. Obviously, the death of my grandparents and my aunt, but you expect that. It's part of life at that point. I'd never had a bad experience. My life was basically okay. It was steady and even and the boat hadn't been rocked, and I was proceeding and all of a sudden I was slapped in the face. This experience slapped me, it startled me, it told me—one, I was out of control. I had no control. I had no control over that. And that probably hurt. I was really fighting at that point for control in my life.

My life has been pretty strange since that time. I've been in a real weird relationship that was a roller-coaster ride in frustrations. And a very loving relationship from my side, from my point of view, but a relationship full of constant turmoil and sharp edges and harassment, personal harassment. The ultimate of not being in control—that relationship was it. So it was like the abortion experience was an initiation rite to a whole series of experiences where I haven't been in control, where that thought has forced me to try to take control of my life. There's been this whole thread of experiences that have been pushing against that. The abortion is one, the relationship is another. Some things at work have been others. It was like a chain of events. The abortion was the first in the chain. I'd never thought about it like that until just now.

I also remember when I was teaching a class in human sexuality and how heated the discussion on abortion was. In many ways, it was just political. I actually . . . I take a very individual position with that. It's an issue between the couple. I really take issue with the question of it being a woman's issue, or a political or legal issue. I don't think it's either of those. I think it's a couple's issue, more than anything, and I think that's a radical point of view. Maybe it doesn't get a lot of acceptance. The women's movement has, I think, fostered the notion that it is a women's issue: "It's my body and I'll do as I please." Which in many ways is healthy because given the kind of perspective we had, perhaps in the fifties and sixties, when the woman's body was a tool for the male's pleasure—whereas I think this (now) is a much healthier point of view and I think in 15 (more) years there will be a much more balanced point of view—and I don't think it's an issue you can legislate.

And I don't think it's a religious issue. I think it's a very personal issue. It takes a lot of discussion between the two people who are involved in it. Again, as I say, it's a very radical point of view, because churches think it's a religious issue. Legislators and more lobbyist-type people think it's a political issue. I think for Colleen it was *her* issue, because it was important for it to be her issue. Most of her life up to that point has been a life based on giving—to her first marriage, her second marriage, not being in control of her life, not doing some work that was important to her. In this time that we knew each other, she was beginning to blossom in her own career. So it was a control issue for her, too.

She wanted control over her life and this meant she could accomplish that goal. She just blocked me out, not a very healthy way from my point of view, but for her survival, perhaps she thought if she opened up to conversation with me, she was afraid I'd sway her the other way and she'd lose control. The abortion was the seed that forced her to deal with that issue herself (of control). And again, a lot of what's happening in this conversation is a lot of synthesis of thoughts and random notions that have been flying around in my head. This is the first time I've ever gone into them in any depth and length.

I have a good memory. I'm a very visual person, so I create images of things. I remember, I can visualize, the conversation on the phone, sitting at my kitchen table, the colors in the room, crying about it afterward . . . I think men fit. Though I'm not sure it can be a forced fit. You could begin to legislate couples' abortion and that is just as dangerous, just as pernicious as religiously saying it's not good or politically saying it's not good or from a woman's point of view saying it's a woman's body—the idea is to sit down and talk it out, just as in the case with Colleen. She couldn't, or didn't want to, she had other things that were more important to her. Perhaps *that* needed to be talked about more than the actual abortion.

It's a complex problem. I don't think there's an easy answer. But it seems to be the most comfortable way and the most supportive way is to allow it to be an issue between the woman and man, however they choose to deal with it, and there are obviously going to be hurt feelings because it's not always going to work out that things will be resolved through dialogue.

I think an interesting question is the whole issue of the sensitive man . . . in touch with the feminine part of ourselves. I don't think that's widespread and I think it takes some sense of that—some willingness to feel and some willingness to share those feelings with another human being before you can even deal with this issue, and that's probably the first step.

Unfortunately, many couples involved in serious relationships do not really agree on what they would do in case of possible pregnancy before one unexpectedly occurs. Tommy had confidence in birth control, and he relied more on denial than on awareness to keep pregnancy and thoughts of pregnancy at bay. He, like other sexually active single men, took too much comfort in the (fallible) technology of birth control. One of the 60% of our men who used unreliable forms, he nevertheless gave little thought to the possibility of an abortion.

Tommy's probing account of his own experience focused on his never-to-be-born 'kid,' and on the fact that he had been willing to change the status of his love relationship and the structure of his personal life in order to be a father. He quickly learned that he might as well have been dreaming, and that the woman he had known intimately for two years could still surprise him with antinatal attitudes he did not recognize or expect.

Tommy:

Gary: How did you react to the abortion experience?
Tommy: With regard to my closest involvement, there was really no decision making on my part. It was simply—I was going out with this girl for about two years and one day she came and said I'm pregnant and I said, "What do you want to do about it?" She said, "I'm going to have an abortion." In retrospect, her mind was made up. She was going to college. We were fairly serious. I at least wanted to talk about it. "Don't you even want to think of having the kid? It's our kid. Don't you even want to consider it?"

"No, I want to keep going to college, I want to be a nurse, too," and all this other good stuff. I assumed that immediately on finding out she was pregnant, she decided to have an abortion. Come to find out it was her sec-

ond abortion and that's what she decided to do. She had been through that
thought process before.

Gary: Was that first one with somebody other than you?

Tommy: Yup, yup. We'd been going out exclusively with each other for two
years.

Gary: Then it was a serious relationship.

Tommy: Yes, we'd been along those lines headed towards engagement, marriage. It was headed along those lines or so I thought at the time.

Gary: So what happened with this particular decision?

Tommy: Well, I would say within six months things deteriorated to the point
where we both started going out with other people. Our relationship becoming less serious than it once was.

Gary: The abortion decision brought it about?

Tommy: It wasn't a direct result, but involving me, I know that this girl that
I was in love with, who was in love with me, was all of a sudden saying,
"It would probably be a great kid, too, but I can't—not can't—WON'T," so
my choices were to leave, say "Fuck you," or to stay, be with, see things
through, which I did. That was pretty difficult in itself.

Gary: Tell me about that.

Tommy: Took the day off from work. Between 9:00 and 10:00 (A.M.) I took
her down there. They wouldn't let me in the place, so I let her off and they
said come back at noontime.

Gary: Was it a public or private place?

Tommy: It was PP.

Gary: They wouldn't let you in, huh?

Tommy: Well, I could have sat around the waiting room and read magazines,
but I preferred not to, so I just went out, walked around, bought some things
and I got back there around 11:30. I was really nervous. I thought, "Holy
shit," you know, what if something happened. I'd heard stories, like they'd
suck their guts out and things like that. I was really nervous about that.

Then all of a sudden she just comes out, gets in the car. We drive away.
She talks about it, starts to describe it to me, you know, and she said she'd
never do it again. And I said, "Is it as painful as having a kid?" and she said,
"It's gotta be."

After that it was like—we didn't talk about it a lot. It was like that chapter was done with, there's no use discussing it. It's in the past. I would think
that she—this is just speculation on my part—that it didn't mean that much
to her. To her it was "Aw geez, I'm pregnant, I've got to do something about
it."

Gary: Were you on some form of contraception at the time?

Tommy: Yeah, she was on the pill until two months before that. She felt it
was making her edgy and nervous. I differed with that opinion, but she went
off the pill and used foams, creams, and rubbers. Apparently, it didn't work.

Gary: It appears to me that the issue didn't exactly get resolved for you. It's another chapter for her, but in your tone it's not that easy to get off your chest, is it?

Tommy: Well, I just didn't close the book that way, I was thinking, "Shit, I really don't want to get married. I don't want to have a family, but if this is our kid, I don't want to see the kid sucked into a tube in the Planned Parenthood office either." But, as I said, her mind was apparently made up before she even told me. I think, but I can't say for sure, that she had already made an appointment when she was talking to me about it.

But I was, of course, involved in the finances. She was always working. She was in school and she said, "$185, and I don't have it. I can't borrow it, I can't ask my parents. Can you do it?"

Why should I pay for it? I was figuring at least a fifty-fifty kind of deal, you know, reluctant in the beginning as I was to do it anyway. And she said, "Geez, I'll pay you back half as soon as I get working." I guess that's still a debt outstanding.

Gary: How long ago was this?

Tommy: Be three years in December.

Gary: What is the lasting feeling with your experience?

Tommy: Kid never had a chance.

Gary: Did you feel you wanted to give the kid a chance?

Tommy: Yeah.

Gary: So, what happened? The abortion experience made a glaring point in the different ways you (two) were thinking about an important thing, like what happens if we get pregnant? You hadn't discussed or talked about it before?

Tommy: Yeah, this is the thing. She'd been on the pill for a long time. They say 97% sure of its effect, so I never thought about pregnancy.

Gary: You're always in the 97%, I guess.

Tommy: Yeah. You just figure 97% covers pretty much. Guess that's my lasting impression—here's this kid of mine that didn't have a chance because the mother thought, "I'll get money from Tom, my parents won't have to know, it won't change my life any. Quick and easy way to do it.'

Gary: Did you talk to anybody about your feelings about this?

Tommy: No, I didn't. Only her, and that was like as I said, the logic that she applied was not at all that overpowering.

Gary: But you were pretty powerless about—

Tommy: It was her body.

Gary: How has this experience changed you, your attitudes toward women, sex?

Tommy: Hasn't, in any way I can think of.

Gary: Are you more careful?

Tommy: Yeah. I think I am. But by the same token, I'm prone to carelessness which negates any carefulness. Usually this is barroom kinds of things, you know. Like, the next morning you wake up and ask, "Oh, by the way, are you on any kind of birth control?" and she says, "Oh, don't worry about it. I'm on the pill." "Oh, that's great!"

Gary: What's your perception and/or experience with other men who've been through abortion experiences?

Tommy: I've only talked to one guy about it, but he didn't even go with her. He paid for it . . . and they've been living together for about six years. He was for the abortion, but he didn't want to know anything about it or to be involved. It was like a business decision. I assume they made the decision together. They are still together.

Gary: What about attitudes women have had toward you regarding this issue? Have women reacted to you or told you about their experiences, etc?

Tommy: Yeah, I've talked to a number. Again, I'm left with this impression of, "Oh shit, I'm pregnant." The last one complained about last summer's abortion and it set her back 200 bucks. Cause-and-effect kind of attitude. Pregnant–abortion. She was a client.

My main thought on the whole issue is that the women I know—there's an attitude that it's an accident, and you repair accidents. You don't tell parents and friends about it. No one knows unless you tell or want them to know. You can wipe the slate clean and start over again."

PROFILE

Brian is a southern white man in his late twenties. At the time of his abortion experience, he was a communications analyst. Brian considers himself to be "pretty religious" and is generally not very communicative with people on personal matters. He feels it is his southern upbringing that makes him "steel up" in the face of hard times. Talking about the abortion experience is a way for him to purge himself some, a way to process it.

Brian:

I was in the process of separating from my wife when my affair with Judy, began. Although I didn't want to get involved in another serious commitment before my marriage was legally and emotionally settled, I found Judy to be very compatible, and soon I was seeing her on a regular basis.

We were driving out into the hills. The warm wind whipped around our heads in the convertible. I felt great. Judy hadn't been acting so hot lately and I was glad that she was enjoying the ride. I was thinking amorous thoughts. Passion had taken over early in our relationship and I guess I was thinking about being with her up on a secluded hill under a tree or something romantic like that when she turned toward me and said she'd had an abortion. Well, I damned near wrecked the car. I had to pull over to collect myself. I was blindly angry for half an hour. The hardest thing was being confronted by a fait accompli.

I guess my sense of honor and responsibility was wounded. I felt deprived of involvement in something I had helped to bring about. I could have exploded, treated her like shit, ended the relationship. A lot of guys' egos would not have withstood it. My marriage (divorce) hadn't been settled yet, so it wasn't a good idea to have had the baby, but I didn't have to pay or to emotionally contribute and I was deprived. It was a shock, even though she and I together would have probably settled on abortion. I held myself in check until we could talk it over. It brought us closer together. Her telling me was the most profound experience of my life because I realized how much I loved her, right then. It brought me closer and our love grew from there.

A year later, we went through the experience of thinking we were pregnant. The rational and fairly easy handling of guilt and other feelings during the first time, the real abortion, totally disappeared. The guilt and trauma from the previous year that we didn't process or share came full flood on us. We went for pastoral counseling because of near hysteria. It turned out to be a panic experience. Pregnancy tests proved negative.

We eventually married and are now expecting our first child. Since we have shared the other alternatives, the pain, the heartache, this means a lot to us and we're calm and serious about it. The abortion has had a heavy influence on me and my relationship. The experience makes the coming of our first child extremely poignant.

Summary

Men waiting elsewhere may be as numerous as those waiting in the nation's abortion clinics. We believe many suffer far more ill effects than anyone now suspects. As social strictures on the discussion of abortion between men loosen, however, opportunities may expand to help such men take some solace from sharing their abortion experiences beyond the clinic walls.

Notes

1. Karen Deborah Brosseau, "Utilizing Male Partners of Adolescent Abortion Patients as Change Agents: Results of an Experimental Intervention," unpublished Ph.D. dissertation (Boulder, Col.: University of Colorado, 1980), p. 101. "Similarly, the woman's decision to be accompanied by her sexual partner could include aspects of all of the above, as well as personality differences related to level of overt dependency needs, discomfort with sexuality, the pregnancy itself, etc."

Chapter 8

Men Who Counsel

Social scientists have relied too heavily on surveys and representative samples of adults in their analysis of abortion controversy to the neglect of those activists who are most involved and committed on this matter. Future research should address this imbalance.

Donald and Beth W. Gransberg, (*Sociology and Social Research*, July 1981, p. 483).

Please try to impress upon those legalistic moralists who condemn abortion out of hand that the man often suffers as much (if in different ways), if not more than the woman. If I think about what is going on right now, I come very close to vomiting. But, neither of us wishes to sacrifice a bright future for an (at this time) unwanted family. This experience hurts and probably will leave scars—I know it will. But since ours is a relationship of love and respect, we will recover and grow together. I know that this all sounds poetic and idealistic, but I think we both mean it. Hopefully, from this experience we can learn enough to help someone else in a similar situation—help them survive and help them feel loved.

Anonymous waiting room male, quoted by Mark R. Smith (Ph.D. dissertation, 1971, p. 199.)

If the males who sit and wait are soon to gain more from their abortion experience, much credit will be owed to a very small number of men now employed as full-time abortion counselors. While their ranks from coast to coast probably include fewer than 15 individuals in over 500 clinics, each such man offers a valuable role model to male *and* female clients alike. Each is also a valuable source of insight into waiting room males for female co-workers at the clinic. And, each is living confirmation that this is a human issue, a woman's issue, *and* a man's issue at one and the same time.

Four of these men—Peter Zelles, Roger Wade, Andre Watson, and Stephen McCallister—prepared short essays for our use about their roles, their clinic-based reflections, and the waiting room reforms they champion. Written independently of each other, their material contains many mutually supportive insights and complementary reform ideas. Eloquent, sometimes jarring, and often very moving, the four men write from a unique vantagepoint, and their provocative field reports are ones we are very proud to share.

Peter Zelles:

My first encounter with abortion was as a late adolescent: a girlfriend told me she had become pregnant in a previous relationship and had had an abortion. Up to that time I hadn't thought a great deal about abortion as an issue—I may have had a vague feeling that it may be morally wrong. After learning of this woman's abortion, I began to think of the realities of unplanned pregnancy, first as they related to her, and later as they related to me. I knew I wasn't ready for a child, yet my relationship had a sexual component, vulnerable to pregnancy.

While there were certainly countless factors that predisposed me eventually to entering a psychology career, it was *this* relationship that mobilized my interests. The emotional and intellectual experiences charged me so that I would never again look at the abortion issue as I once had, and my view of emotional problems became one of understanding rather than judgment.

My subsequent contact with abortion was limited to intellectualization until late in my freshman year at college: the woman I was dating feared she was pregnant. Words cannot describe the fright I felt when she told me of her suspicion. I was unsure of her stand on abortion, but I feared that she would opt to continue the pregnancy.

We waited almost a week before learning if she was pregnant, or merely late; I recall this as the longest week of my life. Fear and a sense of powerlessness over the ultimate decision were with me always. The effects of becoming a parent would be disastrous to my future. By this time, I had already decided on a career in psychology, and was all too aware of the intense commitment required: the "extended adolescence" of graduate school, internships, and attaining state licensure. My goal was a career as a psychologist, and a child was definitely not part of the picture—especially during my training.

The impact an unplanned pregnancy would have on my parents was also troubling. I was conscious of the fact that they had just begun to feel some of the freedom that comes with completion of child rearing (I was the youngest of two children, and had recently moved away from home). I didn't want to burden them financially or emotionally with my problems. Also, I feared their judgment of me— like all people, I wanted to please my parents and make them proud of me. In retrospect, I'm sure they would have given their support, that no matter what happened they would still accept me, but rightly or wrongly, I felt that I should not go to them, despite the fact that we are and always have been very close.

Luckily, I had the support of a few very close male friends who would listen and offer their advice as needed. I feel very sad for the many men I see who don't have *any* friends with whom they can share sensitive personal issues.

Due, perhaps, to my exposure to other people's experiences, I wasn't tremendously troubled by the moral question of abortion; I was comfortable with the "rightness" of such a decision. Because I feared her ultimate authority, however, I chose to avoid discussing alternatives with my partner during this waiting period. When we knew for sure, I thought, we could work toward a decision.

After what seemed like forever, a mutual friend informed me that my girlfriend had started her period; she was not pregnant. The hug I gave to this messenger of glad tidings was of Homeric proportion.

This tremendous sense of relief was followed by the sobering realization that some decisions regarding my future needed to be made if I was to avoid a repeat of this scenario. Specifically, the type of sexual relationship I felt comfortable with needed to be defined: under what circumstances, with whom, how deep a commitment, the responsibility for contraception, and an understanding of the abortion option all must be explored. Again, I realized I had undergone a deep change from a relationship. The manner in which I viewed sexual relationships had matured, and I was attuned to new issues in my life.

Later in my college career, I met the man who held the position I now have as director of male counseling at an abortion clinic. He was a professor, and taught me about male issues in general, as well as the male abortion experience. After graduation, he gave me the opportunity to work with him as a counselor, and later I assumed his role as program director of the male counseling service.

As director of one of the country's only male-to-male abortion counseling programs, I have now counseled over 2,500 men whose partners are having (or thinking about having) abortions. Despite the repetitive nature of my case load, I am still struck by the emotional intensity I see in the men who use my service: sadness, anger, powerlessness, all coupled with isolation from any support system. All this in people who are often seen as uninvolved, unfeeling, and uncaring.

Not a lot has changed over the years. A very few people are becoming aware of the impact abortion can have on men, but this public awareness is generally limited. People hearing of male abortion counseling for the first time often respond in one of two ways: complete surprise that men would need to talk about their partners' abortions (". . . after all, it's the *woman* who suffers") or recognition of male abortion counseling only as instruction on how to be better support people.

Many men fall victim to a stereotyped image by attempting to be a strong, cool, controlled figurehead. My experience with these men, however, has been that they are all affected by an abortion, and I am doing a disservice if I don't probe under that first layer of composure, a placid mask of manhood.

Sadly, even professionals in the family planning community are only minimally aware of the need for male abortion counseling. A study of National Abortion Federation member clinics found that while nearly all clinics provided counseling for female patients as a routine part of an abortion workup, counseling for male partners was offered as requested, if at all. This lack of services fails to recognize the woman as part of a couple—a system—which should be treated as a unit.

It is preferable to meet with the couple together, at the same time and in the same room, but considering our history of treating only an individual regarding the abortion (i.e., the woman) this may be too large a contextual shift for most clinics to handle; an alternative is to provide a male counselor to meet with the male client/partners who accompany their wives or girlfriends to the clinic. While individual sessions do not provide the wide perspective available in couple sessions, they can incorporate a systems perspective, and provide a symbolic inclusion of the male in the process. By making the male counseling session a planned segment of the clinic visit, staff members communicate to the couple an understanding of their relationship.

The Process of Male Counseling

Counseling men in an abortion clinic presents difficulties from the outset, since many clients haven't explicitly identified problems, but are only aware of a free-floating state of anxiety. In addition, most men don't anticipate seeing a counselor; they have come to support their partner, and expect all attention to be directed toward that primary patient. This, coupled with the social stigma surrounding seeing a counselor (especially strong for men), makes engaging men in the session tricky business.

There are, of course, many men who anticipate and welcome counseling, but with as many as ten (unscreened and unknown) clients in the waiting room, it behooves the practitioner to approach all sessions cautiously and gently. Keeping the session casual, inquiring about the woman's well-being from his perspective (which acknowledges his self-identified role as support person), and slowly moving into how the abortion has affected *him*, will serve to create a relaxed and cooperative atmosphere.

The next task for the counselor involves investigation of problem areas: mutuality of decision, communication between partners, presence of a support system, moral concerns, and so on. Since many men haven't talked with *anyone* about their situation, this contact breaks down isolation and allows for initial expression of emotion.

Because of the time limit on sessions, counselors should be directive; experienced counselors are adept at identifying key issues early in the session and moving into a work phase. The counselor draws on his experience with relationships and knowledge of dynamics to bring some understanding to the information being presented. Men benefit from alternative perspectives, direct support, and planning strategies to deal with specific problem areas.

As the session draws to a close, most men report they have benefited from talking. Outside support systems can be explored, re-emphasizing the benefits of remaining open to discussing issues with the partner.

Underlying Values in Abortion Counseling

Since the vast majority of men in an abortion clinic are in agreement with the decision to terminate the pregnancy, one must look beyond the obvious to identify the source of distress. Exactly what the counselor looks for will be a function of his/her values, and my values are made transparent by this article. I believe it is necessary for *all* counselors to realize, however, that the circumstances and manner in which a decision is made can have more impact than the decision itself.

Abortion is a *woman's* choice, and while I agree with the logic, sense, and necessity of this, I realize there is an inherent feeling of unfairness in it. Even in the most egalitarian relationship, the male must realize it is his partner who makes the final decision to abort or continue a pregnancy, and the most he can do is offer his suggestion. If he disagrees with his partner's choice he will likely experience a sense of desperation and anger. Regardless of which option the male is opposed to, it is likely based on long-held, powerful values, and the prospect of having them violated will mobilize his defenses. My intent is not to be grim—many couples will reach a comfortable resolution, but not until *both* partners are fully cognizant of the unequal balance of influence. This type of scenario occurs over and over again in all relationships; fortunately most of them are not as intense, and the position of greatest influence trades off between partners.

In a similar vein, anger can be present even when a couple agrees on the final decision; again, this is due to the imbalance of influence. This may manifest itself in the form of regret either as compensation for an absence of influence ("If only I had been more responsible") or guilt ("She has to suffer with this abortion, and I get away easy"). Both of these positions sound perfectly rational, but they should alert the counselor to issues of powerlessness.

Our data here suggest that emotional isolation is evidenced in more than half of male partners. Because the abortion is "her choice" (and hence, her business) many men don't feel they have the right to share their experience with someone. Others say they don't have a close friend they can trust with such delicate issues. In light of this aloneness, the counseling session takes on a special importance.

Men feel they need to be strong for their partners: to be firm, logical, and emotionless to avoid upsetting them. Being supportive is important, but it doesn't have to preclude having feelings of one's own. Sadness and loss are feelings evident with any abortion decision, and to get beyond them they must be expressed. It is natural and healthy to want to make a crisis "history," but not before it has been psychically processed.

Finally, we must look at the most prevalent underlying issue for both men and women: the morality of abortion. There are few "new" words to be said on this, and newspaper editorial pages are filled with attempts every day. The opposing idealogies are easily understood, but counselors must be aware of their own beliefs, opinions, and biases in order to maintain boundaries with clients.

Abortion patients and client-partners are often encountering conflict with familial values for the first time. The task of the counselor, then, is to help clarify values and start the client onto what may be a re-examination of long-held values. The age of the average client—between 18 and 25 years old— makes her/him an appropriate candidate for this potentially uncomfortable process.

A Different Perspective:
Strategic Abortion Counseling

While it is common for mental health professionals to speak in terms of the symptoms of a particular individual, I propose a different approach based on a circular (rather than linear) epistemology.[1] Instead of trying to understand the experience of an individual, we must look at the couple (or whole family) as a system; this represents the purpose of bringing men into the abortion arena. The actions of each individual in this system are so intimately wound together that trying to discern "ultimate causes" or "good guys" and "bad guys" becomes nonsensical. Instead of discussing a person's attitude *causing* their partner's trauma, we might discuss the *relationship* between the issues, perhaps suggesting it is the reaction that must change to affect the attitude.

Stereotypically, abortion is a situation that is viewed by counselors much like sexual abuse; there is a perpetrator (the bad guy) and a victim (the good guy). Depending on your viewpoint these roles can be filled by either sex, but once they have been put into place the damage has been done. Several assumptions and judgments accompany such roles, as does a simplistic style of intervention based on reforming the perpetrator and saving the victim. This is true linear thinking: A causes B. When making any type of change, one must remember that our actions have effects which are more than immediate. An analogy regarding the environment is illustrative: If I dispose of poisonous chemicals by burying them, I may end up with a contaminated water supply—the solution is not a solution.

When examining a system, the counselor should realize that s/he has become a part of it, and has thus *changed* the system. Another analogy: When an audience listens to a musical ensemble, the performance is affected even though the audience has done nothing more than *be* there. Having an audience of readers for this paper changes the way I write it compared with a piece I might write to amuse myself. Likewise, my presence in the consulting room changes the clients I am with, as well as the situation they are experiencing.

The implications of this view for abortion counseling are tremendous: a woman entering a clinic would no longer be viewed as an *individual primary* client, but as a part of a *system* needing counseling. The male partner would be viewed as an integral part of the system who (ideally) would be counseled along with the woman, or (at least) be provided with an individual counselor who understands the ecology of relationships.

Abortion counselors frequently encounter clients who present a traumatic and emotional crisis. In the context of a counseling session, practitioners often aim their intervention at trying to help the client feel better in the short term, rather than looking at the larger view of the client and her/his relatedness to a system.

Behavior never occurs in a vacuum, but always in relationship to others, and abortion is anything but an exception to that rule. We find that abortion often provides a clear analogue for other issues in a relationship, and the abortion clinic is often a highly effective point of intervention for these couples. The amount of direct contact time with a counselor is limited, but by perceiving the couple as a system and using highly directive strategic interventions, there is much a counselor (or counseling team) can do in one or two sessions.

Strategic intervention involves the use of directive techniques based on the systemic (or structural) perspective. These techniques are used to disrupt problematic patterns, and include "reframing" (e.g., ". . . it's *good* that the two of you fight so much; it shows you're really commited to working things out"); "paradox," ("I'd like you to go home and have an argument lasting an hour or so"; the couple will either not fight or have a more constructive fight); or "metaphor" (literally, the telling of stories which relate strongly to a client's situation, and have "embedded" in them an alternative perspective).[2]

As exciting as these techniques are, remember that the underlying precept is the systemic perspective, which necessitates the understanding (if not the actual presence) of both partners. Ignoring the male partner in abortion is a philosophical, theoretical, and practical mistake which defies the ecological realities of a relationship belonging to *both* partners. The goal isn't to just serve males, but to efficaciously serve both partners.

The current political battle over the "rightness" of abortion inhibits the availability of counseling services (especially for men), because counseling draws attention to the tragic nature of abortion. Many members of the pro-choice movement fear that acknowledging the emotional difficulties often present in abortion will drive people away from the belief of the necessity for safe, legal abortions. When the opposition to abortion diminishes, the abortion establishment will be free to view emotional aspects of abortion as realistic responses to a difficult choice which affects men *and* women, and the provision of emotional support services for both sexes will become routine rather than the exception.

Roger Wade:

In 1973, when I began abortion counseling with men, I had no models or guidelines, since none yet existed. I made plenty of errors at first, but as a consequence, learned things I otherwise might not have. I look back with some pain at my first awkward approaches to the men sitting in the lobby of our clinic. Their squirming and tightly crossed limbs made it clear they were very uncomfortable, but many of them refused counseling. I began to suspect men had a negative reaction to the term "counseling." So, I dropped the word, and instead offered to explain the abortion procedure, and aftercare instructions. This educational approach worked much better, and suddenly about 80% of the men accompanied me to the counseling room. (This percentage stayed the same during the five years I worked as a counselor.)

Male resistance to the psychological was further demonstrated once in the counseling room. When I asked leading questions such as, "How did you feel when you found out about the pregnancy?," or, "How do you feel about the abortion?" I would get responses like, "Okay," or other equally unrevealing answers. A small minority were eager to talk, but in many sessions little of how the men felt emerged. Dissatisfied, I cast about for techniques which would open things up.

After some experimentation, I hit upon the icebreaker, "What do you do?" I had read and heard that men's identities are tightly bound up with work, but I was still surprised when otherwise listless men became animated while discussing their jobs. The more interest I showed in their work lives, the more relaxed they became. It was then possible to move to topics the men were less secure with, such as how they felt about the pregnancy.

Gradually, I began to realize the key to effective counseling was to avoid any impression that it was a counseling session. If I avoided sounding like a counselor and worked leading questions into what otherwise seemed like an exchange of information, the men responded more candidly. Instances when I was overly persistent in digging out feelings produced angry responses from the men. I was asked, "Who are you, anyway?" or, "Why do you want to know anyhow?" or in other ways told to back off.

Most men are on guard against counselors and others who would try to "figure them out." I suspect this is because they have learned to hide their vulnerabilities lest those they are in competition with, which is generally all men, take advantage of their "soft spots." I have had the experience myself of opening up to a buddy only to have him tease me in front of others about my concerns. One of the main reasons men cannot go to each other for support is fear their confidences will be used against them.

What I was learning in the counseling room jibed with comments of the women I was working with. Our staff was overwhelmingly female, and for the first time in my life, I was exposed to women as they are when out of the shadow of men. In their "bull sessions," they talked about men a great deal (more than I would have ever believed). One of the persistent themes was that men never expressed their feelings. Some women even wondered if men had feelings. I was coming to see how they could believe that.

Most of the guys I counseled were searching not for help in unraveling feelings, but for the rules as to how they "should" behave. They did not ask directly for guidance, but their confusion emerged as they described failed efforts to help their partners cope with the situation. Over and over, I heard men say, "I don't know what to do. She gets mad no matter what I do. I've tried to help her." Guys would do housework, or take the woman out to dinner. Others tried to be amusing and humorous in order, as they saw it, to take the woman's mind off the pregnancy. When these well-intended efforts failed to stop the anger and crying, men sometimes explained away the "bitchy" behavior by theorizing it resulted from hormonal changes accompanying pregnancy. Men without a handy explanation became confused, threatened that they were being rejected by the women.

Seldom did men realize the real source of the women's behavior was ambivalence and apprehension about the pregnancy. Instead of opening up conversations which might help the women express these feelings, and the men theirs, the majority of males tried to stay away from the topic. I have come to believe that diversion and delay are typical male methods of dealing with emotional issues. Men do not learn how to slog through an upsetting discussion and would rather avoid tough talks in hopes the feelings will go away.

I asked the men if they had told their partners what they felt about the pregnancy and abortion. In a great many cases they had not. Some guys claimed they did not want to influence the woman's decision and therefore held back. They didn't realize that most women desperately needed to know what their wishes were. Not expressing their feelings about the situation was frequently interpreted by their partners as a sign the men didn't care about them, or want to help.

Many women gave up on involving the men (and, in a number of cases, also gave up on their relationship with the guys). Unfortunately, these women seldom made it clear what they were upset about, or just how angry they were. This probably, or at least partially, explained why I encountered so many befuddled men who told me they felt excluded from what was going on.

Another source of the feeling of being excluded was the attention paid to the woman by clinic staff. I suspect even some of the most liberated of our staff still somewhere in their minds held the men culpable for the pregnancies. Ask most women directly and they will acknowledge that women are responsible for their own sexuality. But lingering about is the old image of the man as the culprit in matters sexual. The pain involved in an abortion also causes resentment and the feeling that "men get off easy." At least at our clinic, the guys got some attention, but at many times they are virtually ignored.

An unplanned pregnancy does require men to play a supporting role, not the starring one. This can be a strange and uncomfortable situation for many. Not only is most all attention focused on the woman, but by law she has the final say in what happens to the pregnancy. A small number of men react with anger to losing power and try to assert dominance by proclaiming that no woman of theirs is going to have an abortion. A few have even gone to court attempting to block an abortion. But most men try to adjust to the situation and offer as much help as they can, even if they don't quite know how to do that.

My years of counseling men convinced me most of them want to do the right thing, but they become confused because there are no well-developed role expectations about how a man should act when an unplanned pregnancy occurs. I used to joke with my colleagues at the abortion clinic that I was going to write a handbook telling guys step by step what they should do. Men act in terms of what they see as their duty, no matter how that jibes with their feelings. I saw this clearly with teenage boys who told me they had proposed marriage when they found out about the pregnancy. It didn't take much to discover that they did not want to get married, and in many cases did not even want to be with the girl, but proposed because they thought it was the thing for a man to do.

As I came to understand this facet of male behavior more clearly, I began to take advantage of it in my counseling. I would suggest, in a circumspect manner, that even though it's difficult for them to express their feelings to the woman, it was manly to do those things which are difficult. I think, judging by the looks on their faces, that many guys took this to heart. I would also say that one of the ways they could take care of the woman was to make sure she followed the aftercare instructions. Most men seemed glad to have me spell out specific ways they could be involved.

Though increasing numbers of men are struggling to toss aside the emotionally constricting traditional male role, very few have completely succeeded. All of us, to one degree or another, are still shaped by it. We spend little time wondering about what is going on inside the heads of others except, perhaps, when we are trying to figure out a way of getting something we want from that other person, or when we are trying to "psych someone out" (like a teacher), so we can anticipate what they are likely to do. In such cases, we are quite adept at reading cues about others.

I do not believe, as some researchers are saying, that men are biologically incapable of reading the emotions of others. No! No! It isn't that we are unable, but rather that, by and large, we have not been taught the value of doing so. I have seen men who are sensitive to the feelings of others, and able to express their emotions. And others are making progress.

One of my pet theories is that the traits identified with male character developed because they were functional for war and work. Compartmentalization of emotions enabled men to shove aside fears which might cause them to panic in battle, or keep them at home instead of traveling out to hunt food. Inability to see what others are feeling allows men to act in aggressive ways toward them without considering the impact of their actions. And the imposition of duty for feeling as the compass which guides behavior further squelched emotions that might have interfered with male functionality in work and war.

Traits which historically served men well are in conflict with the demands of modern society. War now means total annihilation, and work requires the ability to get along with others and to communicate. Men are being forced to change to survive, not just because of the changes in women.

Getting in touch with feelings does not, as many fear, mean giving up one's intelligence and a return to barbarism. The darker side of human character, which so many are fond of pointing to, indeed exists, but the hope is that the fear and misunderstanding of others which fuels male violence will be diminished as men learn how to see themselves in others and express their feelings.

Underneath the cultural male is a human being capable of compassion and love giving. Such a change will not come easy, and is by no means guaranteed, but it is needed.

Andre Watson:

Men and *family planning* are words few people use together in the same context. When you think of family planning, you think of women; when you think of abortion, you think of women; and when you think of reproductive health, you also think of women. Society has taught us well that some things are strictly for a woman. But somewhere involved in each of those processes is the invisible man. It wasn't until I began working for Planned Parenthood of Metropolitan Washington's Men's Center that the role men play came to light in my mind.

Contrary to popular belief, men have significant concerns about family planning and abortion. Since 1978, PPMW's Men's Center has provided family planning and reproductive health services, including medical, educational, counseling, and referral aid, to area men of all ages. As a counselor there, I have encountered numerous men seeking advice, clarification, information, and education relevant to abortion.

The men who seek abortion counseling are usually motivated by one of the following reasons: a need for information or education; a need for venting feelings; or, a need to attempt to persuade their partner to have an abortion. At times, of course, the counseling session would be motivated by any combination of these reasons, and several others, as well.

Most men involved with an abortion want basic information about it, particularly its safety. What actually happens? Is it painful? Will it prevent future pregnancies? Since there are few avenues men can travel to obtain this information, PPMW's Men's Center became the logical place to go. To learn that abortions are safe can be a real relief to a man concerned about his partner's health.

A man, whose partner has decided to terminate her pregnancy, then wants to know, "How can I help?" Since no handbook or set of guidelines exists that specifically spells out the supportive man's role, most men feel powerless and helpless. This can be quite devastating to a man accustomed to having control over situations and providing assistance. Receiving a few tips on how to be supportive can be as helpful and encouraging as lighting a darkened room. Further, this counseling prepares him for the abortion, and his support helps the woman through the procedure.

Although few men consciously come to a counseling session to vent their feelings, this is often what many end up doing. Pregnancy, planned or unplanned, is an extremely important and delicate concern for the men and women who have sincere feelings about their role in this process. Yet, many men are convinced they aren't supposed to show emotions. A counseling session where a man has displayed his emotions may find him relieved, yet embarrassed, since men believe they should always be in control—rational, cool, aloof, self-contained, and restrained.

As a counselor, it became my role to help men vent their feelings. This wasn't very easy. Many men tend to intellectualize and rationalize their emotions about abortions. It is extremely important for a man to release these feelings, or they will manifest themselves in other undesirable ways. These suppressed emotions can also undermine the future health of the relationship.

The emotions men have toward abortion are many. Some are angry and upset with themselves and/or their partner for being in this situation. Others may be afraid or feel guilty: believing abortion is murder, they fear being an accomplice. I mentioned earlier how some men may feel helpless and powerless, not knowing what to do and having little input. A general sense of sadness and regret is prevalent among men who prefer the woman to carry the fetus to full term rather than carry out her decision to abort. Many men vow never to be in this predicament again. The emotions men feel, when faced with an abortion, are limitless. What is important to remember is that they *do* have genuine feelings and concerns about abortion that need to be expressed.

Counseling sessions with a man and his partner about an unintended pregnancy often found him trying to convince her to have or not to have an abortion. Many times these sessions became confused and misdirected, with the man attempting to use me to impose his feelings on his partner. The woman was usually decided, rather than opposed, and it became clear that she needed her own private counseling session to sort out her feelings about the pregnancy.

During counseling sessions where the woman was opposed to the abortion and the man favored it, or vice versa, a recurring theme began to surface: A man has no rights as partner in the decision to abort or carry to term, but many responsibilities as father if she decided to carry the fetus to term. This, added to the sense of powerlessness that many men felt, led many males to think the situation unfair. Consequently, the man's role in family planning cannot be stressed enough.

Stephen McCallister

Interest in the topic of men and abortion is evidence of a long overdue insight: decisions about unplanned pregnancy don't just affect the pregnant woman. But men's feelings don't magically begin the moment the woman decides to have an abortion. The abortion itself is the culmination of a decision-making process from which men are often excluded. This isn't to say that men must be making the decisions about a pregnancy. It is only to observe that the emotional products of leaving men out of pregnancy decision making and counseling are often mixtures of powerlessness, alienation, and isolation.

During the last five years, I've worked developing family planning programs for men at two different agencies. Most recently, I've developed male education and counseling services for Planned Parenthood of Snohomish County, Washington. Men and unplanned pregnancy has been a special focus of this work, which has produced the first pamphlet for men involved in an unplanned pregnancy and a counseling model for integrating men into pregnancy counseling services. The longer I work in family planning, the more I've become convinced that male involvement is central to finding the best possible solutions to some of the worst possible situations.

Leaving men out of pregnancy counseling and abortion isn't just a problem for the man. A pregnancy that isn't expected or wanted is both an individual crisis and a crisis for the relationship between the man and the woman. Thus, male noninvolvement can have ill effects for the woman and the relationship between the couple. If this sounds a little grandiose, consider the following quotation from a study of women's reactions to having an abortion:

> Frequently women were more concerned about the relationships with their male partners than with any other aspect of the abortion. They needed and tried to include their partners in their experiences. In almost all instances in which the respondents experienced substantial emotional distress, it was because they lacked emotional support from their partners.[3]

Saying that men needn't be a part of pregnancy counseling makes about as much sense as saying that one spouse needn't be concerned with the other spouse's decision to seek a divorce.

So, why aren't men involved? My purpose here isn't to provide a detailed analysis of male noninvolvement, but I will offer a few observations. I see at least three elements to male noninvolvement. One element is the way men deal with their emotions. Another element is the attitudes and philosophy of pregnancy counselors and abortion providers. Finally, men involved in unplanned pregnancies often face no positive choices and, therefore, many simply choose not to be involved.

Men, for the most part, aren't very comfortable with their emotions. As they grow up, men learn to deal with emotions like wild horses: if you can't tame them, then at least keep them in the corral. Society has often painted a picture of unplanned pregnancy being a major crisis for the woman, while men are portrayed as the ones who "got her pregnant and walked away."

Unfortunately, the net effect is that most men don't even consider that a pregnancy might concern them. When a pregnancy occurs, most men find themselves with deep and unexpected feelings. Not in control of either the situation or their feelings, many men simply repress their emotions.

Discussion of male participation raises philosophical questions for pregnancy counselors and abortion providers. Without too much exaggeration, it's possible to say that the first axiom of pregnancy counseling is that the decision is, ultimately, up to the woman. Consequently, many see male participation as irrelevant and men as potential interlopers trying to interfere with the woman's decision. These philosophical concerns are reinforced by the fact that pregnancy counselors have heard hundreds of stories about irresponsible, uncaring, and even abusive men. The compassion and empathy of the counselors for the women they serve can make it difficult for them to view men without suspicion or distrust.

When a man becomes involved in an unplanned pregnancy, he often discovers that he has no positive option. The traditional example is the "shotgun wedding," a mandatory marriage that made the man the victim of the pregnancy. All too often, his alternative was to walk away from the woman and the pregnancy. As a 16-year-old girl told me, "The girl gets the baby and the boy gets the blame." Of course, there have been many changes: legal abortion, acceptance of single parenthood, modern female contraceptives, and accurate paternity tests among them.

Still, these changes haven't brought men new, positive choices. Today, instead of a shotgun wedding, it may be a court order obtained by the state welfare office to do blood tests for paternity to establish child support. Or, the woman may decide to have an abortion that the man feels is murder. The net effect has been a proliferation of ways for men to be the victim of an unplanned pregnancy. Being the villain, on the other hand, has become a little harder.

All these elements taken together overwhelmingly push men toward not being involved in pregnancy counseling or abortion. A man repressing strong feelings who finds himself confronted with uncomfortable or hostile professionals and no positive role to play in resolving the pregnancy doesn't have much incentive to involve himself or make his feelings known. Yet, we know from both women and men that involving the man is important. New avenues and opportunities for involvement of men in pregnancy counseling and abortion need to be adopted. Men will not be a part of what is, in essence, a no-win situation. Men—and women—need roles other than those of victims and villains.

Male participation in pregnancy counseling and abortion doesn't mean that men will take the decision whether to continue or terminate a pregnancy away from women. Participation can mean sharing one's views and gaining information without coercing the woman. But concerns about men trying to force their opinions on women are real. One of my most vivid memories is of a man whose first words to me were, "My wife and me are gonna get an abortion, but she's not sure yet." Similarly, there must be a recognition that men do have responsibilities should the pregnancy be carried to term. Bluntly speaking, advocacy of male participation doesn't mean advocacy of men defaulting on child support or other obligations.

Ideally, men and women will deal with the pregnancy together. A mutually agreeable decision on a pregnancy option may not always be possible, but it is desirable. In most cases, the woman does want to know the man's feelings and intentions. These may play a large role in her decision. We may say that the decision is the woman's, but she can hardly decide on her own that her partner will marry her and raise their child with her.

In the cases where the man and the woman cannot agree, counseling men is still important. The man may have needs for additional counseling. He may have inaccurate or incomplete information about the choice the woman has made. He may simply need to know that he has had a chance to voice his feelings. In the end, although they can't agree, he may at least gain an appreciation of the difficulty of the choices the woman faces.

Since the woman will make the final decision regarding the pregnancy, what are the goals of involving men in pregnancy counseling? Individual men will have widely varying needs, but there are at least three goals for pregnancy counseling with men. These aren't intended to address all of the questions and concerns, but they do represent a sort of "minimum" for counselors. These areas are: information about pregnancy options, permission to explore feelings, and a chance to decide if he can support the woman's decision.

Information about pregnancy options is one of the most crucial needs men have. In the case of abortion, anti-abortion groups have distributed graphic descriptions of second trimester abortions and often-misleading information about abortion side-effects. These can be very disturbing to a man whose partner is deciding to have an abortion. Men are often very concerned with possible ill effects the woman might suffer as the result of an abortion. A common concern is the effect of the abortion on the woman's future ability to have a child. Accurate information about pregnancy options and objective responses to men's concerns can be a great help.

Sometimes the information needed isn't related to the pregnancy, *per se.* A 16-year-old boy may come to the clinic terrified because the parents of his pregnant 15-year-old girlfriend have threatened him with a statutory rape charge. In Washington state, however, this situation doesn't meet the legal definition of statutory rape. If he is able to conquer his fears enough to come to the clinic, accurate information can obviously be of great assistance to him.

The second area of need is permission to acknowledge and explore feelings evoked by the pregnancy, including negative feelings. As stated before, many men find it difficult to acknowledge emotions. Many men have negative feelings such as anger or sorrow relating to the pregnancy. These feelings aren't comfortable for most men, and they eventually develop into feelings of guilt. Furthermore, the emphasis placed on the decision being the woman's, some men fear that expressing their feelings to the woman would be unfair or inappropriate. As the man stands silently, the woman may interpret his silence as an indication that he has no feelings. Almost inevitably the result is conflict between the couple.

The fact that men aren't readily willing or able to communicate their feelings can be very intimidating to pregnancy counselors. For the most part, pregnancy counselors are concerned that the man will explode in an outburst of anger and hostility. Although hostility does occasionally occur, it is usually not difficult for the counselor to control as the counselor represents an authority figure in most cases. That men's behavior in counseling is individual was evidenced in one clinic meeting where two "problem cases" were discussed. One of the men went through the entire clinic visit without saying a word; the other man wouldn't stop talking.

If the man is given encouragement to acknowledge his negative feelings about the pregnancy, a lot of pressure can be taken off the woman and the relationship. Indeed, it is only natural to feel frustration, sorrow, and even anger in such a situation. The important thing is that the man is helped to channel these feelings appropriately. It may not be pleasant for a pregnancy counselor to have to deal with conflict between a couple, but it is better that such conflict, if it is present, is dealt with in a structured and controlled environment.

The third major area of need, once options and feelings have been discussed, is how the man can support the woman's decision. If there is a mutually agreeable decision for the man and the woman, then the man can be a valuable source of support. The man may provide back-up and encouragement for the woman to act on follow-up instructions. For example, the man may help the woman through the abortion with emotional support, a financial contribution, and with the logistics of getting to and from the clinic. Further, he can be an important encouragement to comply with abortion aftercare instructions and in making sure that she remembers to follow through on a post-abortion check-up appointment. If the woman chooses to carry the pregnancy to term, informing the man about proper nutrition for her and avoiding drugs and alcohol during pregnancy is important. That way he can be supportive of good prenatal health habits, rather than unwittingly undermining them.

Some men are entirely excluded from the pregnancy by their female partners. For whatever reasons, some women will choose not to tell the man of the pregnancy and have an abortion without his knowledge. Emotionally, this can be a devastating experience for the man, mixing strong emotions about the pregnancy with a feeling of loss of trust with the woman. This became evident to me when a young childless man related that his girlfriend had an abortion without telling him some months earlier. He was seeking a vasectomy, "Because I never want that to happen again."

Many, if not most, couples never discuss the possibility of pregnancy until it happens. Often each will be surprised by the other's view, and this can be upsetting and disorienting. "It's like I was talking to someone I didn't even know," one man said. These couples may need time and encouragement to communicate and talk through the situation. It's possible that they will have very different opinions about the best pregnancy option, and that they will have very different individual needs for counseling and referral. While a mutually agreeable decision on a pregnancy option is desirable, it's important to accommodate the special needs of both the woman and the man.

PROFILE

At 19 years of age, Buddy, a high-school dropout and construction worker, lives in an economically depressed region of the country. Like many other couples, he and his lover based their abortion decision on "hard" reasoning, the kind that allows for little equivocation.

Buddy reacted solidly, and found justification for the abortion in light of his future plans for marriage and children. Over 90% of our men responded to their abortion experiences by promising to use family planning measures in the future, and Buddy's reasoning helps explain why many are likely to do their damnedest.

Buddy:

We're still very much in love and planning on marriage, couldn't be better. It was a trying experience for her, but I think we did the right thing. If we could have brought the child into the world, we would have.

We've often wondered what it would be like right now to be parents, for me to be a father. I was feeling guilty for a while. . . I'd done away with something that had been mine. We both felt the same way, but we learned to live with it. If anything, it's brought us that much closer. It was a learning experience. It made us think we should take special precaution.

I was impressed with the clinic. They showed husbands and boyfriends a little film which helped us. Sandy was impressed with the treatment she got. They took the feeling about taboo out of abortion and made us feel more comfortable.

They offered counseling, a nurse explained the procedure, other nurses put on a slide show. I hadn't known how they did it (the abortion procedure). The more aware the public is of the procedure, the less it would be looked down on.

I would liked to have gone back there in the procedure room with her. I didn't inquire, but I wish I could have joined her. In the recovery room she should not be interrupted in her rest.

Abortion should really be looked at. . . weigh the differences. If you can raise a child, provide for it and give it *all* your love—do it. If you can't, you shouldn't bring a child into the world.

Notes

1. A fine discussion of this distinction is found in Bradford Keeney, *Aesthetics of Change*, New York: The Guilford Press, 1983.

2. See Jay Haley, *Problem Solving Therapy*, New York: Harper & Row, 1976.

3. Ellen Freeman, "Abortion: Subjective Attitudes and Feelings," op. cit., p. 155.

Chapter 9

Men Who Want More

I can imagine no circumstances under which I would have an abortion; I consider the fetus a human life. But, I would also consider it immoral to bend my efforts to stop any other human being from having an abortion she deemed necessary. I hate the idea of abortion, but I hate even more the death of a woman by coat hangers or lye. I hate, that is to say, the idea of murder twice done.

Harrison, Barbara Grizzuti, *Off Center* (New York: Playboy Paperbacks, 1980, p. 77.)

...the public discourse about abortion is posed entirely in "male" terms of abstract rights— "the right to life" versus "the right to choose." The public men speak a different language than the private women. The male legislators misunderstand and, therefore, devalue the moral standards underlying the decisions of the prochoice women.

Carol Gilligan, as reported by Judith Kegan Gardiner, "Morality on a New Scale," (*In These Times,* October 20–26, 1982, p. 19.)

At one time or another most of our 30 cooperating clinics have been picketed by anti-abortionists, and the males who accompany abortion patients through the picket line often take away vivid memories of that encounter. In this chapter, we focus on a pro-choice activist, Bill Baird, and on an anti-abortionist, Joe Scheidler, whose diametrically opposed positions help illuminate the morality debate that sooner or later touches nearly every male in the clinic waiting room.

Baird and Scheidler are nationally prominent, energetic, and thoroughly committed activists. While we do not agree with every attitude and policy recommendation of theirs, we do endorse Baird's insistence on legal, safe, and affordable abortions. We also agree that Scheidler sometimes strikes a nerve, and finally compels an open-minded listener to recognize more personal confusion and unhappiness over abortion than is comfortable.[1]

Most of our waiting room men were of two minds here: On the one hand, they were very supportive of the 1973 Supreme Court decision, and wanted abortion-on-request to remain the law of the land. Their appreciation of pro-choice services was considerable, especially since 85% felt both parties had jointly reached their decision for abortion. At the same time, however, only 15% believed the fetus was not human until birth, and another 25% were convinced the question of personhood had to remain unanswered. As many as 60% were troubled by the irrevocable ending of the life they had helped set in motion.

To resolve this dissonance between the positions of Baird (pro-choice) and Scheidler (anti-abortion), many of the men seem to adopt a poignant, pain-embracing position similar to that taken by feminist Mary Kay Blakely:

"Pro-life" is the euphemism chosen by the people whose definition of life is purely fetal. Life, for them, is a concept that stops at birth. They are the people who...have no compassion for the fully developed lives of the women whose circumstances have brought them to the front door.

Those are the "pro-choice" people, another misnomer. The "choice" they face is either an abortion—a decision none of them will celebrate—or, a range of bleak alternatives, from martyred motherhoods to unrelenting poverty. There are no pleasant "choices" in the range of possibilities.[2]

Like Blakely, these waiting room men side with women who have final responsibility for the termination decision, albeit these men want to shoulder as much of that burden as a loving and trusting woman will permit.

Overall, the men who wait ponder much on clinic day, and long thereafter, about the sharply contrasting values and policies of Baird and Scheidler. Unhappily, as it is possible to hold conflicting emotions and moral tenets at one and the same time, many such men are finally left with considerable emotional and moral ambiguity—a residual toll that pro-choice or anti-choice activists alike might use in support of very different public policy implications.

William R. Baird, Jr.[3]

If you ask Bill Baird, the self-styled "father of abortion rights," about men and abortion, as we have done often since we first met him in 1982–1983, you should brace yourself for strong reactions!

Born in 1933 into a poor family of six children in Brooklyn, New York, William R. Baird, Jr., traces the start of his pro-choice crusade back to a time in 1963 when he was working for a national drug firm. While making a sales call at a New York hospital, he watched a woman "stagger in covered with blood, and holding her stomach":

> I heard the most piercing scream of pain and agony. She was begging 'please, my children, my children.' She had an eight-inch piece of coat hanger poking out of her uterus. Wrapped around with adhesive tape—to gently push and scrape the wall of the uterus and produce enough blood so the doctor could legally do the abortion to preserve the life of the woman. This mother miscalculated by about half an inch. She died right in front of me . . . . [4]

Baird later learned that the woman had been 29 years old, quite poor, and the mother of eight. Given the strict ban against legal abortions in New York in 1963, the woman had become another grim statistic in the annual column of mortalities traceable to a botched self-abortion attempt.

Persuaded at that instance that this was insane, Baird began a life's work of speaking out against the anti-choice situation and on behalf of birth control education and options. Arrested in 1965 and 1966 for these then-illegal activities, Baird pioneered in the concept of bringing medical information and materials to the poor by going directly into low-income neighborhoods with a 30-foot converted truck he called a "plan van." He decorated the interior like a comfortable living room and consulting room, painted the sides with the message, "Free Family Planning," and drove it night after night into ghetto areas. In May 1965, he gave out contraceptives from the van and insisted on being arrested, since the New York State law only authorized physicians, nurses, and professional personnel to do so. Less than a month after Baird was held overnight in a Long Island jail, the high court overturned such laws— "a reform possibly hastened by Baird's arrest."

Later, in 1965, Baird established the nation's first abortion and birth control center on a college campus (Hofstra University on Long Island). When the New York state legislature in 1967 repealed an anti-birth control law Baird had challenged, he opened the first of what later became three such centers.

In 1967, Baird traveled to Boston to deliberately challenge the constitutionality of the state's "crimes against chastity" law. Under its provisions, only married couples could receive birth control information or materials, which only physicians could provide. After spending 36 days in the Charles Street Jail, Baird was released by a federal ruling. He continued his case and, in 1970, won in the U.S. Supreme Court, thereby legalizing birth control for single persons (Baird v. Eisenstadt). In 1973, when the Supreme Court overturned state laws prohibiting abortion, it favorably cited the Baird decision six times.

Baird reappeared before the High Court in 1979, when he successfully challenged a Massachusetts law that would have required minors seeking abortions to get the consent of both parents (Baird v. Bellotti). One of very few Americans to ever figure into more than a single major Supreme Court ruling, Baird is very proud of this distinction—and of his record of eight jailings in five states on behalf of his ongoing crusade for birth control and abortion rights.[5]

Building on his role in these landmark court decisions, Baird has appeared on every leading national TV news or celebrity talk show, and has been written about in Newsweek, Time, Life, and newspapers around the country. As well, according to his personal public relations packet, he has spoken before standing-room-only audiences at colleges and universities from coast to coast.

Indeed, Baird alone, of all major pro-choice leaders, has made a practice of attending and picketing every national meeting of the National Right-to-Life Committee. In 1982 he registered at the convention hotel (the Hyatt in Cherry Hill, New Jersey) so he could picket the tenth annual meeting without being charged with trespassing. Two local news reporters noted he had "surreptitiously registered as a convention delegate so he could attend sessions and challenge speakers. 'I'm a great believer in confronting my enemy,' Baird said. 'I believe you fight for freedom in a nonviolent way.' "[6] That said, he joined eight pickets outside the 1,500-delegate meeting in carrying a 6-foot-high cross with signs depicting anti-abortion groups as crucifiers of women who suffer unwanted births.

Typical, perhaps, of the actual confrontations that Baird manages to have with anti-abortion delegates was one at the Cherry Hill meeting that had him rise from the floor at a session and directly challenge an exhibit area sensation:

Baird asked why one of the women (at a booth of a group known as Methodists for Life) carried a 12-week, 6-inch fetus (floating in a covered glass jar of formaldehyde).

'If she has a great respect for human life, why isn't it buried? Could you imagine you and I as adults walking around with a cadaver?'

'I am being very reverent in my attitude toward this child,' the woman replied. 'This child is a martyr. It shows the reality of abortion. What good would it do in the ground?'[7]

The newspaper reporter chose not to comment on the impact on, or significance of, this exchange for the onlookers.

Again, in 1983, Baird showed up as a registered delegate (and bête noire) at the annual national Right-to-Life convention. Valuable media attention was given once more—exactly as he expected—to his pro-choice point of view. A month before the July meeting in Orlando, for example, he asked the Florida attorney general to investigate the pending anti-choice convention for advocating "criminal acts," a complaint later discounted by police authorities, who Baird, in turn, castigated as "right-wing reactionaries."[8] During the three-day gathering of about 2,000 anti-abortionists, Baird urged reporters to recognize they had "witnessed here a national conspiracy to violate the civil rights of women . . . they brow-beat them, pressure them, and try to brainwash them."[9] Baird insisted some anti-abortion leaders were preaching violence, as when they urged followers to invade abortion clinics and interrupt ongoing surgery. Once again, as often in years past (and directly to Art Shostak after their February 1982 TV panel appearance), Baird closed by telling reporters he feared for his life and expected to be assassinated.[10]

(Anti-abortionist leader Joe Scheidler, in turn, rebutted his longtime acquaintance and protagonist by dismissing Baird's charges as being out of hand. Scheidler insisted that the use of violence had never been traced to the Right-to-Life movement: "The violence is in the clinics, not outside of them," he concluded, but not before boasting that his group had succeeded in closing down six abortion clinics in Chicago in recent months.)[11]

As if sharp differences in social change style and tactics were not enough, Baird has been outspoken on explosive topics that many pro-choice advocates prefer to discuss only in private.

- Baird has indicated that he is personally opposed to abortions, though he feels the decision "is the woman's, not the state's or mine. . . . I am not pro-abortion. I am pro-choice. I want to give everyone the right to intelligent sex education to reduce the need for abortion."[12]

• Baird has condemned the Catholic Church as "the most savage critic I have," and "the single greatest enemy of the rights of women." He has asked the Church to "recognize there are decent people who are pro-choice, and stop firing up the anti-abortion lunatic fringe."[13]

• Baird has urged supporters of the right to abortion to let anti-abortionists know "that violence will be met with violence."[14] While he recommended strong self-defense measures, he pointed out that "so far no one has firebombed a Right-to-Life headquarters, no one has firebombed a Birthright headquarters, no one has firebombed a Roman Catholic headquarters, but that does not mean that persons are not contemplating the possibility."[15] After detailing 40 incidents of violence that year against clinics, Baird told delegates to the 1983 National Abortion Federation meeting, "It's war! Never shuffle or beg! Go right through them! Tell them—'My sisters must be free!' "[16]

Given these, and other very controversial pronouncements, it is little wonder that an admirer in 1978 described his relationships with organized feminist and pro-abortion groups as "love-hate. He's a nut, but an inspired nut, too much of a maverick to be a dependable ally."[17]

Long an embarrassment to certain pro-choice feminists (and their male allies) who insist on decorum, civility, conventionality, and evolutionary ways, Baird presses instead for radical change. A "master manipulator of screaming headlines and incendiary issues," Baird's energy in never granting the opposition a moment's peace sets a frenetic pace that few other pro-choice leaders can keep.[18] Ingenious at poking the most exposed nerves of society, Baird takes seeming pleasure in accumulating detractors, even among pro-choice activists. Typical is the dismay of Planned Parenthood, which he indicts for fearing to arouse antagonism. Baird has called the organization a "wasteful, hidebound bureaucracy," "afraid of its own shadow."[19] Baird was hailed in 1974 by a male comrade-in-arms, pioneering activist Lawrence Lader, for daring all in a "crude, inflammatory approach" (confrontation politics), one that seemed "the only way to shake the country...the only strategy that could produce immediate results."[20] Baird's histrionics, at least as viewed then by Lader, "seemed justifiable considering the prison terms he risked—and eventually served. His strategy always brought progress in the long run. His style added a wild, unorthodox zest that was essential to the campaign."[21]

Tagged by the press as the "father" of the birth-control and right-to-abortion movements, Baird takes a strong position on the role of males in the abortion context:

- *Male participation* is highly desirable, and Baird insisted in a 1969 press account of his Hempstead clinic that men be brought along by clinic clients "to make sure they know what the girl will be going through. And I want them to take care of any costs."[22]

- *Male leadership* is a valuable supplement to the style of many feminists in the pro-choice movement—"too many of whom take a melba toast approach."[23] As well, "we need each other, truly. You sure don't have to be a woman to fight for women."[24]

- *Spousal consent* is an unacceptable interference with a wife's right to an abortion—and Baird provided legal fees for a 1972 test case whose winner, a divorce-seeking 19-year-old wife, praised Baird as "the only one fighting for women's rights. I got no help from any of the women's liberation groups."[25]

- *Males as family life educators* must assume greater responsibility with their wives for the sex education of their children: "I would particularly urge fathers to take the initiative and talk with their children about sex. While they have sometimes discussed sex with their sons, . . . they have almost totally neglected any discussion with their daughters."[26]

- *Males as co-conceivers* must resist the popular practice of judging this or that reason a female has for wanting an abortion; males should learn that females have a right to be wrong, an absolute right.

- *Males as pro-choice activists* must guard their language as it is a critical tool: The enemy is *not* to be designated "pro-life," but "anti-abortion;" co-conceivers are not "expectant fathers," but "impregnators" until a baby is born; the fetus is *not* a "child," but a fertilized egg, smaller than a microscopic egg ("an acorn is *not* an oak").

Bill Baird, in sum, remains one of the most mind-stretching and spirit-lifting figures on the scene;[27] a man who shows the way to valuable gains for *all* drawn into the abortion vortex, gains still absent from the scene, though certainly not for lack of Baird's 20 years of all-out effort.

Joseph M. Scheidler[28]

My first encounter with abortion came when I was in active service in the U.S. Naval Reserve in 1945–1946. There were several occasions when young men would be collecting money from their shipmates ". . . to help some poor slob get an abortion for his girl." It was never money for oneself to pay for "his" girl's abortion, but was always at least once removed.

I never gave any money to such funds, having a firm moral conviction that any cooperation in the evil of abortion was a serious (mortal) sin, and was excommunicable in the Church I was a member of (Catholic). I also knew from considerable reading that abortion was the unjust and deliberate taking of a human life. I wanted no part in murder.

Throughout college, the topic of abortion was discussed in classroom situations, but I don't recall anyone I knew ever having an abortion or even being involved in one. I knew one or two young women who became pregnant out of wedlock, but there was usually a rapid planning session and marriage before the baby was born. That was in the late 1940s at the University of Notre Dame.

Even as a newspaper reporter for the *South Bend Tribune,* where some of the staff were not exactly moral paragons, I still did not encounter anyone struggling with the problem of abortion and I went innocently on my way believing that this was a problem that rarely troubled people—the *need* to abort an unwanted child.

In the seminary I attended, we discussed abortion at length, both as a moral evil and as a canonical impediment. We studied St. Thomas and the other Fathers on human life and although there was a whole range of interpretations of when "ensoulment" took place, the conclusion was always that abortion deprived a human being of life and was not only a form of homocide, but was an especially grievous sin and always caused one to lose membership in the Church, even if one were not performing the abortion or having it, but was an accomplice. The only things that could relieve one of serious guilt were ignorance of the seriousness of the sin or grave, paralyzing fear.

Following my philosophy and theology courses, I left the seminary just before ordination and returned to "the world," as we called life outside the walls. I taught, dated, and continued my studies at the University of Chicago, and elsewhere, but through all my contact and travels, I rarely encountered the subject of abortion or paid much attention to it as a social or personal problem. I read accounts of liberalization of abortion in the Soviet Union, Japan, and England, and was aware that certain states had changed their restrictive laws on abortion, and I once wrote letters to the *Chicago Tribune's* "Voice of the People" protesting an effort in the Illinois General Assembly to liberalize Illinois' abortion law.

My real involvement against the crime of abortion came with the U.S. Supreme Court's twin decision on January 22, 1973, legalizing abortion for the full term of a woman's pregnancy, and striking down all state laws restricting abortion. The ruling was sweeping in its scope and even caught the pro-abortionists off guard. Nobody had expected such an extensive ruling that gave no quarter to the unborn child, no rights to the parents of minor children, no notification to the father of the child. It was the most blatant exercise of "raw judicial power," as a dissenting justice called it, that could be imagined. It was so sweeping that even the generally pro-abortion media misreported it and to this day has not understood its full dimensions.

But many of us did. The ruling put me into a kind of shock, from which I have never recovered. I knew about genocide, having traveled extensively in Germany following World War II. I saw the death camps of Europe and I saw the remains of what had been cities in the countries where those death camps had operated. I realized in 1973 that America was no better off than a Nazi dictatorship, as far as the unborn children were concerned, and that it would be difficult to save many of them from this new, sweeping decree of the Supreme Court.

I immediately resigned my job with a public relations firm and set up the Chicago Office for Pro-life Publicity, believing that if Americans knew about the humanity of the unborn child and the dangers of abortion, they would resist this new ruling. That office functioned for one year, when I was hired to direct the Illinois Right-to-Life Committee. After four years leading that group, I felt that it was too restrictive and overburdened with people who were willing to take a soft approach to abortion. I resigned and formed Friends for Life, which I directed for two years when the same problem arose: too much compromise, too many restrictions. I left Friends for Life, and founded the Pro-Life Action League, trimmed down the board and made provision that there would be no halfway measures in fighting abortion.

As a pro-life activist I have frequently run into the problem of the fathers of children to be aborted, or those already killed by abortion. I have had dozens of phone calls from men who were desperately trying to prevent a girlfriend or wife from aborting a wanted child. I have had an equal or even greater number of calls from men who have found out by one means or another that their child's mother has already had an abortion. All were at least somewhat angry, very confused and bewildered. Most wanted to know what legal action they could take. One man had found an abortion clinic receipt on his wife's dresser, one found the bill on his charge card. Some have said they could no longer live with the woman who had destroyed their child without even consulting with the child's father.

One such desperate father said he had already filed for divorce. He could not live with a woman who would kill his child. I could sympathize with him. I can't even imagine loving someone who would murder a child, let alone a child I had fathered and wanted to protect. I often wonder how couples stay together when the wife has had an abortion, or how a woman can live with a man who is urging her to abort. I suppose it takes all kinds of people to make up a society, but I thank God for giving me a loving wife who abhors abortion as much as I do.

I am constantly amazed at the casual way men treat abortion. We run into them at the abortion clinics, pushing the girl into the clinic, cursing us for trying to explain the danger of abortion to the young woman, the pain the unborn child will feel, the humanity of the child, the responsibility parents have toward their own child. They frequently call us obscene names and tell us to mind our own business. Some call the police and accuse us of harassment. Some will come out of the clinic later, after dumping the girl there to have the abortion, muttering that it is the end of *that* affair. Frequently, the girl goes home from the abortion alone. Many of these affairs break up after the abortion, if not before.

I believe any man who would allow the mother of his child to have that child aborted is sick, morally and emotionally. It is unthinkable that a man would urge an abortion, but it is nearly as bad for a man to sit by idly and allow a woman to abort his child without doing everything in his power to protect and save that child. I believe it speaks ill for our society that men are so weak, spineless and self-centered that they pervert the father instinct and allow this destruction of their own offspring. I have no pity for such creatures and believe they cease to have any claim on real manhood. They certainly will make rotten fathers, if they should ever decide *not* to have their children aborted. What kind of a father will allow some of his children to be exterminated?

At the clinics, I frequently talk with the father of the child about to be aborted, and I have found a wide variety of concern. Most of it is extremely negative attitudes toward the "pregnancy." Some will say they just want to get rid of "the damn thing." Several have been actively shoving the young woman, cursing at us while encouraging her not to listen. They will try to hide the photographs of interuterine life that we are attempting to show the young woman, calling these pictures distortions and lies. We have taken a number of blows and much verbal abuse from these "fathers."

I have a habit of calling them all "Dad," and on occasion will pull out my wallet and show them a few pictures of my seven children, and then contrast these family pictures with photographs of aborted babies, suctioned out and showing arms and legs and collapsed rib cages in a mass of placental matter. I'll say something to the effect that here is my son and daughter, and here's yours in a few minutes. You'll never play baseball with *that*.

Several years ago, I attended a coroner's inquest involving an abortion in which the woman died. The abortionist was from a notorious clinic in Lincolnwood, Illinois, and had aborted a young married woman in her eighth or tenth week of pregnancy. He thought he had removed that baby, but the woman continued to show all the signs of being pregnant, so about three months later, she went back to him. He performed a second abortion on the woman. She went home, delivered a lacerated baby with two amputations from the first abortion attempt, and died of loss of blood. The doctor had severed an artery in the second abortion. Her husband, who had not even known that she was pregnant, returned home to find his dead wife, and the aborted baby.

The day following the verdict, "death from legal abortion," I was getting gasoline at a local filling station not far from the clinic when a young man about eighteen asked me for directions to the clinic. I tried to tell him about the death that had occurred at the clinic, but he drove off. I drove to the clinic and waited for him. When he arrived, I told him I didn't like for people to run off in the middle of a conversation, and I asked if I could sit with him and his girlfriend for a few minutes to tell them something about abortion, their baby, and the abortion clinic they were about to visit.

The young man was very receptive. He said he didn't want his girl to have the abortion, said he wanted to marry her and would raise the baby. She was adamant and dumb. She sat mute, chewing her gum, and seemingly unmoved by his protests of deep love and affection. I suggested all kinds of help that I could get them, both in Chicago and in their hometown in northern Indiana. I suggested that they take the day in Chicago to think about their decision. I offered to take them to lunch, pay for a movie or play. He was eager to discuss the matter while she didn't say anything. Finally, hoping to draw her into the discussion, I asked her how far along she was. Her reply was, "I'm a sophomore." I don't think I talked them out of the abortion. I will never know because I had to leave to give a talk and they didn't meet or call me as I had requested. But at least that young man was *trying* to save his son or daughter.

Some years ago, a young man contacted me and said he wanted to do something to make amends for an abortion he had funded. His girlfriend had gotten pregnant by him, and while he tried to discourage her from having an abortion, he was unable even up to the time she went into the operating room. He had driven her to the clinic, and went in with her, all the time trying to talk her out of having the abortion. He paid for the abortion and sat in the waiting room with her, still talking about the baby and offering marriage or at least allowing the baby to live and promising to take care of it. When she went ahead with the abortion, they broke up, but he had not been able to reconcile his part in the death of his child.

Together we formed "Fathers United Against Abortion," and this young man went on a few radio shows and a television program or two trying to garner support and encouraging other men to join. He never had much luck, and so far as I know the organization no longer operates. But while he was active he did some interesting work with my own pro-life group, and was instrumental in launching one of the most damaging exposés against abortion clinic operators that has ever been done. He would take abortion clinic counselors out to dinner and quiz them on their clinic programs, and put these interviews on tape. Later, we used these tapes to encourage a twenty-part series on abortion in the *Chicago Sun Times* and launch an all-out investigation by the *Sun Times* and the Better Government Agency into abortion clinic practices in Chicago. The series was later reprinted in tabloid form and our pro-life group purchased and distributed 4,000 copies to other pro-life groups in an effort to launch similar investigative reporting in other cities.

As the father of seven children, I cannot have anything but contempt or pity for the man who doesn't fight to protect and save his unborn child in the same way he would fight to save and protect his born child. The only difference between the two is that the unborn is more defenseless and needs his protection more, even, than the born child does. He is father of both.

It is an indictment against our society that so many men are irresponsible about sex, care nothing for the mother of their child, and will allow their children to be murdered. I consider the man who buys an abortion for his girlfriend to be a moral pimp and worse, a criminal who pays for a hit on his own offspring. There are no adequate expressions in the English language to describe such a person. I do realize, however, that even this form of low life can repent and regret what he has done and can change and do good for others. Nobody is consigned to hell before he dies, and good can come out of evil. However, to treat abortion as an option, to place the life of one's own son or daughter in the balance against one's pleasure, or convenience, is to sell a life very cheaply.

"Deciding an abortion together" is plotting the death of one's child together and is a despicable evil. It cannot be "enhancing" in any way. Simply to share the crime so that neither can totally blame the other when it is over may seem like a good idea, but there will still be blame and disgust for one another from time to time and will irritate the less sensitive one. Nothing is solved and the guilt can only grow with time.

There is a horror in every abortion that cannot be described. It is not only the dismemberment of a child, which is horror enough, but is the destruction of new generations; killing the child is also killing the father of future generations. It is the murder of one's inheritance. It kills the past, the present and the future of one's heredity. It wipes out nations. It is both suicide and genocide. It takes away not only a child's sight, hearing, laughter, and dreams, but cuts off a family tree at the root, ends a line of men and women, and cries out to Heaven for vengeance. There is no greater evil than this evil, the aborting of man.

If one pretends to be religious, his religion ends with the aborting of his child. Religion is a right relationship with God. How can one have any relation with a loving God who knows his own and has granted men and women the power to share in his creative act, and then kill God's most helpless and defenseless children? How can one pretend to believe in God and deny God the love of a child, destined to come to know, love and serve Him and share eternity with Him in Heaven. Those who abort God's children are atheists in their hearts.

The only way a man should be brought into the abortion decision is as an advocate for the unborn child who may have no advocate elsewhere. He should be brought into the decision as the father of this child who wants his son or daughter to live. To talk about "making a hard decision together" is too foolish and bizarre to discuss. Just picture a mother and father of a three-year-old discussing plans to kill their little child, and deciding that this mutual decision is somehow life-enhancing. They'd be carted off to the looney bin. Abortion is just the murder of a younger child, and "discussing abortion" is plotting this murder. Play with semantics until you work out a nice sounding excuse and the facts will remain the same. This is almost 1984, and we are all set for "doublespeak," using words to mean what we want them to mean, using illogical conclusions as though they make sense and calling good evil, right wrong, life death.

Through it all, there will remain a few who know the difference, who are not taken in by the twisted semantics of the age. And these few will know clearly that society is living a lie. We will hear your arguments that confuse and impress many, and we will know that you are living a lie. And we will not even have to condemn you. You will have condemned yourselves.

PROFILE

Anthony represents 30% of our men who found the abortion helped them and their partners bring their love further along than ever before. Anthony's experience also confronts us with questions which go far beyond a couple's ability to achieve a supportive abortion experience.

Specifically, how fair is it that couples who seek legal abortion services are sometimes physically hassled by anti-abortion pickets? And why, when the couple attains the safe quarters of the clinic, should they receive inconsistent professional treatment and demeanor? It was disconcerting to listen to Anthony's account, and to know that he was not sensationalizing an isolated incident.

Anthony:

We have an excellent relationship. We're still living together. We were both really burned out for two weeks. It bothered me a lot, the whole thing was, I didn't like the idea of my baby being killed.

We've got another year of college and couldn't support ourselves yet. I offered to quit and work, but we ruled out adoption, which would have hurt a lot more. She really decided to have it and I finally, after three weeks, agreed after we muddled around and looked at it from all sides. We were so close to getting out into the real world.

I think it's too much responsibility for us. Maybe a bad thing to say at 24, but I've seen too many friends whose kids have got nothing because parents had to get married.

We've gone out for five years and marriage is a matter of time. It was no one-night fling. Our relationship is stable. We have just started living together. I am concerned most that she is going to be able to have another child. I don't know why I'm so fearful. There haven't been any problems. . . .

The clinic could have done a lot better. We spent six hours there. I finally asked what was going on, what was happening. I couldn't go in to procedure or recovery.

There was no counseling at all, including for me. I would have felt a hell of a lot better. She wished I had been able to go with her. I learned more from her than I did from the preoccupied counselor. I didn't like her attitude at all, it bummed me out and stopped me from asking questions. They should have gotten us together at some time to inform us or check our decision.

There were four protesters, nuns outside. It was traumatic enough without being hassled and heckled. One guy grabbed me. I tried to be real nice, said, "No, thank you." He grabbed Anita, and I told him to leave her alone.

They had signs and pamphlets all over the street and yard. I'm surprised they can get away with that. It's a horrible thing for a girl to have to go through that crap. They had gone by the time we were done, luckily. We had been in there from ten to four.

The waiting room had a lot of magazines. All over the walls were plastered posters about birth control. The message was like, "You really messed up this time, don't do it again!"

I was anxious and nervous the whole time. If they had put up bright, cheery pictures instead of the sarcastic, demeaning poster of a guy and girl arm in arm with the guy crossing his fingers behind his back. . . . It's lousy in an abortion center.

The waiting girls were talkin' and making natural chatter. All the guys were sitting around, heads down, quiet, bummed out. Seven or eight guys. Two were pissed off; they didn't want to be there, didn't even know if it was their kid. There were two other guys like me, in college, two older men in their mid to late thirties—looked like factory workers. They didn't say anything to anybody. One slept most of four hours. I went out and walked around for two hours. We waited and waited. Everybody was smoking cigarette after cigarette.

The clinic should take the initiative to start counseling, even though there are guys there who probably didn't care. Maybe I needed an emotional crutch, but both of us wished I could have been there in the procedure or recovery room.

It's not going to happen again, I can tell you that. Anita didn't want the pill because of side effects. I wish somebody there (clinic) would have talked to us about it. We both sat there a long time, a lot of sitting. I thought we'd never get out of there.

Deep down inside, I still feel guilty about having put her through that. I just wish people would think more about what they're doing. I wish I had. Sex is so much fun until *it* happens.

PROFILE

Family planning is a high priority with many couples, but even the most consistent use of birth control is not 100% effective. Legal abortion makes it possible for couples like Charles and his wife to compensate for the margin of failure inherent in all forms of birth control.

Charles reminded us that not all pregnancies result from carelessness. He also emphasized the positive aspects and indispensible contributions a good clinic experience can make to the welfare of a couple.

Charles:

We've had no subsequent problems. We're planning on having a child next year. The biggest reason we had the abortion was that a child did not fit into the plans of our timetable. It was the right thing to do and given our circumstances it was best at the time. There have been no physical or psychic repercussions. It's been a private matter and there's been no need to discuss it with counselors and so on.

I personally feel it was right for us, but maybe not for others. It was a good experience for us. Given the term of pregnancy, I just don't feel it was a living child. There wasn't any attachment or guilt or remorse. It was a first trimester, ten weeks. If it had been later, I would have felt it, it would have weighed heavier on my mind, but we didn't feel that way. If it had been second trimester, neither one of us would have opted for the procedure.

I thought the clinic did an outstanding job of providing a conducive atmosphere. It meant a lot to me. I felt comfortable, my wife felt comfortable. Nice people, nice place.

I'm thankful that this country can provide the services. There's nothing worse than having unwanted children.

Notes

1. Feminist Jean Bethke Elshtain warns that "without allowing right-to-life women to speak the truth as they understand it; without engaging them from a stance that respects their human possibility for the creation of meaning through uncoerced dialogue; which requires of the investigator a stance of empathy, openness, and a willingness to entertain and explore alternatives she may not share, we will continue to treat them in distorted, presumptuous, and prejudicial ways..." Jean Bethke Elshtain, *Public Man, Private Woman: Women in Social and Political Thought*, p. 312. Princeton, N.J.: Princeton University Press, 1981. Similarly, Carmen and Moody, as far back as 1973, insisted that "it is of supreme importance...that we limit the 'warfare' by a resolution to refrain from the language of extrem-

ism that writes off our opponents as evil adversaries, unworthy of being heard." Arlene Carmen and Howard Moody, *Abortion Counseling and Social Change,* p. 115. Valley Forge, Penn.: Judson Press, 1973.

2. Mary Kay Blakely, "Hers." *New York Times,* April 9, 1981, p. C-2. Blakely quotes poet Marge Piercy's argument that "a woman is not a pear tree," and goes on herself to insist that "human reproduction involved much more commitment and nurturance than a nine-month gestation period."

3. All of the quotations in the Baird section, unless otherwise indicated, are from a public relations packet provided by Mr. Baird at Art Shostak's request (a collection of newspaper and magazine articles in photocopy format, the pages of which were generally unnumbered). We are very grateful to Mr. Baird for his cooperation in sharing this press file.

4. As quoted in Gayle Pollard, "Baird on Baird: 15 Years of Crusading." The *Boston Globe,* April 4, 1982, p. B-2. See also Mildred Hamilton, "The Fiery 'Father of the Abortion Movement.' " *San Francisco Examiner,* June 25, 1980. (unpaged)

5. According to Laura Scharf, Director of Communications (in 1980) for the Bill Baird Center, he has "succeeded in getting more laws changed in the fields of birth control and abortion than anyone else in the history of this country." (Public relations packet: May, 1980, p. 1.)

6. As quoted in Walter F. Naedle and Timothy Dwyer, "Both Sides Brandish their Symbols as Anti-Abortion Convention Opens." *Philadelphia Inquirer,* July 16, 1982, p. 6-A.

7. As quoted in Karen Curran, "Pro-Lifers Advocate Activism." *Camden Courier Post,* July 17, 1982. p. 4-A.

8. As quoted in Ike Flores, "Abortion Foes told to Picket Clinics." *Philadelphia Inquirer,* July 16, 1982, p. 6-A.

9. Ibid. In 1980 Baird explained to reporters covering the annual Right-to-Life meeting, "I go to their convention every year to call attention to the bigotry of their crusade. Calling a fertilized egg a person is as ridiculous as my saying an acorn is really an oak tree." Hamilton, op. cit.

10. Typical is this 1978 quote: "Let me tell you what it does to your life. . . . Not a week goes by without death threats. Police take me to and from speaking engagements. I have bars in the windows of

my clinics in Boston and New York." As quoted in Georgie Ann Geyer, " 'Father of Abortion Right.' " *Los Angeles Times*, May 15, 1978. (unpaged)

11. Flores, op. cit.

12. As quoted in Donna Furlong, "Bill Baird Continues Fight for Women's Medical Rights." *Daily Evening Press* (Lynn, Mass.), August 22, 1980 (unpaged). "I look at it this way. I am a pro-life advocate. I have saved the lives of countless women who may have died through dangerous and illegal abortions by helping to make abortions legal and safe."

13. As quoted in Hamilton, op. cit. Baird, in 1966, conducted the first pro-choice protest ever held in front of New York's St. Patrick's Cathedral. His signs read, "Rome fiddles while the world yearns for birth control." Lawrence Lader, *Abortion II*, p. 52. Boston: Beacon, 1974. In 1980 Baird asked, "Can a religious belief be used in this country to force its tenets, by law, on others? My battle is not about abortion. My battle is whether a woman is free to do what is best for herself." Hamilton, op. cit. In 1981 he insisted "there is a war declared by Rome. The biggest sexist leader of the world is that Pope... I'm as fed up with organized religion because I've seen so much hatred from them." As quoted in Karen Garlock, "Abortion Rights Non-Sexist, Activist Says," *Cincinnati Enquirer*, January 24, 1981 (unpaged). Baird has long urged that the courts rule illegal the church's use of its tax-exempt status from political activity and lobbying. See, for example, Robert H. Kramer, Jr., "Baird Predicts Advocates of Abortion May Lose the Fight because of Apathy." *Providence Journal*, May 1, 1978 (unpaged). Baird warns, "I'm not preaching anti-Catholicism. But if we lose this abortion law, we'll go back to the Dark Ages." As quoted in Marvin Pave, "Catholics Can End Abortion, Baird Warns." *Boston Globe*, January 17, 1974 (unpaged).

14. As quoted in Anonymous, "Catholic Church Spurs Violence, Pro-Abortionist Says." *Cleveland Plain-Dealer*, February 20, 1981, p. 1. " 'The lawlessness of the anti-abortion side has to stop,' he said."

15. Ibid. In a paper by Baird entitled "Abortion Center Survival: A Partial Guide," he writes, "We are not suggesting this, but it has been considered that sugar be placed in their gas tanks, air let out of tires, calls made to homes in the middle of the night." Baird calls it "a bitter irony that the pro-choice people, all using non-violent methods, often are nervous about offending the anti-abortion forces, with their firebombing tactics." Hamilton, op. cit.

16. As recorded by Art Shostak from the CBS-TV *Morning News*, April 13, 1983. It should be noted that Baird reminds reporters, "I have been punched, kicked, spat at, called every name, and never once responded physically." As quoted in Vera Glaser, "He's Victim of 'Religious War.' " *Miami Herald*, August 7, 1978, p. 4-D.

17. Glaser, ibid. Baird "nevertheless thinks those groups should help finance his activities."

18. Lader, op. cit., p. 51.

19. Ibid., p. 51. " 'I teach more people in a day than they reach in a month,' he proclaimed, 'and I do it free.' " Baird's first major victims came in 1968 when Planned Parenthood officially adopted a right-to-abortion stand after a Baird-organized sit-in in their headquarters.

20. Lader, op. cit., p. 16. "It was also a dangerous approach, considered by many we were trying to reach, and even by some in the movement, nothing more than outright law-breaking. It could have failed. Yet it succeeded because it had justice and humanity on its side, and was the only strategy that could produce immediate results."

21. Ibid., p. 51. "We needed the unexpected and irreverent. We needed tumult. We had to create a sense of danger and urgency. The risks were considerable, but the movement was built on risks." (p. 55). Baird "proved the effectiveness of public shock tactics. It was these tactics...that would produce a wave of anger across the country, particularly among women, and usher in the next phase of the abortion movement. We could not move the country from moderate reform to complete repeal without such anger."(p. 80).

22. As quoted in Harry Roden, "Abortion Clinic: Crusade Goes on Amid Controversy." *Long Island Press*, September 28, 1969 (unpaged).

23. Hamilton, op. cit. In 1973 Baird criticized feminists Gloria Steinem and Betty Friedan as "intellectual egg-heads who mouth the problems, but do not put themselves on the line." As quoted in Susan Everly, "William Baird Will Seek Release of Doctors Jailed for Abortions." *San Francisco Gazette*, January 25, 1973 (unpaged).

24. As quoted in Garlock, op. cit. In 1982 Baird explained his complaints about certain women's groups with these words: "They will say to me, 'You're a man,' I will say, 'Phyllis Schlafy is a woman'...It's not your gonads. It's where your head is at.' " Pollard, op. cit., p. B-2.

25. As quoted in Bruce Drake, "Abortion Case Triumph Thrills Wife." *New York Daily News*, June 1, 1972 (unpaged).

26. As quoted in UPI, "Boston Abortion Patients Catholic." *Clinton Daily Item*, January 8, 1981 (unpaged).

27. For an account of the respect, and also the hatred Baird has earned from different anti-choice individuals, see Merton, op. cit., p. 194, 209–210. As long ago as 1974 Baird seemed to a reporter to "have grown increasingly and irritatingly fond of hearing himself cry 'betrayal' and 'oh, how I've suffered,' and has occasionally gotten self-righteous about imagined snubbing by those whom he assumes owe him uncritical loyalty on demand. . ." Lader, op. cit., p. 54. In 1978 a journalist noted that "Baird is a hero largely only to his patients. Indulging in their own 'devil' theory about men, the militant woman's movement has refused to recognize his substantial contribution. Admittedly, he has a touch both of fanatic and the martyr. But Baird also has the prophetic gift of having been sometimes too right." Georgie Anne Geyer, op. cit. When asked in 1982 how he wished to be remembered, Baird replied, "As a loving, gentle man, who would never surrender." Pollard, op. cit., p. B-2.

28. This original essay was prepared especially for this volume by Mr. Scheidler. We thank him for his contribution to the range and depth of our volume. For the views of pro-choice writers on Mr. Scheidler's campaign, see Connie Paige, *The Right to Lifers: Who They Are, How They Operate, Where They Get Their Money*. New York: Summit Books, 1983. See also, Merton, *Enemies of Choice*, op. cit. In 1984 Mr. Scheidler attended the convention of the pro-choice National Abortion Federation, much as Mr. Baird regularly attends anti-abortion gatherings.

Part III

New Insights

In 1982, one of the leading survey research organizations in America, the University of Chicago's National Opinion Research Corporation (NORC), asked more questions about abortion in its annual poll of Americans than at any time before in its 20 years of exploring abortion attitudes. And, also in 1982, Carol Gilligan, a cognitive psychologist with a special interest in how males and females make moral decisions, published her research findings and analysis in a remarkable book aptly entitled *In a Different Voice*. Her searching interviews with women waiting to have abortions led Gilligan to conclude females and males do *not* view a pregnancy termination in the same moral terms, even though the classic literature on the development of moral reasoning taught just the opposite.

In Chapter 10, we use NORC's broader-than-ever survey data to ask:

- Is there a distinct female point-of-view? A male point-of-view? How do these perspectives resemble or differ from one another?

- Are more males or females pro-choice? Anti-abortion? How has this been changing over time?

- Are some explanations for having an abortion more acceptable than others? To males? To females?

We approach the NORC 1982 survey data from a very particular angle: In every case we are curious about how public attitudes influence the mind and mood of over 600,000 men who annually warm seats in clinic waiting rooms.

In Chapter 11, we take advantage of Gilligan's bolder-than-ever theorizing to ask in a highly tentative way:

• Is there a distinct female moral domain? A male moral framework? How do these perspectives resemble or differ from one another?

• Are more males or females inclined to assess pregnancy responses in absolute or situational terms? How does this shape the outcome?

We use the Gilligan analysis, in conjunction with the related work of counseling psychologist Arnold Medvene, to ask, How does any of this help explain the difficulty the sexes have explaining themselves to one another? How does moral development contribute to the problems couples have maintaining a relationship after an abortion experience? And, what might abortion counselors learn from the Gilligan/Medvene perspective?

Writing in Chapter 8, counselor Peter Zelles identified morality as "the most prevalent underlying issue for both men and women." Chapters 10 and 11 help shed new light on the subject's moral ambiguity, and may clarify the position of men who agree with writer Barbara Grizzuti Harrison that "there seems to be no morally tenable position one can take, no 'pure'position."[1]

Notes

1. Barbara Grizzuti Harrison, *Off Center*, p. 78. New York: Playboy Paperbacks, 1981. "Young Bolshevist revolutionaries once said that murder was sometimes necessary, but never justifiable. That thinking informs my thinking about abortion—and makes it no easier to come to a comfortably unambiguous conclusion about it."

Chapter 10

Climate of Opinion: Male and Female Attitudes

We are in the middle of a collective American history in which the established configuration of sexual roles is shifting, cracking, glacially yielding to a different configuration. For women, the movement has been occurring long enough that one can discuss it confidently. For men, the movement is so incipient that one wonders, sometimes, if one is hearing the sounds of actual change or merely the echoes of women's voices, or simply the murmurs of dreams.

Peter Filene, *ed.*,
Men in the Middle (Prentice-Hall, Englewood Cliffs, New Jersey, 1981, p. 28).

If we are to understand the experience of 1,000 men who sit and wait, we must explore the climate of public attitudes and opinion that shapes and informs that experience, the world of views that count.

Some 75% of our respondents spoke to no one other than their sex partner before reaching a decision about the pregnancy and its resolution. Given this restriction of dialogue, they leaned heavily on their impression of what "everyone feels" and what "we all know" But how do the sexes actually view the legalization of abortion? And its morality? On the different reasons (health related or otherwise) offered by women seeking abortions? And, do the attitudes of the sexes suggest a consensus is emerging, a convergence in viewpoints independent of gender? Above all, how does any or all of this influence the men who sit and wait?

Table 10-1. Attitude toward Legality of Abortion, by Sex, 1975, 1981

"Do you think abortions should be legal under any circumstances, legal under only certain circumstances, or illegal in all circumstances?"

	1975		1981	
	Male	Female	Male	Female
Legal under all circumstances	20%	22%	22%	23%
Legal under only certain circumstances	54	53	54	50
Illegal in all circumstances	22	23	19	24
No Opinion	4	4	5	3

Source: The Gallup Poll (Vol. Two), 1978 (April 1975), p. 509; The Gallup Poll, July 1981, Report No. 190 (May 1981), p. 18.

Public Judgment: Pro-Choice or Anti-Abortion?

While the American public agrees by two-to-one that the public good is adequately served by legalized abortion-on-request,[1]

Table 10-2. Attitude toward Legality and Morality of Abortion, 1982

"Abortion should be—	legal	illegal	not sure	
	62%	31%	7%	Date: 1/82

"If you personally believe abortion is wrong, do you think it should be illegal?"	Is not wrong	Is wrong, but should not be illegal	Is wrong and should be illegal	Not sure
	44%	22%	27%	7%

Source: AP/NBC Survey, released on 1/82, 8/82.

many men and women remain considerably troubled by critical moral questions. Their unease explains much of the strained atmosphere of clinic waiting rooms.

Americans worry about the alleged personhood of the fetus. Some deny the reasonableness of elective surgery as a fall-back birth control option. And many doubters fear that abortion reform undermines tight-knit nuclear family values and traditional sexual morality. Some go on to indict the women's movement and the Supreme Court for viewing the abortion option as "fundamentally involving a conflict among the rights of individuals, quite apart from their rights and obligations as family members. Yet such an atomistic view of society conflicts with the way these people see the world."[2] Accordingly, moral censure and political opposition persists in those of either sex with a special commitment to the culture's more traditional morality values.[3]

Bill of Particulars

To judge from the anti-abortion recall discussed earlier, moral indecision is especially great where the question of the "personhood" of the fetus is concerned. Impressed by first one side, and then by a counter-argument from the other, some concerned Americans look hopefully to the scientific community for an expert resolution to the morality of the dilemma...only to be taught a critical lesson about the limits of scientific authority:

Table 10-3. Abortion Attitude Resoluteness, by Sex, 1982

"How firm are you about your opinion on abortion? Would you say you are—	Males (612)	Females (841)
Very likely to change?	3%	2%
Somewhat likely to change?	15	10
Somewhat unlikely to change?	25	20
Very unlikely to change?	58	68

Source: General Social Survey, NORC; *Codebook,* 1982. p. 159

> Even many doctors who believe that abortions are justified will con-
> cede that life begins at fertilization, and that the fetus becomes hu-
> man at any point the anti-abortion groups care to specify; the prob-
> lem is not determining when 'actual human life' begins, but when
> the value of that life begins to outweigh other considerations, such
> as the health, or even the happiness of the mother.[4]

And, on *that* question, science is appropriately silent—but not the
American public. While science defers to moralists, legislators, lawyers, protagonists, and the democratic process, the American public opts instead to take sides, and creates a distinctive opinion profile of its own (see table 10-4). Pro-choice partisans can take little
comfort from the majority opinion that life begins at fertilization,
or, "quickening" (when the expectant mother feels the fetus
move). Anti-abortionists will be similarly discomforted by the attitudes of one-fifth of the nationwide Gallup sample who hold
decidedly pro-choice sentiments.

Reasons for Abortion: "Hard and "Soft"

People appear curious about why a female or a couple wants to
terminate a pregnancy, and their curiosity is seldom neutral. Instead, there is a decided tendency to play judge and jury; to rush
to judge the wholesomeness, reasonableness, and just plain good
sense of this or that explanation offered by abortion seekers. As
made clear by national polling data that predates the 1973 legalization decision, the public insists all explanations or reasons are
not equally worthy.[5] Some are far less acceptable than others—
these being the ones most often cited by waiting room males!

Table 10-4. Attitude toward Start of Life, by Sex, 1973, 1975, 1981

"Some people feel that human life begins at the moment of conception. Others feel that human life does not begin until the baby is actually born. So you yourself feel that human life begins at conception, at the time of birth, or some point in between?"

	1973		1975		1981	
	Male	Female	Male	Female	Male	Female
Anti-abortion answers:						
At conception						
}	55%	73%	58%	74%	55%	67%
At quickening						
Pro-choice answers:						
When the unborn baby can survive if born early					11%	9%
At birth	20%	8%	20%	9%	21%	14%
Don't know or no opinion	N.D.	N.D.	N.D.	N.D.	13%	10%

Source: The 1973 and 1975 Gallup data are from Judith Blake, "One Supreme Court's Abortion Decisions and Public Opinion in the United States," *Population and Development Review,* **3,** 1977, pp. 55–56. The 1981 data are from *The Gallup Poll,* Report No. 190, July 1981, p. 19.

Between 1965 and the mid-1970s, for example, the public showed a decided tendency to approve reasons over which a female had little or no control ("hard"), and to disapprove of abortion situations where the choice was much more optional ("soft"). Typical of the polling used to measure these attitudes is this six-item question from NORC's General Social Survey, a question employed with some slight variation from 1965 through 1982:

"Please tell me whether or not *you* think it should be possible for a pregnant woman to obtain a *legal* abortion—

1. If there is a strong chance of serious defect in the baby?

2. If she is married and does not want any more children?

3. If the woman's own health is seriously endangered by the pregnancy?

4. If the family has a very low income and cannot afford any more children?

5. If she became pregnant as a result of rape?

6. If she is not married and does not want to marry the man?"

Between 1965 and 1976, the NORC survey showed a sweeping increase in approval, though almost 50 percentage points continued to separate highly acceptable from barely tolerated reasons for an elective abortion (see Table 10-5).

When examined two years later, the NORC data confirmed a long-term trend: three-fourths or more of the respondents in 1978 favored abortion for the top three "hard" reasons, while less than half were favorable when "soft" reasons were offered.[6] In 1982, the picture was very much the same: the "hard" reasons won approval by 92%, 87%, and 85%; the "soft" by only 52% (low income), 49% (married), and 49% (single).[7]

Table 10-5. Attitude toward Reasons for Abortion, by Approval Percent, 1965, 1972, 1976

	1965	1972	1976
"Hard"			
Health danger to mother	73%	87%	91%
Rape	59	79	84
Defect	57	79	84
"Soft"			
Too poor	27%	49%	53%
Single	18	43	50
Married; no more children desired	16	49	46

Source: National Gallup Polls, as reported in Raymond Tatalovich and Bryon W. Daynes, *The Politics of Abortion: A Study of Community Conflict in Public Policymaking* (New York: Praeger, 1981), p. 118.

As for male and female attitudes, the 1982 data reflect a convergence profile true of earlier years as well—men and women see eye-to-eye in this matter, as is shown in Table 10-6. All of this suggests that waiting room males confront a judgmental public generally twice as accepting of "involuntary" as of "voluntary" excuses for an abortion; a public consistent in its ranking over time and across the sexes, though, also, a public capable of making more refined judgments along critical lines of demarcation (sweeping approval or disapproval; pick-and-choose; and hard reasons only).

Table 10-6. Attitude toward Reasons for Abortion, by Approval Percent, by Sex, 1982

	Male (615)	Female (832)
"Hard"		
Health danger to mother	93%	91%
Rape	88	86
Defect (fetus)	85	84
"Soft"		
Too poor	52%	52%
Single; doesn't want a child	49	49
Married; wants no more children	51	47

Source: General Social Survey, NORC, *1982 Codebook*, pp. 154–155.

Summary

When as many as a million or more American men annually learn a pregnancy they share may end in abortion, the largest number choose to keep it to themselves: only one in four of our 1,000 waiting room males talked with anyone besides their sex partner before the decision was made. Instead, the males silently process their subjective notions of what "everybody knows," of what "everybody feels," of what the climate of general opinion seems to recommend.

To judge cautiously, then, from public opinion data, males who sit and wait may wrestle with three critical attitude clusters:

1. *Both sexes generally support the legalization of abortion on request;* neither sex, however, considers this an unqualified right, and both males and females respect the regulatory role of the state in this matter.

2. *Both sexes generally support the right of the prospective parents to decide the fate of the fetus;* neither sex, however, believes any and every reason offered to explain a termination decision is comparably worthy and morally acceptable.

3. *Both sexes generally subscribe to the same or similar attitudes toward abortion;* neither sex, however, agrees with the other about when human life ("personhood") begins—males, in particular holding a more pro-choice attitude than females.

These ambivalent views undoubtedly take their toll on waiting room men sensitive to the public's uncertainty and remorse about abortion.

PROFILE

Raymond's interview shows the incredible pressure that can be brought to bear by family attitudes and public opinion. Although he and his fiancée probably wanted their pregnancy to proceed to term, their concern about what others would think and feel helped prevent them from doing so.

Is the vote of parents, friends, and clergy worth more than that of the couple? Our men, in three of four cases, seemed to answer by consulting no one but their partners. Still, every man was affected or shaped by widespread American ambivalence about abortion's morality, along with majority support for abortion-on-request.

Raymond:

There were some hard feelings right afterwards. For two weeks we didn't say much, pretended it didn't happen. We got married and are trying to have a baby now.

The abortion saved her and my families a lot of bad feelings. We watched her folks go through the other brothers and sisters getting married because of pregnancy. It made them happy [the abortion]; they didn't know nothing about it.

My wife's sister is pregnant and big with a guy who won't marry her. My wife came home upset. Overall, we're both glad we did it. She has a kid from when she was 15, but we'd never do it again now, unless a doctor recommends it.

We had planned on marriage. She lived with me for several months. We couldn't get an earlier wedding date, so she wouldn't be showing.

Both of our dads were having a lot of trouble. One was really depressed at the time, the other was having marital stress and we did it for them. I didn't force it. We waited quite a while before we did it and it hurt her to wait. I hope she's pregnant this month.

I'm a hunter, a sportsman. Her family is against hunting, but she's going with me now. I like to take her five-year-old out and he likes to go with me, and I think about what that other kid might have been and how he'd have enjoyed it.

If we didn't have her kid, it would be very tough for us. I'd be thinking about it all the time. My family isn't as close and caring as hers and this is why it hurt her more. Doing it with all her family's kids around really bothered her.

The day we had it done, we went 150 miles. No one knew. On the way home it became a relief. The stress and arguments stopped and things have just been getting better since.

We couldn't go to our small-town family doctor for a check-up, so we were worried for awhile. We just burned all the records in the sink a couple of weeks ago, so no one would find them. We feel guilty and some embarrassment about it.

Our minister told us she didn't want to walk up the aisle with her belly hanging out. We wanted a big wedding. When we talked about the wedding, he asked if she were pregnant, and she said, no. After that night we started talking about the abortion. I made the first move by calling a help line. The minister asked again if she were pregnant and she said she didn't know. The next time (after the abortion), she said, no.

It's a small town and congregation, so he wanted to save embarrassment for them and himself, so he wanted to know. He's a young guy; great guy to talk to. Everybody knows everybody's business, but their own.

Things are going really good for us right now. We want to have a baby. You can't put it out of your mind totally. It's there, but it's like a bad dream now and there's nothing I can do about it.

The clinic was scary at first. The first place we had called was ornery. The second was okay. Getting through that door was damned hard. All those people in there. Some people were talking about having had them before. It hurt to hear it.

They talked to both of us. They didn't make you feel like you was killing a baby. The counselor talked to me; he was a nice guy. He explained what was happening, was very warm. You can't ask for more than that.

It seemed like an eternity, but we were there for an afternoon. What got me was listening to some of the lower class people talk in the lobby like this was nothing. One couple came in and had a little boy with them, seemed like real nice people, and we were going to ask them why they were doing it, but didn't.

The clinic staff let us know what was happening all along the line. They didn't make us feel guilty or let us sit there and wonder.

Everybody's situation is different, but you gotta make up your own mind. I wouldn't want to go through a one-night stand marriage. I don't want to ever look on it as a way out. . . . We'd like to start our life here.

Notes

1. "Two-thirds of a national sample agree that any woman who is pregnant should be able to decide whether or not she wants to have an abortion." Market Opinion Research, "New Attitudes about Government Involvement in the Abortion Issue," p. 2. Washington, D.C.: National Abortion Rights Action League, 1981. "On abortion, 75% said that the decision to have an abortion should be left to a woman and her doctor." Witt and Evans, "Poll Shows Little Change in Opinions." *Philadelphia Inquirer*, June 7, 1981, p. 15-A. "Two out of three Americans think abortion should be a matter for decision solely between a woman and her physician." Anonymous, "The Gallup Poll Surveys Abortion." *Philadelphia Evening Bulletin*, September 5, 1972, p. 10.

2. Peter Skerry, "The Class Conflict Over Abortion." *Public Interest*, Summer 1978, p. 81. "If we accept for the sake of argument that abortion *is* a moral issue, then the nature of the class conflict over abortion is more apparent. Scientific knowledge and analytic skills are simply not as capable of informing this issue as they are certain others, such as pollution or nuclear power. The members of the knowledge class. . . are thereby really not any better equipped to deal with the matter of abortion than are the members of any other group." (p. 84)

3. Typical of those with anti-choice attitudes are evangelical conservatives who, in a 1980 poll, were 41% in favor of banning all abortions versus all voters (31%). Allan J. Mayer et al., "Evangelical Politics." *Newsweek*, September 15, 1980, p. 36. Donald Granberg has found that opposition to abortion may reflect a more general political conservatism, especially in terms of opposition to divorce, sex education, dissemination of birth control information, premarital sex, and pornography. Issues of personal morality appear *the* major source of difference in attitudes between anti-choice and pro-choice activists. Donald Granberg, "Pro-Life or Reflection of Conservative Idealogy? An Analysis of Opposition to Legalized Abortion." *Sociology and So-*

cial Research 62 (1978): 414–429. On the attitudes of Catholic males in our sample, see Arthur Shostak, "Catholic Men and Abortion," *Conscience* (January/February 1984): 5–6.

4. Jerry Adler and John Carey, "But Is It A Person?." *Newsweek*, January 11, 1982, p. 44.

5. See in this connection, Benjamin I. Page and Robert Y. Shapiro, "Changes in Americans' Policy Preferences, 1935–1979." *Public Opinion Quarterly* Spring (1982): 31; Judith Blake, "The Supreme Court's Abortion Decisions and Public Opinion in the United States." *Population and Development Review* 3 (1977): 55–56; Judith Blake, "Abortion and Public Opinion: The 1960–1970 Decade." *Science* 171 (February 12, 1971): 540–549; Alice S. Rossi, "Public Views on Abortion," in Alan F. Guttmacher, Sr., ed., *The Case for Legalized Abortion Now*, pp. 26–53. Berkeley, Calif: Diablo Press, 1967; Lucky M. Tedrow and E. R. Mahoney, "Trends in Attitudes toward Abortion: 1972–1976." *Public Opinion Quarterly* 1979: 181–189; Theodore C. Wagenaar and and Ingeborg W. Knol, "Attitudes toward Abortion: A Comparative Analysis of Correlates for 1973 and 1975." *Journal of Sociology and Social Welfare* 4(6, July 1977): 927–944.

6. Helen Rose Fuchs Ebaugh and C. Allen Haney, "Shifts in Abortion Attitudes: 1972–1978." *Journal of Marriage and the Family* (August 1980): 493.

7. Sharon N. Garnartt and Richard J. Harris, "Recent Changes in Predictors of Abortion Attitudes." *Sociology and Social Research* 66(3, April 1982): 324.

Chapter 11

Men—What Do They Want?

To be responsible for oneself, it is first necessary
to acknowledge what one is doing. The criterion
for judgment thus shifts from goodness to truth
when the morality of action is assessed not on
the basis of its appearance in the eyes of others,
but in terms of the realities of its intention and
consequence.... The needs of the self have to
be deliberately uncovered.

Carol Gilligan,
In a Different Voice (Cambridge, Massachusetts,
Harvard University Press, 1982, pp. 83, 84).

In addition to the impersonal climate of public opinion, our background analysis of the male abortion experience includes the highly personal process of developing a moral core, of forming the moral center of one's being.

How have clinic waiting room men earned their moral resolutions? How do they make moral decisions? And what are their central moral concerns? Above all, how does their moral framework compare with that of their sex partners? And how significant is any disparity, or convergence, in their respective moral domains?

These questions received especially helpful treatment from the field research and analysis of Carol Gilligan, a cognitive psychologist who, in 1982, authored an aptly titled book, *In a Different Voice*.[1] From our reading of Gilligan's work, we have gained a clearer understanding of the moral background of our 1,000 waiting room men.[2] A campus-based counseling psychologist, Arnold Medvene, closes this chapter with some thoughts of his on two distinct approaches males seem to take to the abortion challenge. His clinic-derived insights complement Gilligan's line of analysis, and shed new and valuable light on the innermost thoughts of waiting room males.

One Morality Or Two?

As Gilligan critiques prevailing wisdom in this matter, she attempts to correct eminent male psychologists (such as Erikson, Freud, Kohlberg, Levinson, McClelland, Piaget, Valient, and others) who may seriously mislead their readers. For a variety of reasons these men have treated both sexes as if they were one, and have created the erroneous impression that only one moral way of being exists.[3] On the contrary, Gilligan asserts, there are two very different moral ideologies, one male, one female. And this duality explains much of the dissimilarity in the abortion experiences of men and women.

Drawing on 10 years of her own field research (including a rare pre- and post-abortion study of 21 women, and a study of 144 individuals—72 males—in which she asked about conceptions of self and morality), Gilligan began to distinguish two ways of speaking about moral problems, two modes of describing the relationship between the other and the self. As she reconstructed the socialization experience of the sexes, males take from childhood an *Ethic of Abstract Rights;* females, an *Ethic of Caring and Intimacy.* While males tend to define moral problems in terms of rights and rules (the "justice approach"), females define moral problems in terms of an obligation to exercise care and avoid hurting others.[4]

Males grow up preoccupied with winning and holding the respect of significant others, especially their childhood peers and parents. Later, the respect of employers and co-workers becomes comparably important. Females, however, are socialized to look for approval by satisfying the needs of others *first,* even while struggling not to entirely betray their own needs. Males learn that respect is earned through struggle, through taking a "proper" stand. Females are socialized instead to demur, to focus on gaining and holding intimate relationships rather than on asserting or defending abstract rights and rules.[5]

At a time, then, when a rapid decision must be made about an unwanted pregnancy, the male relies on his Ethic of Abstract Rights. Many, however, perhaps for the first time, struggle to balance a moral absolute—"the baby must live!"—against a newly discovered contradiction—"My sex partner has a right not to go through with the pregnancy; it's *her* body!"

Females, in turn, struggle to achieve an "understanding that gives rise to compassion and care."[6] Reared to want to sacrifice themselves to protect the unborn child, they must learn, with their sex partner's help, how to protect their *own* rights as well.

Both males and females alike are compelled to recognize that there are life situations in which it is impossible to avoid hurting others.

Keeping One's Distance versus Gaining Intimacy

Along with its emphasis on unavoidable hurt, Gilligan's analysis illuminates the tension between abortion clinic couples who move toward, and yet, also away from one another in often erratic ways, barely understood by either of them.

For the male, much of the difficulty derives from his emotional reticence and macho pose which helps bottle up his feelings. Raised to respect a stiff-necked Ethic of Absolute Rights, many men seem to view morality dilemmas (such as the abortion question) as primarily a matter of what they think life and society owe their hapless pregnant sex partner. Since the U.S. Supreme Court has twice decided the fairness question in favor of an unfettered right to an abortion on request (1973, 1983), certain males conclude the "right thing" for them to do is repress any emotions or thoughts of their own in the matter. They assure their sex partner that *anything* she wants is okay with them ("If only she wouldn't be so upset!").

Females look elsewhere for moral guidance. They make little, if any, use of the male insistence on absolute right and wrong. As their childhood taught them to view morality in terms of caring, and resolving conflicting responsibilities, they focus on making and holding onto loving attachments. Many males, in contrast, are preoccupied with "making it." "Power and separation secure the man in an identity achieved through work, but they leave him at a distance from others who seem in some sense out of his sight."[7] So pervasive is this male drive for prowess that many view the female emphasis on gaining emotional attachment as perilous: Intimacy is thought to pose a "danger of entrapment or betrayal, as being caught in a smothering relationship or humiliated by rejection and deceit."[8]

Females, sensitized to a different world view, follow a script complete with its own ethic and moral preoccupations. Many come to see the distancing ways of males as perilous, as posing a danger to females of unwanted isolation, loneliness, rejection, and deceit.

Each sex seeks to counter threats seemingly posed by the other—threats neither sex actually perceives itself posing. Males remain suspicious of opportunities to lose themselves in love relationships. Many prefer to guard their options, to keep their distance by playing the field. Females are deprived thereby of deep romantic relationships, and endure the heartache of searching for a White Knight. Each sex, ironically, actually needs more of that which it thinks it fears the most—males need *more* emotional investment; females, *less* emotional dependency (". . . we know ourselves as separate only insofar as we live in connection with others, and we experience relationship only insofar as we differentiate other from self.").[9]

Achievement of the ability to be intimate is regarded by Gilligan as indispensable if the maturing male is to mitigate excessive isolation. Intimacy, she contends, is ". . . the critical experience that brings the self back into connection with others, making it possible to see both sides—to discover the effects of actions on others as well as their cost to the self."[10] For this reason, intimacy is "the transformative experience for men through which adolescent identity turns into the generativity of adult love and work,"[11] and, for this reason, abortion clinic counseling for males should be dramatically revised and expanded to include intimacy-gaining skills.

Gilligan's insights, in sum, could guide counseling in the direction of more and more empathy between the sexes. It is important here to emphasize the explanatory power of her two-mode approach. If Gilligan's understanding of sex-specific moral domains is sound, much of the inability of the sex partners to understand one another becomes itself more understandable—and far more amenable to reform than has been previously considered or imagined. Waiting room men may be capable of achieving far more moral and personal growth from their experience than is presently understood. As one of Gilligan's female respondents explains, "Abortion, if you do it for the right reasons, is helping yourself to start over and do different things."[12]

Arnold Medvene, Counseling Psychologist

In my psychotherapy experiences with men facing abortion, their resolution of loss revolves around two pivotal issues: (1) openly confronting and working with one's emotional experience, and (2) disclosing these feelings and emotions on an intimate level with others to work against the sea of isolation and personal withdrawal that men often experience following this benchmark emotional event.

As a male therapist my goal is to form a strong therapeutic alliance with my brother to fully examine the male experience. Issues of trust, openness, decision making, power, separation, control, equality, and feelings of anger, sadness, hurt, and loss are central themes which are explored without judgment or evaluation. My purpose is greater clarity and understanding of the male dilemma so men can truly make free choices, and not be fettered by cultural beliefs, traditions, and values that define what a man really is.

Abortion is a male crisis of vulnerability. At a time when he wishes to be omnipotent there is a pervasive sense of powerlessness and helplessness. Abortion brings the man close to forces of life and death and shatters his fantasies of invulnerability. Unwanted pregnancy demands that a man confront an experience for which he has limited resources and skills. This sense of helplessness and frustration leads to bewilderment, anxiety, loss of self-esteem, and despair. A highly significant life happening is occurring, yet it is one often responded to by little or no emotion by the male.

Since Western male culture places strong emphasis on growth, competence, and overcoming adversity, there is little understanding of and support for an inward emotional glance that says to the man, "trust your feelings, share your feelings, expand your feelings, be your feelings." This emotional denial of natural grief responses is energy draining, and often leaves the male exhausted and feeling without reserves or resources. Living does include sadness, hurt, and pain. The capacity to reach inside and touch that part of oneself and not shrink away from painful thoughts and feelings is a beginning to fully living.

The men I work with are essentially *Personalizers* or *Controllers* in their abortion experience. I will list the kinds of responses and reactions each group brings to therapy as they better try to understand their way of coping with a highly significant life event. Their capacity to heighten self-awareness, to explore and extend previously surface-level ideas and feelings, to trust another person with their doubts, fears, anxieties, humor, anger, and feared humanness is an indication of their self-acceptance and capacity to be intimate in a personal relationship.

Personalizers

1. Acknowledge the abortion as an intense emotional experience.
2. In-depth exploration of their feelings.
3. Integration of thoughts and feelings about this loss, and how it corresponds to other transition points in their lives.
4. Respond to the woman in terms of her feelings, values, and self-experience.
5. Struggles with being too female-identified, and fear losing the respect and admiration of their male friends.
6. Embarrassed by having too many feelings.
7. Cherish individuality for both sexes.
8. Mood swings are common.
9. Loving and affectionate to the woman and feel a keen sense of

Controllers

1. Hard to be in a supportive, non-starring role.
2. Angry and resentful about their loss of control and sense of powerlessness.
3. View the experience as a power struggle with a winner and a loser. It is a test case of who is more dominant and forceful.
4. Tend to focus on solutions and make the problems concrete and solvable to move away from their feelings.
5. View the woman in an impersonal and objectified way.
6. Tend to denigrate her being to render her powerless and insignificant.
7. Fear being stigmatized and losing esteem among other men.
8. View abortion as right or wrong—no feelings involved.

loss in their life together.
10. Creative problem solvers.
11. Search for meaning in their experience.
12. Try to maximize this experience as a benchmark in their adult development.
13. Feel guilty that the woman pays such a high price for their mistake; feel guilt about destroying life; feel anger at failed birth control.
14. View powerlessness and helplessness as a means toward greater self-awareness.
15. Struggle with their male-conditioned response to blame the woman and to hold her responsible for their problems.

9. Ambitious, acquisitive and view self-disclosure as a threat.
10. Resist shared decision making with the woman as she is seen as less competent and too emotional.
11. Insensitive to feelings—theirs and the woman's.
12. Tend to trivialize the meaning of the experience for self and the other person.
13. Feel outside and peripheral to an internal experience.
14. Feel isolated and wary of the interest of other people.
15. Restless overactivity.

Personalizers try to look at their experience of loss as a way to know themselves in greater depth. Their journey is one of authenticity and enrichment though this trip encompasses grief, anger, pain, and sadness. These men often choose growth over safety and, in doing so, risk the security, power, and influence endemic to being male in our culture. Their capacity to travel unfamiliar roads connotes a great deal of inner wonder and a willingness to be pioneers in the male experience.

Controllers are basically angry with the woman having the abortion as she is seen as a threat to their control, power, and dominance. These men use a great deal of energy in emotional denial, and their reluctance to grieve produces a sense of safety and security; but it also fosters severely restricted personal growth. Coming to terms with their feelings of sadness, hurt, and pain is a way to be whole and not split off from themselves, and it is their quintessential developmental task in this experience.

We cannot really hide from our pain as it is a part of life. But when we begin to face the meaning of our feelings, we can learn a great deal about how to live and the meaning of life. George Bernard Shaw once wrote that "Heartbreak is life educating us," and our ability and courage to trust and explore within allows us to live as fully as we can.

PROFILE

Although we discussed abortion with a number of articulate women and formally interviewed a select few, we have presented only male interviews as a matter of thematic and editorial strategy. The climate of opinion chapter, however, has explored the male and female domains and whet our appetites to see how the perspectives offered in the chapter might apply in a given male-female situation.

Bob and Rita were interviewed on separate occasions. Each talked sincerely and openly about their abortion experiences with the other one. The parallel split interview format demonstrates many tenets of male and female domains, contrasts, comparisons, and conflicting perceptions.

Bob

I don't find myself scarred from it. It's been reduced to another of life's problems. It is now resolved. I have been to Nam, and I know the sense of power from looking down the barrel and deciding on a life. The abortion of a fetus is lower on the scale of phenomena. But I no longer use absolutes—all or never. I think the controversy over abortion is based on poorly defined absolutes.

I found out on long-distance while she was out of town. She was very elated. She loved the idea of being pregnant. She determined that on approval from me she'd have the baby. . . . I got caught up in the idea from her effervescence. My reaction was conditioned by hers. I had a lot of reservations, but I said, "Why not?"

Rita

I'm very intrigued that men are shocked at my opinion of them. Two male friends were upset with me because I said they didn't care about pregnancy or abortion. They said they had feelings, but what do they have beyond that?

I've had my own abortion experience. . . . Being pregnant was absolutely mind blowing in a primitive way. I mean, it (sex) really worked! Afterward, I talked to a lot of women about what it felt like. Men seemed to be out of that whole ballpark. They listened sympathetically, but the men never talked about their regrets, or their connections to the pregnancy or the abortion.

Bob was so out of touch with what being pregnant was like that he never asked how I felt, only what did I want to do. He wasn't in love, didn't want a baby, but he said he'd marry me—to make it honest, I suppose. One morning I woke up and realized my relationship was a fraud and that marriage and pregnancy didn't go together. I had to take over by myself.

Was I willing to sacrifice to be a good father? I came from a broken home. I had been denied a lot and I was looking for a lot. As a father I didn't know if I'd be able to sacrifice my ambitions to give and cater to it. And an absentee father is not my idea of a good one. It is a conundrum for me.... She wasn't self-sacrificing enough for children. Ideas, not realities of nurturing and daily routine of raising a child, were what she had.

I accept that conception is the beginning of life. Whatever you want to call it. It's human, of humans. What degree of responsibility do we as a society have to women, to embryos? I believe we have to protect the rights of those who are developed. On the other hand, abortion should not be used as a birth control device. It should be used as an emergency tool rather than a standard birth control device. The ideal, of course, is birth control. In that absence we need abortion to cover technical or use failures. Funerals are for the living; so, too, are abortions. It's cultural. I can't see the fetus as a cultural human being, although it has the potential from conception.

There was a sense of fantasy about the whole thing as we worked it out over the phone.... I don't remember who was first, but we began to talk about not going ahead with marriage and children.

It was peace and calm after we reached the decision. It was right and we felt it. I probably felt more at

When I said I was getting an abortion, Bob said, "Whatever you want to do...."

The irony of the whole thing was that I thought I could get support from anyone *but* him. I could not do it with a man—my sister, mother, friends, but no man I know is open enough to share something as heavy as pregnancy and abortion.

I don't know how men feel about pregnancy. My feelings are strong about being pregnant. I was overjoyed. I still want it more than a husband, or a ranch house, or anything.

... he had no understanding of what I had been through and what I had to go through right afterward, even though I told him. Bob did all the gesturing, but we never sat down and talked. For him it was over. He went on about his job. I wanted to move out. He showed no emotion about breaking up. I never slept with him again and we never discussed the abortion, although I ran into him several times after I moved out.

peace than she did. The idea of having a human being inside her was
awesome to her. "Little Johnny's
gone," she'd say in public as a spoof,
but there was a cutting sense of loss.

I wasn't ready to marry before
the pregnancy and I wasn't ready afterward. She knew that and eventually it became a determining factor in
the decision. . . . I sense that she
feels rejected, especially after the
abortion because I could have supported the decision to have the kid
and she'd not have changed. I'd be
a father—last month [January 1983].

I've been seeing a new man for
awhile and he's pretty nice, but we
don't really talk about sex or birth
control. Except one night when we
were first going out, he said to me,
"If you never want another abortion,
you'd better stop playing Russian
roulette with your birth control pills,
because I have no intention of marrying you."

I always feel like I have to protect my man. Saying, "I don't want to
ruin *your* life." If I imagine telling
him that I'm pregnant, I think of soft
candlelight and wine, breaking the
news gently. I'd want to reassure
him. Why do I feel that way?

Parental Advice

Only one survey we found in the abortion research literature explores the
kind of advice parents think they would offer an unmarried son or daughter
trying to decide how to resolve an unexpected pregnancy. Drawn entirely
from white, middle-class, well-educated "mainstream" respondents, the survey has highly restricted generalizability. Nevertheless, to judge from our encounters with waiting room males, the advice profile below is one in broad
general use, almost regardless of race, class, or style of life:

Sex-role stereotypes are obvious above, the men urging their sons to do
the "right thing" and marry the girl (26%), even while advising against any
new-fangled notion of single male parenthood (6%). In contrast, they would
advise their daughters to undertake single parenthood (21%) rather than marry
the "s.o.b." who "knocked her up" (13%). Women, in turn, are far less endorsing of single parenthood for either gender, and also think very little of
the marriage option. Instead, unlike the men, they urge the adoption route,
or, slightly more often, the abortion resolution.

	Father's Advice for Daughter/Son	Mother's Advice for Daughter/Son
Have an abortion	20%/17%	23%/19%
Have the baby; give it up for adoption	13%/12%	23%/22%
Have the baby and keep the child; or seek custody of it	21%/6%	14%/5%
Marry and keep the child	13%/26%	6%/11%
None. Would leave it entirely up to her/him	17%/19%	19%/22%
Other	17%/19% (N = 605)	20%/23% (N = 8,076)

Source: A Report on American Families from the Editors of Better Homes and Gardens, May 1983, pp. 136–137.

Sharp distinctions between fathers and mothers in the advice they would offer a son or daughter confronting pregnancy may go far in explaining why only 11% of our 1,000 waiting room males actually took their parents into their confidence—and weighed their advice in reaching a resolution of the pregnancy: Only one other source of advice—the clergy—was less seldom used by waiting room males.

Notes

1. Carol Gilligan. *In a Different Voice: Psychological Theory and Women's Development.* Cambridge, Mass.: Harvard University Press, 1982.

2. To be sure, Gilligan focused entirely on female respondents (29 expectant mothers, 21 of whom were interviewed again at the end of the year following their choice of the abortion option). We alone are responsible for this effort to apply her theorizing to the male partner in the abortion experience.

3. Gilligan contends these men devised models of human development in which women appeared deviant or morally stunted. See, in this connection, Phyllis Chesler, *About Men.* New York: Simon and Schuster, 1978.

4. Gilligan cautions on page 2 that the gender linkage to the two themes "is not absolute, and the contrasts between male and female voices are presented here to highlight a distinction between two modes of thought and to focus a problem in interpretation rather than to represent a generalization about either sex." See in this connection Raye H. Rosen and Lois J. Martindale, "Sex Role Perceptions and the Abortion Decision," *Journal of Sex Research* 14 (November 1978): 231–245.

5. Gilligan's model of women's moral reasoning appeals to responsibilities, rather than to rights. Women are thought to fear isolation, rather than aggression, and to emphasize caring for others before oneself. An admiring critic concludes this line of analysis "builds a moral megaphone that enables us to hear women's voices with all their complexity and integrity." Judith Kegan Gardiner, "Morality on a New Scale." *In These Times*, October 20–26, 1982, p. 19.

6. Gilligan, op. cit., p. 165.

7. Ibid., p. 163.

8. Ibid., p. 42.

9. Ibid., p. 63.

10. Ibid., p. 163.

11. Ibid. p. 163. Mark Gerzon concurs, and advises that "a crisis in masculinity is also an opportunity. It compels us to find new maps of the world we live in. It encourages us to find wise traveling companions. It inspires us to learn to read the compass of our heart...men want access to what they have forfeited: intimacy, nurturance, friendship, mutuality." Mark Gerzon, *A Choice of Heroes: The Changing Faces of American Manhood.* Boston: Houghton Mifflin, 1982.

12. Gilligan, op. cit., p. 78. For a dissent from Gilligan's perspective, see Judith O. Smetana, *Concepts of Self and Morality: Women's Reasoning about Abortion,* op. cit. For a negative view of gender convergence, at least in the marketplace, see Rachael Flick, "The New Feminism and the World of Work." *The Public Interest* (1983): 33–44. For a skeptical view of Gilligan's perspective, see Carol Tavris, "Women and Men and Morality." *New York Times Book Review,* May 2, 1982, pp. 14–15; Anne Colby and William Damon, "Listening to a Different Voice: A Review of Gilligan's *In a Different Voice,*" *Merrill-Palmer Quarterly* 29 (October 1983): 473–481.

Part IV

Reform Possibilities

In this closing section of our book, we are preoccupied with the single most compelling question we have: "How could it be done any better?"

We are sensitive to the major reasons offered in defense of the status quo; for example, "The female, after all, is *the* patient, and *must* be our major concern!" "Funds are in short supply, and *must* go to subsidize the abortions of indigent women." "Men in our waiting room never complain, at least, not that we have heard." "Until the anti-abortionists stop threatening our clinic's very existence, we cannot be distracted by *any* new reform efforts." Each of these arguments was made repeatedly, only to have many speakers later note that certain clinic staffers *were* troubled by their relative neglect of male partners, by the number of relationships that seemed to flounder after an abortion (perhaps unnecessarily) and by the increasing incidence of male repeaters.

In Chapter 12, we explore the standing of men in the law, and discuss how, since the 1973 Supreme Court legalization of abortion-on-request, men have had no rights in a contested abortion situation. Special attention is paid to three legal reform possibilities: spousal consent requirements; spousal foreknowledge requirements; and the revision of child support requirements—the pros and cons of which are laid out for the reader's own assessment.

In Chapter 13, we move rapidly through a large number of reforms that bear on the preclinic phase of the experience. For example, we discuss the role of sex education courses in secondary schools, the impact the media could have, the contribution that might be made by the men's movement—and the women's, as well—among many more such potential sources of aid.

Finally, in Chapter 14 we focus on the clinic day experience. Drawing on many reform ideas suggested by our 1,000 men, and on programmatic changes espoused by our contributing abortion counselors, we outline several practical, low-cost, and promising changes in clinic realities. Should these soon earn an experimental trial, we might finally achieve the sensitive and rewarding quality of services for men favored by many clinic staffers.

After traveling across the country in 1980 and visiting numerous clinics from coast to coast, journalist Linda Bird Francke concluded many such providers were "increasingly becoming disturbed because they offer little besides free cups of coffee to the men who sit and wait."[1] Perhaps the time has finally arrived to go further—much, much further.

Notes

1. Linda Bird Francke, *The Ambivalence of Abortion*, p. 158. New York: Dell, 1978. See also Linda Bird Francke, "Abortion and Men," op. cit., pp. 58–60; Carole Joffe, "What Abortion Counselors Want from Their Clients," *Social Problems* 26, 1 (1978): 112–121.

Chapter 12

Standing in the Law

In reappraising traditional abortion laws, we are reassessing our views and our evaluation of man...the abortion decision is a rethinking of what man is, what society is, and what the relationship between the two must be for the maximization of human potential.

> David Granfield. *The Abortion Decision.* (Garden City, New York Doubleday, 1969, p. 10.)

In civilized life, law floats in a sea of ethics.

> Chief Justice Earl Warren, The *New York Times*, November 12, 1962.

When an abortion conflict arises between father and mother, the court faces the classic faulty dilemma: one set of rights inevitably (at least in criminal law) tends to cancel out the other.

> Rick and Robin Blackwood, *The Journal of Legal Medicine*, October 1975, p. 35.

What rights, if any, do males have in deciding the fate of the fetus they have co-conceived? How have lawmakers and the courts treated the male role in abortion questions? And, above all, how might a man's standing in abortion law help explain the abortion experiences of 1,000 waiting room males?

"Where Do I Stand?"

To begin this discussion on a personal level, in the fall of 1982 we received a long-distance call from a very distraught, middle-aged, single man who had heard of Art Shostak's research. The caller's former lover was a single woman he had not expected ever to hear from again. But she had just reentered his life—unexpectantly pregnant with their child.

The woman insisted she wanted nothing from him, no financial or emotional support of any kind for herself or for their child. Instead, she was firmly intent on proudly bearing and rearing the child as an unwed mother. She felt compelled to inform the natural father only out of a sense of "doing the right thing." She declined, however, to hear him make a case for an abortion. She also declined to put in writing her verbal assurance never to ask him to support financially or participate in the rearing of "her" child.

That's when he called to learn his legal rights. While it had taken him close to an hour to tell his story, it took barely 60 seconds to explain he had no rights.

The caller was incredulous. Why had he no right to explain his reasons for not wanting to be a father at this time? His reasons for not wanting a child of his reared without him? His reasons for not wanting to share parenthood with this particular woman? His reasons for not feeling ready to become a father? And, for wanting a choice about when and with whom to assume fatherhood?

But his ex-lover did not want to hear any of this, and she had every (legal) right to deny him an audience. The law of the land since *Roe v. Wade*, in 1973, had cordoned off the woman and her physician. Thus, at the discretion of the woman the wishes of the natural father might or might *not* be considered.[1]

As for his financial liability for helping meet the costs of rearing a child whose birth he had opposed, the law remained what it had always been. Despite a male's willingness to pay all costs entailed in an abortion, no expectant father may escape legal and financial obligations to his offspring if his sex partner chooses childbirth rather than the abortion he has advocated.[2] He is liable for a fair share of the costs of rearing the child to age 18, whether or not he chooses to have any parenting role.

A few months later, we listened to another tale, one with a very different goal but with a similarly stressful impact on the man directly involved.

On learning from his lover of "their" pregnancy and her determination to have an abortion, a young man had been steered by anti-abortionists to a lawyer eager to enlarge male rights in this matter. Together, they had secured from a New England state court a well-publicized injunction to delay the abortion of "his" child. However, as with scores of other such cases since *Roe v. Wade*, while appeals were being filed by attorneys for both sides, the expectant mother went to a nearby state and had her abortion—an irrevocable act that forced the court to declare the entire case now moot.

Angered by this victory of the pro-choice forces, the attorney for the expectant father loudly assured reporters he would seek many more such cases. The young man, however, struck observers as less the enthusiastic crusader, and more one who had been utterly devastated by his loss, both of his lover and his "child."

Generally, when a couple amicably settles any differences of opinion about the fate of the fetus, the state and the courts are not drawn into the matter—a much-preferred scenario by all. But when there is a clash of wills, the state and the courts decide the matter in a clear and compelling way: Since *Roe v. Wade*, in 1973, the natural father has had *no* legal standing in any such controversy. By a 6–3 vote the High Court asserted, for the first time in the nation's 197-year history, that one sex alone could decide the fate of a fetus in the event of a couple's disagreement in the matter.[3] The decision also wrote into the federal judicial record a remarkable sociological role prescription for males. Hereafter, they were to have *no* role with any enforcement authority behind it.[4] Only the female and her physicians were to decide whether termination of a pregnancy was the preferable course of action.

Males Without Standing

In the 24 months immediately following the Supreme Court's 1973 decision, 62 laws directly related to abortion were adopted by 32 states. Twelve of these 32 passed *spousal consent* rules, which were initially struck down by lower courts in eight states: They all received a Supreme Court test in 1976, and the Court declared unconstitutional any absolute veto by the child's father of the mother's assessment of her own needs (*Danforth v. Missouri*).[5]

In its decision, the Supreme Court expressed keen sensitivity to the case for a voice for husbands:

> We are not unaware of the deep and proper concern and interest that a devoted and protective husband has in his wife's pregnancy, and in the growth and development of the fetus she is carrying. Neither has this court failed to appreciate the importance of the marital relationship in our society. . . . Moreover, we recognize that the decision whether to undergo or to forego an abortion may have profound effects on the future of any marriage, effects that are both physical and mental, and possibly deleterious.

Notwithstanding these factors, however, the Court felt it could not agree the State had constitutional authority to "give the spouse unilaterally the ability to prohibit the wife from terminating her pregnancy, when the State itself lacks that right."

While the Court thought, ideally, the decision to terminate a pregnancy should be concurred by both the wife and her husband, the Court rejected spousal consent statutes as the proper way to promote this.[6] Reminding Missouri that *Roe v. Wade* three years earlier had stripped the states of abortion-hindering power, the Court observed that even if the State had the ability to delegate such power to the husband, the Court thought it "not at all likely" such action would bolster the marriage relationship: "When the wife and her husband disagree on this decision, the view of only one of the two marriage partners can prevail."

In the view of the Court, since the woman physically bears the child and is directly and immediately affected by her pregnancy, "as between the two, the balance weighs in her favor." Accordingly, the high court ruled spousal consent statutes were inconsistent with the standards enunciated in *Roe v. Wade* and were, therefore, unconstitutional.[7]

Males as Pre-notified Parties

A second legal controversy over the rights of males in disputed abortions concerns state laws that would require clinics to advise a husband before terminating his wife's pregnancy, an idea supported by 65% of our respondents.

Proponents of these highly controversial measures are convinced such laws might achieve five desirable results:

1. They could provide a very short "cooling off" period in which both parties might further explore the decision.

2. They could encourage the wife to reconsider her decision if it was made solely in response to a temporary problem in the couple's relationship.

3. They could encourage the husband to reconsider and improve his pledge of emotional and financial support for bringing the fetus to term and rearing their child.

4. They could help a wife stop guessing what her husband's reaction is to her pregnancy before she has had a chance to hear his side.

5. They could help a husband gain a better understanding of his wife's final decision and the status of their relationship, even if he disagrees with that decision.

Above all, proponents argue that in order for men and women to negotiate effectively, they must both feel they have some power and a stake in an equitable decision.[8]

Opponents warn that a prenotification requirement would especially threaten women in marriages that lacked mutual trust and communication skills. They worry about the human hardship that could occur in cases where:

- the husband is not the co-conceiver;

- the husband is likely to threaten or use violence;

- the couple had separated before the estranged wife became aware of the pregnancy; or,

- the wife's mental health would be seriously threatened by the anguish and stress.

These opponents reject the spousal prenotification idea as a dangerous erosion of the hard-earned *total* authority women have had since *Roe v. Wade.* They argue that the 1973 Court decision assured women *complete* privacy and *total* freedom from hindrance. And they insist that spousal prenotification would compromise privacy and create a cruel hindrance to solitary and reflective decision making.[9]

Child Support

Along with spousal consent and spousal prenotification, the legal controversies include a question of the fairness of imposing financial responsibility where there is no longer ability to exercise control.

Whether or not a child will result from a pregnancy is now a choice that belongs exclusively to the female, though the courts continue to hold the natural father responsible for child support payments. An opponent of this legal precedent argues that "to saddle a man with at least eighteen years of expensive, exhausting child support liability on the basis of a haphazard vicissitude of life seems to shock the conscience and be arbitrary, capricious, and unreasonable, where childbirth results from the mother's free choice."[10]

Going even further, it is argued that when a man is forced to discharge support obligations toward a child whom he did not anticipate or want, and over whose birth or personhood he had no control or responsibility, he may justly charge discrimination. As Karen DeCrow (former president of the National Organization for Women) has argued in the Serpico child-support case:

> Justice...dictates that if a woman makes a unilateral decision to bring pregnancy to term, and the biological father does not, and cannot share in this decision, he sould not be liable for 21 years of support. Or, put another way, autonomous women making independent decisions about their lives should not expect men to finance their choice.[11]

Defending a client in exactly this legal bind, DeCrow argued that if her client was "willing to share the financial responsibility of an abortion and the woman refuses to have one, then he should not be forced to support the child." That is, if he does not wish to be a "social" father, he should not have to pay child support on the grounds that he has been denied an equal right to choose parenthood. "Men should not automatically have to pay for a child they don't want. It's the only logical feminist position to take."[12]

Opponents of this line of argument (including 48% of our respondents, though only 37% of the married men) are cheered by appellate decisions that consistently uphold the claim by mothers for child support. The Colorado Supreme Court, for example, has refused to invalidate a state law's "irrebuttable presumption" that both parents who participate in the conception of a child should share in the duty of financial support. The state's tacit accommodation of the mother's decision to have the child, while ignoring the father's desire to terminate the pregnancy, is "the only constitutional course open to the state," at least since *Roe v. Wade*. Finally, the father's right to be free from discrimination via gender-based classifications is outweighed by the state's need to protect a mother's fundamental right to make decisions relating to her pregnancy, and also, to the state's interest in ensuring children receive adequate financial support.[13]

Unmarried Males: Some Men are More Equal

Shunted to the sidelines in this legal debate are males without the honored status of *spouse* (albeit some with a "living-together" status are slowly gaining a standing in law similar to that of legally wed husbands). Males who are "merely" lovers, sex partners, or otherwise, lack any substantial legal standing in a contest over a pending abortion.

Attorneys who have tried to help erase this double standard insist the emotional ties of unwed fathers to the fetus resemble those of husbands in every significant way. They insist the situation is best seen as a controversy between a male and a female, regardless of whether or not the couple had wed before co-conceiving their disputed pregnancy. And, they note with approval a steady widening of the unwed male's rights in his sex partner's decision to put the child of their (marriageless) union up for adoption. (Some states assure prenotification, and some require his consent if he has kept up "family ties.") Unwed males, or so their lawyers maintain, warrant the same say in the decision to terminate a pregnancy as may ever be gained by married men. And, if an Equal Rights Amendment were to pass, unwed fathers might finally gain rights similar to those held by a married father.

Critics of premarital relations vehemently disagree, of course, and oppose every legal change that dilutes the advantages of the married status.[14] Others less zealous about chastity before marriage question the impact on the American family of equating an unwed male and a husband's desire to participate in a contested abortion decision: "If he cares so much," they conclude, "why doesn't he marry her, and thereby assure some degree of meaningful child support and co-parenting?"[15]

Summary

Ethicist Daniel Callahan believes it is "one thing to emancipate women from discrimination and tyranny; it is quite another to emancipate them from all human claims and obligations toward the rights of others."[16] Exactly how the state and the law can serve society best in this matter remains controversial in the extreme.[17] All that is clear is that since 1973, in matters of spousal consent, spousal prenotification, and unwed fathers' rights, men have had no standing in abortion law...as many waiting room men know.

...We agree with the Court that a woman has a legal right to an abortion, though we would hope it is a right that will never be exercised routinely. We look forward to the day when those who oppose abortion will give up the legal battle by which they intend to use the coercive powers of the state to enforce their norm, and instead use moral suasion to promote the view that abortion, while no longer a crime, is not morally neutral either.

The Editors, "The Abortion Perplex" (*The New Republic*, July 11, 1983, pp. 7–8.)

PROFILE

Vince's letter and subsequent TV talk-show appearance with us highlighted the total absence of a husband's rights in whether or not a potential child of his will be aborted. More significantly, Vince typifies the ultimate impact of fatherhood lost, and, in turn, marriage lost. Although a father now by a new wife, thoughts of his first "child" are still with him. (In all, 81% of our waiting room men had thoughts of the fetus and 69% of our follow-up men had occasional or frequent thoughts of the fetus.)

Vince:

In March 1979, my wife became pregnant. This was not a planned pregnancy. My wife was not using any form of birth control as she got sick from the pills and an IUD was painful for her.

My wife did not want the baby because of her age (33) and the fact she felt she had already raised three children (ages 8 to 15, from a previous marriage) at the time and did not want the pain of childrearing until she was in her late fifties. She also was just starting her career as an accountant.

I stressed to her . . . I loved her, would share the child raising, and I was beginning to love the baby.

In June 1979, she aborted the baby without my knowledge or consent. She had been both ill and very depressed during the pregnancy, and on the day of the abortion she was in high spirits while I was sad, angry, and cried much that day.

I tried for months to control my feeling on the abortion, but found myself thinking about it at work, on the road, and at home. I called it 'the murder' when I talked with my wife. I found it affected my feelings for her more than I could control.

The only one outside my marriage who knew was my boss at work. Talking with him helped, but really in retrospect not enough.

The marriage ended on December 8, 1979, in divorce. I had loved my wife deeply 'til that point, but I could not get out of my head that the abortion killed our love.

Notes

1. Prior to this decision "the father's interest [in the fetus] had been sheltered within the criminal sanctions imposed by the state to protect its own interests . . . the state prohibited abortions to such an extent that a father's interest was sheltered by the prohibition . . . the *Roe v. Wade* decision eliminated until the final trimester of pregnancy the shelter which had protected his rights in the past." Richard A. Gilbert, "Abortion: The Father's Rights." *University of Cincinnati Law Review* 42 (1973): 442–445.

2. See, in this connection, Marshall B. Kapp, "The Father's (Lack of) Rights and Responsibilities in the Abortion Decisions: An Examination of Legal-Ethical Implications." *Ohio Northern University Law Review* 9 (1982): 369–383. Kapp insists that our "most deeply-held values of ethics and law" require freeing the father of his support requirement (p. 383).

3. Two critics insist that "when such profound interpersonal rights are in conflict (as in divorce and child custody disputes), the courts have always sought to *balance* the interests and accommodate, as much as possible, both sides rather than adopt a 'winner-take-all' approach." Lynn D. Wardle and Mary Ann Q. Wood, *A Lawyer Looks at Abortion,* p. 78. Provo, Utah: Brigham Young University Press, 1982. See *Roe v. Wade,* 410 U.S. 113 (1973); see also *United States Supreme Court Reports,* 35 L Ed 2d 735, Rochester, NY: The Lawyers Co-operative Publishing, 1983, pp. 23–25.

4. Where sociological underpinnings are concerned two critics charge that "current law reinforces very outdated and sexist stereotypes. Do 'women still have most to lose by an unwanted pregnancy'? Are men 'bungling parents'? Are 'women always in the end responsible alone for their children'? And are 'men untrustworthy in their commitments'?" Bill Wishard and Laurie Wishard, *Men's Rights: A Handbook for the 80s,* p. 70. San Francisco: Cragmont, 1980.

5. See *Planned Parenthood v. Danforth,* 428 U.S. 52 (1976).

6. For an example of pro-consent reasoning, see Joseph Parker Witherspoon, "Impact of the Abortion Decisions Upon the Father's Role." *The Jurist* 35 (1975): 32–65. "It seems perfectly clear that to subject the father of an unborn child to the uncontrolled discretion of its mother with respect to having an abortion is to convert the father into a partial slave who is indistinguishable from those who, after being freed from the *de jure* status of slavery were still faced with denials in particular instances of the fundamental civil rights of the freeman." (p. 59). For the argument that a physician should require the husband's written consent, see Russell S. Fisher, "Criminal Abortion," in *Abortion in America.* Harold Rosen, ed., p. 5. Boston: Beacon, 1967.

7. In disagreeing, two lawyers contend that "approaching the abortion issue from the perspective of whether the individual wish of the husband or the individual wish of the wife should prevail ignores the threshold question of whether either partner to a marriage has the right to make a unilateral decision about an act that will necessarily involve the taking of the life of a jointly conceived child." Wardle and Wood, op. cit., p. 83.

8. Sociologist Amitai Etzioni argues that "the principal sociological rationale for requiring consultation with the spouse is to encourage an airing of the feelings between the couple *before* any irreversible action is taken. Husband and wife may not necessarily end up with the same views, but alienation resulting from one person taking a

unilateral and clandestine step will be avoided... Our main point is that the law does not merely regulate our lives, it articulates and symbolizes our values and mores. In an era when the family has been rendered increasingly vulnerable to dissolution, we should not gratuitously add to the stress by enshrining in the law the starkly individualistic view that a child in the making, a future shared project of the family, is wholly and completely a 'private' matter for the woman to determine, with no concern at all for the wishes of the father—when he is her husband." Amitai Etzioni, "The Husband's Rights in Abortion," *Trial*, 12 (November, 1976): 58. See also Gerald F. Slattery, Jr., "Constitutional Law-Abortion—No Requirement of Spousal or Parental Consent to Woman's Decision to Abort." *Tulane Law Review* 51 (1977): 1279–1286. Cf. Frederick Avamsino, Jr., "Abortion: The Future Cases: Fathers' Rights." *University of San Francisco Law Review* 8 (Winter 1973): 472–492.

9. See, for example, Stephen G. Anderson, "Abortion and the Husband's Consent." *Journal of Family Law* 13 (1973–1974): 311–331; Brian D. Shore, "Marital Secrets: The Emerging Issue of Abortion Spousal Notification Laws." *The Journal of Legal Medicine* 3 (1982): 461–482. Cf. Debbie Wiemers, "Spousal Notification and Consent in Abortion Situations: *Scheinberg v. Smith*." *Houston Law Review* 19 (1982): 1025–1039. For a very current anti-notice argument, see Gaylene Rogers, "Spousal Notification Requirement is Constitutionally Permissible Burden on Woman's Right to Privacy in Abortion Decisions." *Texas Tech Law Review* 13 (1982): 1495–1511; Judith Greene, "Spousal Notice—Weighing the Burden of a Women's Abortion Decision," *Stetson Law Review* 12 (1982–1983): 250–264.

10. Kapp, op. cit., p. 376. See also Wesley D. H. Teo, "Abortion: The Husband's Constitutional Rights," *Ethics* 85 (1975): 337–342; L. M. Purdy, "Abortion and the Husband's Rights: A Reply to Wesley Teo." *Ethics* 86 (1976): 247–251.

11. Karen De Crow, "Letter to the Editor." *New York Times Magazine*, May 9, 1982, p. 108.

12. Karen De Crow, as quoted in *Washington Post*, March 28, 1982, pp. 4–12.

13. *Scheinberg v. Smith*, 482 F. Supp. 529 (S.D. Florida 1979). See also *Charles v. Carey*, 79 C 4541 (N.D. Illinois, November 16, 1979) (order granting preliminary injunction), *aff'd in part, rev'd in part*, 622 F. 2d 772 (7th Cir. 1980) (interlocutory appeal); *Doe v. Deschamyss* 461 F. Supp. 682 (1976).

14. See, for example, Rick Blackwood and Robin Blackwood, "What are the Father's Rights in Abortion?" *The Journal of Legal Medicine* (October 1975): 28–36.

15. See, for example, a 1978 Court decision that held, "Once the reputed father of an illegitimate child is found guilty, and adjudged its father, he is liable for the care, maintenance, and education of the child, and to all penalties for failure to perform those obligations, the same of a father of a legitimate child." *Harris v. Alabama* 356 So. 2d. 623, February 24, 1978.

16. Daniel Callahan, *Abortion: Law, Choice and Morality*, p. 82. New York: Macmillan, 1970. Nathanson contends that as pregnancy is "the result of the act of two people, it seems manifestly unfair to say that women have exclusive rights when the consequences of abortion involve both sexes." Bernard Nathanson, *Aborting America*, New York: Doubleday, 1979, p. 257.

17. Helpful here is Jean Gray Platt, ed., "Survey of Abortion Law." *Arizona State Law Journal* (1980): 67–216; Richard A. Gilbert, "Abortion: The Father's Rights." *University of Cincinnati Law Review* 42 (1973): 441–467; Joseph W. Dellapenna, "The History of Abortion: Technology, Morality, and Law." *University of Pittsburgh Law Review* 40 (1979): 359–428. Note also that as of June 1983, Lexis, the computer-driven law search service, listed 3,000 federal and state court decisions bearing on abortion matters.

Chapter 13

Before the Abortion:
A Better Way

There is no conflict between seeing men as
hurt—as human beings trapped in roles they do
not need or really want—and yet acknowledging
that women are even worse off. It is not necessary for any group to be more hurt or oppressed
in order to deserve carefully designed programs
of help and support.

Bruce M. Rappaport, "Family Planning:
Helping Men Ask for Help" (*Public Welfare*,
Spring 1981, p. 25).

I think that women are going to start saying,
"Look at men. They're suffering a lot. Let's pay
some attention to men!"

Margaret Atwood (Canadian writer and feminist) (*New York Times*, March 28, 1982,
p. 21).

I never thought that men were the enemy.

Betty Friedan (*People*, November 24, 1981).

.y the time men arrive in a clinic waiting room, a good deal of harm has been done that *might* have been prevented or reduced if they had learned something from a school-based abortion program, a contraceptive outreach program, a media exploration of male roles in abortion, and/or new programs sponsored by the women's and men's movements.

1. *Educational Coverage.* Until the typical high-school curriculum includes a bracket of course work on teenagers and conception, contraception, abortion, and abortion alternatives, we will not be meeting the need, not even by half:

> According to a recent survey, adolescent boys listed 'getting a girl pregnant' as their third biggest worry, just after 'going to jail' and 'flunking out.' Girls ranked pregnancy their second biggest fear, second only to the death of their parents.[1]

> Sex-related stress was the single largest response written by students...in a survey of 4,400 Ohio high schoolers. Girls said they didn't know 'how to say no,' while boys felt pressured into getting girls to say yes.[2]

Little wonder that 91% of our waiting room men felt that "adolescents should get more information about birth control at school."

Unfortunately, the nation continues to ignore both the need *and* general opinion support:

> *1972* A Gallup Poll found 73% of the public in favor of better dissemination of sex education.[3]

> *1982* A Gallup Poll found 70% of the public in favor of sex education in the public school.[4]

> *1982* A NORC Poll found 84% of the public in favor of sex education in public schools.[5]

Only six states, however, require schools to teach some form of family life or sex education. While other states encourage such courses, they leave the decision to require them up to individual school districts: A survey in 1979 found that only a third of all high schools taught anything about human reproduction, sexuality, contraception, or abortion.[6]

Teenagers are *not* pleased with what is being passed off as sex education in many school districts. While almost all agree the subject should be offered, 58% in a 1981 poll of over 160,000 high schoolers did not feel their courses went far enough, or provided useful insights into the emotional complications involved. Not surprisingly, the curricula is drawn up without any input from the teenagers themselves, and it primarily reflects the community's fear of a teenager "getting into trouble"; hence, there is a stern focus on preventing venereal disease and encouraging abstinence.[7]

To underline the seriousness of all this, it is vital to recognize that 71% of this 160,000-teen sample did not feel they could discuss contraception with their parents. Indeed, 52% did not feel they could discuss *any* aspect of sex or sexuality with either parent. (Some 44% of this 13–18-year-old group were sexually active, although only 38% of the boys and 50% of the girls were using birth-control methods.)[8]

On rare occasions when a high school sex education course includes abortion as a study topic, the content appears as ill-chosen, as in the case of sex coverage per se:

A 1980 project funded by the Federal Government was hailed as "the single largest sex education research-and-development program" of the period. Its various materials met or approached ideal criteria determined by a survey of 100 sex-education professionals.

Its exploration of the implications of abortion was initiated by a videotape of children who were severely retarded, followed by a "right-to-life" film.[9]

Far more relevant and helpful, in our opinion, would be a film about abortion clinic realities, complete with positive role modeling of mature male and female reactions to the abortion challenge (see the project proposal, "Videotape Profile," in Appendix).[10]

If we are soon to reduce the rate of teenage pregnancies and terminations, we must reconsider the neglect of this rare and timely educational opportunity. Teens tell sensitive counselors, educators, and therapists that they want and need help sorting out their attitudes and expectations of sex and sexuality. Drawn to use sexual expression as a vehicle for communicating caring and intimacy, their sexual values are "neither casual nor indiscriminate."[11] All the more vital, therefore, is their introduction to the subject of abortion and its myriad impacts on *both* sexes.

In this same vein, a comparable program should be implemented for *parents:*

> A public education program...perhaps on a yearly basis and through their children's schools, would appraise them of local community statistics on sexual activity, contraceptive use, abortions, and the venereal disease rate among minors—all in a spirit that would encourage them to speak with their child about these issues in a way that would help the child think through their own values and become conscious of her or his own responsibilities.[12]

Such a program could include a sensitive and constructive review of what has been learned about abortion's many meanings for females *and* males, thereby helping parents close a significant gap in their grasp of teenage realities.

There is no denying the fact that political, social, and organizational impediments to implementation are formidable. And, it is vital to respect the variety of motivations, tastes, needs, and moral values of target audience members. Still, the opportunity offered for educational gains here warrant every patient, realistic, and pragmatic effort possible.

2. *Contraception Outreach Program.* The situation here could hardly be worse, as very little emphasis is placed on the role of the male on teenage sex:

> In addition to his being ignored by research, it is still the exceptional family planning or parenting program that reaches out to include him; and government policy—in attempting to claim financial support from him—undoubtedly contributes to his seeking to stay firmly out of the picture.[13]

At least in this regard, a specialist warns, "law and public policy foster irresponsibility in the male partner of a teenage pregnancy."[14]

Fortunately, a few influential voices are being heard on behalf of male needs. Typical is a 1979 indictment by Professor Catherine C. Chilman, a specialist in adolescent sexuality research and policy design:

> The usual focus on females as being *the* person responsible for contraception is a flagrant example of sexism. This focus is frequently

excused by such statements as, "It is the female who gets pregnant," or "Male methods of contraception are less effective; besides, males don't like them." (What female ever said that she *liked* her methods?) It also is said, "You can't trust a male to use a contraceptive."[15]

This very attitude, Chilman warns, "is apt to become a self-fulfilling prophecy."[16] Indeed, as far as she is concerned, "all of the above attitudes would seem to undermine the male's sense of responsibility as a copartner in reproduction control."[17]

All the more welcomed, therefore, are field trials of innovative outreach programs predicated on very different (pro-male) values. A program at a San Francisco Bay area hospital, for example, provides general medical services to teenagers:

> ...all male patients are routinely rotated through our family planning counselors before they see the regular medical staff whether they are at the clinic for a sexually related concern or not. In other words, a young man does not have to acknowledge sexual naivete in order to gain access to accurate information and counseling.[18]

Frustrated by characteristic male reluctance to admit ignorance through the raising of questions, the staff of the Men's Support Center invented a "myth card game" to help break the ice and get the questions out:

> Our set of 3×5 cards have brief and usually false statements designed to promote discussions on sexuality and family planning issues. We developed the cards by researching the typical questions asked by teenagers, during presentations to public school classes. Statements like, "You have to be 18 to buy condoms" or "Women mean 'yes' when they say 'no' are examples...."
>
> The young man is given a stack of these cards, asked to read them, and then put them in one of three compartments in a cardboard box. The compartments are marked 'true,' 'false,' and 'don't know.' ...the counselor corrects any misinformation, validating what knowledge the young man has, and discussing subjects in more detail where some real interest is shown."[19]

This game allows counselors to ask the questions *for the client*, thereby respecting his need not to appear naive. As well, it gives guidance about sensitive areas that warrant more discussion.

Another welcomed type of outreach program utilizes the offer of free or low cost physical exams in exchange for a birth control and/or sex education discussion. A variation on this has the counselor go where the action is:

> ...we sent two staffers who are ace basketball players out to the public courts...where young men congregate.... After they impressed the kids with their skills, Tim and Bob would tell them they were from the county health department and wanted to talk to them about birth control.[20]

Other topics, especially the options open to young males suddenly immersed in an unexpected abortion drama, are readily included in this kind of impromptu "classroom" exchange. Outstanding exceptions to the general rule of male neglect, these few pioneering outreach programs warrant far more imitation across the country than they have begun to earn.

3. *Media Exploration.* Only one movie in recent years, a 1972 film (*Play It as It Lays*), has even touched in passing on our subject. (And then, it pictured a husband forcing his adulterous wife to have an illegal abortion.) Despite the extraordinary human drama involved here, the variety of ways men react to the abortion challenge eludes the kind of Hollywood film treatment that could provide valuable "adult education."

Television's record is just as disappointing. To the best of our knowledge (and that of scores of clinic staffers we asked), none of the rare TV dramas on women and abortion have paid more than fleeting, unflattering, or patronizing attention to males on the scene. "Soap operas" are no better, and possibly worse. Their scripts rehash every shopworn cliché imaginable about men caught up in an abortion drama (they desert, abuse, philander, and, in other ignoble ways, demonstrate only pathetic inadequacies).

Print media have a slightly better record, though only by comparison to the film and TV "blackout." Somewhat surprisingly, magazines for women have seldom explored the significance of putting the male sex partner on the sideline. A few, *Glamour*, *Mademoiselle*, and *McCall's*, to their credit, have had relevant feature articles with sensitive and constructive advice for readers.[21] Others, however, like *Cosmopolitan*, *Essence*, *Redbook*, and *Women's Day*, according to a 1983 computer search, have totally neglected the topic—as have almost all the magazines aimed at a male reading audience. Two articles are exceptions to the rule, one having appeared in a 1981 issue of *Esquire,* and another, in a 1982 issue of *Hustler.*[22] Both demonstrate the substantial educational content such publications can share with their distinct male following, and together whet the appetite for more such feature writing.

General readership publications have as checkered a record as do women's and men's material. Despite a single strong article in a 1983 issue of *Time* ("Sharing the Pain of Abortion"), and in a 1982 issue of *The Progressive* ("Whose Freedom of Choice?"), the record is otherwise bare.[23] Overall, the magazine shelf has offered a male or female reader almost nothing on this topic proportionate to the 1,600,000 females and 1,600,000 males annually involved in it.

A major bright spot—and model for emulation by *all* media types—concerns a small number of paperback handbooks of advice, for example:

The Planned Parenthood *Handbook* in 1973 urged its readers to recognize that "...a man can have just as painful and conflicting emotions about a pregnancy in which he is involved as a woman."[24]

The 1978 guidebook, *Men: A Book for Women,* points out that "the man's side has been overlooked in the abortion debate...whenever there is a relationship that will continue afterward, the man is involved, too.... Few men remain unaffected by the decision not to bear what would otherwise have become their child. The strain of abortion often lingers long after the actual operation."[25]

The 1982 paperback, *Your Choice: A Young Woman's Guide to Making Decisions About Unmarried Pregnancy,* advised readers to recognize that "a man's feeling often runs deeper than he's able to show. Help him to open up by approaching the subject with an attitude that says, "I know you're concerned about this, too. What do you think we should do?"...If you can suggest specific ways he can help—with money, transportation, his presence at a clinic or while you talk with your parents—he'll probably feel better, too."[26]

The 1982 guidebook for teenagers, *Mom, I'm Pregnant,* advises a reader to "expect your boyfriend to have feelings of his own. Often a boy has trouble expressing his true feelings openly.... Fatherhood can be very scary to someone who is not prepared for it."[27]

The 1983 handbook, *A Woman's Guide to Safe Abortion,* gently counsels taking "the man who made you pregnant" into one's confidence: "You may be surprised to find out when you talk to him that he very much wants to help in any way he can."[28]

While males benefit indirectly from these female-oriented publications, they can profit directly from pamphlets by counselors Ann Baker, Roger Wade, and Peter Zelles, along with a 1980 leaflet of the Planned Parenthood Federation, "A Man's Guide to Sexuality."[29] Until these items are in much wider circulation, however, their full potential will remain unrealized.

Regrettably, males can learn very little about the abortion experience from the fast-growing body of men's literature. Best sellers like Herb Goldberg's two books, *The Hazards of Being Male* (1976) and *The New Male* (1980), Joe L. Dubbert's *A Man's Place: Masculinity in Transition* (1979), Robert A. Lewis's essay collection, *Men in Difficult Times: Masculinity Today and Tomorrow* (1981), and Andrew Tolson's *The Limits of Masculinity: Male Identity and the Liberated Woman* (1977), have no reference whatsoever to the subject of men and abortion.[30] Quite different is Warren Farrell's pathbreaking classic, *The Liberated Man* (1975), which recommends our topic for men's group meetings ("Do we know anyone who has had a vasectomy? An abortion? How did they feel about it later? How do we think we would feel?").[31] We earnestly hope authors of forthcoming books in this genre will take Farrell's example to heart and begin to explore the annual experience of 1,400,000 abortion-confronting men.

Perhaps the strongest media performance to date is that of newspaper advice columnists (like Ann Landers and Dr. Joyce Brothers), who have focused on men and abortion, along with radio talk-show hosts who have discussed this book on the air, and newspaper feature writers who have occasionally covered the subject. All three types focus on tough and engaging questions, often using snappy, realistic, and memorable answers likely to stay with a reader or listener for some time thereafter. Their techniques for "teaching" how to reduce losses and maximize gains in the abortion drama merit much applause, and much more utilization.

These bright exceptions to the contrary, the media record en toto profoundly disappoints—but, hopefully, will shift soon in the direction of far more adequate coverage of the subject.

4. *Men's and Women's Movement.* A workshop that Art Shostak

was invited to run in 1981 on men and abortion for the New Jersey branch of the National Organization for Women first set us thinking about the role of such organizations.

The National Congress for Men (NCM), for example, links approximately 125 men's, fathers', and divorce reform organizations nationwide. At its third annual convention, the delegates discussed a wide range of topics (exploitation through stereotypes; prison reform; nonsexist draft; paid paternity leave; and so on). Especially relevant was:

> *Abortion*—from the male perspective. Considerations for the prospective father who desires to preserve, protect and raise the child; the dilemma for the anguished father denied participation in a decision to continue or terminate life.''[32]

NCM, which has women on its advisory board and welcomed women to its three-day meeting, boasts that its current president is also the president of the Joint Custody Association, a gender bridge-building effort. Should NCM soon encourage some of its 125 or so affiliates to conduct forums on men and abortion, the gain in ''consciousness-raising'' could be quite substantial.

A fine example was set on May 26, 1983, when a Washington, D.C. organization, Free Men, held its first-ever public forum on the question, ''Can We Help Men Confronted with Abortions?'' Speakers included Art Shostak, counselor Andre Watson (see Chapter 8), writer Judith Patterson, and Dan Logan, Free Men's executive director. Dan, in particular, rattled some in the audience with his strong defense of Karen DeCrow's legal position in the Serpico case (see Chapter 12):

> A man should have the opportunity to reiterate his choice not to parent while it's safe for the woman to have an abortion. If he does, he shouldn't be legally considered a parent, and should not be held financially responsible...to harness such a man to up to twenty years of child support is akin to rape.[33]

Much debate ensued, of course, and the audience (60% female!) exchanged thoughtful views long into the night.

A new organization, the National Men's Organization, was formed in 1982 with members from 39 states (7%, female).

Avowedly anti-sexist, NMO intends to help lift the "sex role burdens that limit and impoverish the lives of men, and the oppression of women at all levels of society."[34] Using a task group approach, NMO formed units to explore homophobia, media images of men, male-female relationships, men's health issues, fathering, and 12 other topics. If and when it acts on a suggestion Art Shostak made in January 1983, and forms a "Men and Abortion" task group, it might begin to make a nationwide contribution in this area that is equal to its considerable potential. Likewise, such a task group might make its own contribution to that "scattered male chorus which, perhaps, will eventually acquire the solidarity and, most of all, the analytic clarity of the women's movement."[35]

As for an explicit contribution the nationwide network of women's organizations might make to the men and abortion subject, four types of help come readily to mind:

> Forums could be held for an open-minded discussion of abortion realities, and the degree to which females are *really* well-served by the male's second-class status in the matter.

> Articles could be included in *Ms.* magazine and other movement publications that explore the pros and cons of an expanded role for men in the abortion drama.

> A portion of a local N.O.W. chapter meeting could be set aside for a review of local abortion clinic norms in this matter, and their possible reform.

Fourthly, and above all, the well-established women's movement could collaborate with the barely-off-the-ground men's movement in campaigning for "men and abortion" reform as a *joint* enterprise, from the very outset.

Males *cannot* expect women to help "rescue" them or assume the leadership role here. Nor will women welcome this new campaign without a sigh of regret. The feminist reform agenda *already* taxes every iota of strength and perserverance, and adding still another fight hardly merits a brass band and cheers of welcome. Certain feminists will insist men assume the largest share of this particular reform campaign, and demonstrate thereby their deep-reaching commitment before the women's movement joins the fray. Perhaps this is as it should be, though progress may be significantly slowed by this development.

Betty Friedan has recently urged the women's movement to usher in a new "Second Stage." An effort would be made to consolidate hard-won gains and move forward to new goals— especially where gender collaboration is concerned:

Don't ask what women are going to do! Ask what women and men are going to do! If you take a question like child care as just a woman's problem, forget it, forget it![36]

This orientation "has sent some radical feminists into a flaming rage and given other feminists a sense of relief,"[37] the latter, women who agree with Friedan that "the women's movement has come just about as far as it can in terms of women alone."[38]

If Second Stage supporters soon signal their availability for a joint reform campaign to concerned men (activists who will take the initiative and assume the burden of a campaign's "nitty gritty" workload), the Second Stage might have as one of its brightest achievements the overdue reform of the abortion experience.

Why might feminists soon bother? They are urged to think of interrelated changes in the male role, and of priorities in such change, as mapped out, for example, by Rosalind Petchesky, author of *Reproductive Freedom: Feminist Theory and the Abortion Issue:*

Men should never have an equal say, but of course they should be included in the abortion decision. But men should be included in birth control, childbearing, and childrearing as well. Men should consider themselves responsible for the consequences of sexuality and the quality of relationships. But to say that they should be more involved in abortion before those other things is putting the cart before the horse.[39]

Perhaps. Other feminists, however, may ask "Which is the cart and which is the horse?" The positive experience a young man *could* have by sharing more fully in the abortion drama *might* help him later choose to be a childbirth labor coach, a "full equality" homemaker, a house husband, or, if it becomes necessary, a joint custody "partner" in post-divorce child-rearing.

Summary

Long before a man joins his sex partner for her abortion clinic appointment, certain reforms explored in this chapter might help him—as counselor Stephen McCallister puts it—identify "the best possible solutions to some of the worse possible situations."[40]

We believe concerned men and women should help upgrade school courses in human sexuality, and insist that "men and abortion" be covered in the curriculum. Contraceptive outreach programs should be expanded and invigorated, attention being paid to abortion's toll on males as a reason for them to become much better contraceptors. The media should substantially improve its coverage of the male experience in abortion. And the men's *and* women's movements (separately and together) should help raise consciousness about this subject and promote a far-reaching agenda of "men and abortion" reforms.

Feminist Mary Kay Blakely suggests that "there is no neat, antiseptic solution to the pain of abortion. There will be no end to the scenes of human misery, without sincere effort to change the conditions of life that produce them."[41] To her list of such conditions as unrelenting poverty, martyred motherhood, and too much despair, we would add conception and contraception ignorance, media blindness to abortion's "untold" story, and the failure thus far of the men's and women's movements to give a damn. Until we make progress on *all* these fronts we will have far more males wrestling far less adequately with a far more costly abortion challenge than is good for any of us, male and female alike.

PROFILE

Andrew, like many of our other men, saw his social environment through his own very personal abortion experience. A brush with a critical identity crisis two years beforehand had left him no choice but to start over.

Now he claims "a whole new outlook" due to the love and respect for life gained through hard-earned self-awareness and his religious growth. Andrew's work as a counselor in the Colorado state prison reflects his dedication to doing something for others much less likely to succeed than himself.

Andrew:
We came close to not doing it at all. We were still discussing it right up to the time of the appointment. We sat outside in the car until the last minute. In fact, the last minute was an hour late. I bowed my head and asked the Lord for direction. Since we were an hour late, I asked Him to let us know. If the doctor was still there, it would mean we were to go ahead with

the abortion. If not, we wouldn't. We just caught him. I was very saddened by the whole thing.

I'd always viewed pregnancy as a bad reason to get married. I don't sleep around. Suzie was involved in a gay relationship before she met me, but things worked out. We went on a cruise during our mutual vacation time. On the first night we slept together and there was a magnificent spark when we touched. I guess that's when things really started to happen between us.

We considered all options carefully. She's involved in a demanding master's program and I wasn't available for babysitting because of my job which has me on the night shift. Both of us were opposed to marriage although we have since considered living together . . . I don't think it's fair to have women carry the burden for birth control alone. I offered to have a vasectomy. She started the pill two days before learning of the pregnancy. Birth control had not been a problem for her before.

I have career goals and life goals. My career goals are not paramount. For life goals, I want a wife who would love me as much as I love her, who would remain equally as faithful to me as I would to her and who would raise a family with me. I was thrilled by the possibility of a child. I wanted it bad. But I want to please. If she'd wanted the baby, I'd have done anything I could. More than anything I desire a family, but I don't want to get married *because* of a family.

I wait for reactions before I react. I saw she was scared by the whole thing. Her desire for a master's is very strong and I wouldn't want to take that away. I guess I just went more with the flow of her intuition. She made the first appointment for counseling at the Birth Control Institute. We went to the session. They talked more about the process of abortion than the options. That's how I'd do it, because nobody can tell me what my options are since I know what they are. Any responsible adult should be aware of their options.

At the clinic they demonstrated the uses of the instruments and discussed anesthesia. If I were them, I would assume that people came to the institute because they knew what they wanted and I would not want to take the responsibility for making decisions. For example, I didn't want to tell Suzie that this would ruin my life. I wanted to see what she would do on her own feelings and thoughts. Two years ago I would have said, "This is really going to destroy me," but luckily, I'm stronger now.

Everything you do in life is a lesson, positive or negative. This has taught me that no matter how strong the urge to make love with a woman is, you have to think about all these things beforehand. I don't throw my affections around loosely and this experience has strengthened that behavior. It has strengthened my heart and my convictions. I won't condemn others for their actions, not even the people I work with. I am not a judge.

If everything works out and at some future point in time we have a child,

I'm sure my emotions will burst, knowing we could have had a son or daughter, now. I might get kicked at work and become sterile and not have another chance to have a kid. The whole thing makes me very sad.

I desire to go on living, not to wallow. If you dig a pit you can choose to lie in it or crawl out of it and have new experiences, new lessons. I say I deal with it. I never forget anything. It's always there as a sounding board, a dent in my tabula rasa for future reference, a bench mark.

The whole ordeal has strengthened my convictions. At this point I know I wouldn't ever consider abortion again. I would not risk pregnancy with anyone else. I would do anything . . . castration, vasectomy, anything! I'm dead set against it.

One of my biggest problems in dealing with the world is that people are so ignorant. I think we ought to start in grade school, learning the possibilities of pregnancy, so that by junior high school children can accept the knowledge; whether they can make the decision is another issue.

I live for the experiences to make somebody happy in my day, to please somebody. Just my desire to experience carried me through the abortion. It was forced on me, but it's my drive and desire to get as much out of life as I can that carried me through.

The experience did bring us closer together. Now that she is on the pill our sex life is fuller, improved, because we are free from the "bond" of possible pregnancy. I can say for 100% surety that this situation will never come up again in my life. If the woman I happen to marry has to have an abortion, to save her own life, I have no qualms about that. Otherwise, I won't put myself in that position. I won't wet my "dip stick" to take the risk.

The clinic experience was informative. I hadn't known about the actual operation. Other than that it was a very cold atmosphere. They know why you are there. It's institutionalized. You put your feet in the stirrups and the doctor comes in. If they had allowed me to participate or go into the procedure room, I would have been there. I sat in the waiting room with six other gentlemen. Occasionally, a woman would stick her head out the door and say, "Everything's okay, she'll be out in half an hour." I sat and read a Stephen King novel.

Basically, I was appalled at the crude, callous jokes some of the other guys were making in the waiting room. Most of them were very insensitive. When you and a woman are dealing with this, you have to be very sensitive to her, her feelings, her needs. These guys were a bunch of assholes. One guy had been through it before. He was singing, "I left my fetus in San Francisco. . . ."

For the most part, in my dealings with men, they are crude when they talk about their women, their wives. I'd say, basically, men are insensitive. I don't forsee any change. Men have been stereotyped for years as macho and women stereotyped as flowers, and the other side of the spectrum. Until the man and woman take away that type of impact on their child's life, there won't be any changing. It's like starting a new race.

The abortion is something I'd never want to go through again. Suzie told me she'd had one previous abortion for different reasons. She didn't want the guy to father her child. With me it was different. She wanted me to, but not then. It intensified my sadness, but at the same time I realized it was not an appropriate time.

Notes

1. Anonymous, "Hersay: Mid-Revolutionary Mores." *Ms.*, August, 1983, p. 18.

2. Carol Clurman, "Study: Causes of Teen Stress Changing." *USA Today*, June 2, 1983, p. 3-A.

3. Anonymous, "A Vote on Abortion." *Time*, September 4, 1972, p. 8.

4. Carol Cassell, "Sex Education Poll," *Planned Parenthood Review* (Spring 1981): 13.

5. NORC, *Guidebook to the General Social Survey, 1982*, p. 161. Chicago: National Opinion Research Corporation, 1983.

6. Jules Archer, *Who's Running Your Life? A Look at Young People's Rights*, p. 113. New York: Harcourt Brace Jovanovich, 1979. See also Arlene K. Richards and Irene Willis, *What to Do If You or Someone You Know Is Under 18 and Pregnant*, New York: Lothrup, Lee & Shepard, 1983.

7. Jane Norman and Myron W. Harris, *The Private Life of the American Teenager*, p. 69. New York: Rawson Wade, 1981.

8. Ibid., p. 67.

9. Constantine Horner, "Is the New Sex Education Going Too Far?" *New York Times Magazine*, December 7, 1980, p. 146.

10. Profoundly disappointing in this connection was the 1983 *Frontline* video production, "Abortion Clinic." Aired on PBS-TV stations on April 18, 1983, and hosted by the late Jessica Savitch, the TV production focused on the "anguish" of four women, two who decided to have their babies, and two who chose abortion. In none of these cases did the male get any sustained or helpful attention. As well, none of the clinic scenes indicated the presence of males in the waiting room, although the director of a clinic used in the film has indicated to us the the TV production crew interviewed several such men on camera. See in this connection, *Frontline* #112, "Abortion Clinic."

(Boston, Mass.: WGBH Transcripts, 1983). Far more valuable is a new videotape production of a moving original play dealing with male decision making in an abortion context, "The Cruelest Month," written by and available for viewing from Herb Jacobson, 1312 Magnolia Way, Denver, CO 80224.

11. Aaron Hass, *Teenage Sexuality: A Survey of Teenage Sexual Behavior*, p. 181. New York: Macmillan, 1979. "We must pay more attention to *their* needs—and we can only achieve this by fully appreciating how intensely they experience feelings associated with love and sexuality."

12. Margaret O'Brien Steinfels, "Ethical and Legal Issues in Teenage Pregnancies," in Theodore Ooms, ed., *Teenage Pregnancy in a Family Context: Implications for Policy*, p. 303. Philadelphia: Temple University Press, 1981. Hass notes in this connection, "As a sex therapist, most of the patients who come to me have been influenced by sexual myths and misconceptions which they harbor. Parents, too, need sex education and an opportunity to clarify their own values before they will feel comfortable interacting with their child." Hass, op. cit., p. 181.

13. Theodore Ooms, "Introduction," in Ooms, ed., op. cit., p. 22.

14. Steinfels, op. cit., p. 298.

15. Catherine S. Chilman, *Adolescent Sexuality in a Changing American Society: Social and Psychological Perspectives*, p. 300. Washington, D.C.: National Institutes of Health, 1979.

16. Ibid.

17. Ibid. See also Bruce Stokes, *Men and Family Planning*. Washington, D.C.: Worldwatch Institute, 1981.

18. Bruce M. Rappaport, "Family Planning: Helping Men Ask for Help." *Public Welfare* (Spring 1981): 26.

19. Ibid. See also Steven Schott, "PP Involves Men." *Planned Parenthood Review* (Spring, 1981): 14–15.

20. Michael Castleman, who in 1976 helped start the first birth control clinic for men in the United States, as quoted in Eleanor Smith, "Counseling Men about Abortion." *California Living Magazine*, January 17, 1982, p. 11. Along with tactics like using basketball there is merit in exploring the use of abortion-related records by Canadian singer Geof Morgan ("No Room in Our Lives") and Judy Collins ("Momma, Momma").

21. James C. Lincoln, "Abortion: How Men Feel About One of the Biggest Issues in a Woman's Life." *Glamour*, February 1980, pp. 164–165, 243; Carol Lynn Mithers, "Abortion: Are Men there when Women Need them Most?" op. cit., pp. 231–232, 250, 253; Janet Chan, "Right Now: Abortion and Men." *McCall's Magazine*, June 1978, p. 3.

22. Linda Bird Francke, "Men and Abortion," op. cit., pp. 59–60; John Tido, "Men and Abortion," op. cit., pp. 31–32, 126–127.

23. John Leo and Val Castronovo, "Sharing the Pain of Abortion." *Time*, September 26, 1983, p. 78; Judith Paterson, "Whose Freedom of Choice?", op. cit., pp. 42–45.

24. Planned Parenthood of New York City, *Abortion: A Woman's Guide*, p. 36. New York: Abelard-Schuman, 1973. "The terrible truth is that every situation is different. It can turn out that the people who are close to you and love you most are the least able to help you at this time, or that your crisis will bring out the best in them. Only you—if anyone—can predict which it will be."

25. James Wagenwoord and Peyton Bailey, *Men: A Book for Women*, p. 346. New York: Avon, 1978. The discussion of types of men (pp. 346–352) is one of the best of its kind to come to our attention.

26. Caryl Hansen, *Your Choice: A Young Woman's Guide to Making Decisions about Unmarried Pregnancy*, p. 51. New York: Avon, 1980.

27. Reni L. Witt and Jeannine Masterson Michael, *Mom, I'm Pregnant*, p. 46. New York: Stein and Day, 1982.

28. Maria Corsaro and Carole Korzeniowsky, *A Woman's Guide to Safe Abortion*, p. 28. New York: Holt, Rinehart and Winston, 1983.

29. Ann Baker, *After Her Abortion*. Granite City, Ill.: The Hope Clinic for Women, 1981; Roger C. Wade, *For Men about Abortion*. Boulder, Co.: Roger Wade, 1978; Peter Zelles, *The Pregnant Male*. Minneapolis, Minn.: Midwest Health Center for Women, 1982.

30. Herb Goldberg, *The Hazards of Being Male: Surviving the Myth of Masculine Privilege*. New York: Nash, 1976; Goldberg, *The New Male: From Self-Destruction to Self-Care*. New York: Signet 1980; Joe L. Dubbert, *A Man's Place: Masculinity in Transition*. Englewood Cliffs, N.J.: Prentice-Hall, 1979; Robert A. Lewis, *ed., Men in Difficult Times*. Englewood Cliffs, N.J.: Prentice-Hall, 1981; Andrew Tolson, *The Limits of Masculinity: Male Identity and Women's Liberation*. New York: Harper and Row, 1977.

31. Warren Farrell, *The Liberated Man*, p. 303. New York: Bantam, 1975. Regrettably, the book has only this one lone reference to the subject of men and abortion.

32. Anonymous, "Men's Issues." Los Angeles, Calif.: National Congress for Men, 1983. On the urgency of male/female collaboration here, see Patterson, "Whose Freedom of Choice?," op. cit., p. 44.

33. Dan has written as much in an essay entitled "Abortion: It's A Man's Business." This essay appeared in the *Detroit Free Press*, the *Syracuse Post-Standard*, and other major newspapers in January of 1983.

34. National Man's Organization, "A National Anti-Sexist *Men's* Organization." Pittsburgh, Penn.: NMO, 1983. Elsewhere NMO explains, "Our focus is and will remain on men's issues and on men's growing role in opposing sexism and sex role conditioning. We would not want to lose our special identity as the distinct voice of the anti-sexist men's movement." National Men's Organization, "Some People Have Asked: Is This Organization Open to Women?" *Brother*, 1 (1, Winter 1983): 11.

35. Peter Filine, ed., *Men in the Middle*, p. 29. Englewood Cliffs, N.J.: Prentice-Hall, 1981. See also Joe Interrante, "Dancing Along the Precipice: The Men's Movement in the 80s." *M*, 10 (Spring 1983): 3–6, 32; Herb Goldberg, "Why is the Men's Movement Not 'Happening'?" *Transitions*, 3 (2, Spring/Summer 1983): 1–2. For an optimistic perspective on collaboration, see Bill Wishard and Laurie Wishard, *Men's Rights: A Handbook for the 80s*, pp. 76–77. San Francisco, Calif.: Cragmont, 1980. See also Robert Brannon, "Inside the Men's Movement." *Ms.*, October 1982, pp. 40, 42, 44.

36. As quoted in Nan Robertson, "Betty Friedan Ushers In a 'Second Stage.' " *New York Times*, October 19, 1981, p. 32. See in this connection, Betty Friedan, *The Second Stage*. New York: Summit Books, 1981. Cf. Suzanne Gordon, "Her Feminist Mystique," *In These Times*, January 13–19, 1982, p. 18.

37. Ibid. The speaker, however, is the journalist Nan Robertson, and not Betty Friedan. See also Mary Kenny, "In The Driver's Seat." *Encounter* 60 (2, February 1983), pp. 25–30.

38. Donna Show, "Betty Friedan: Feminist Turns Family Advocate." *Philadelphia Evening Bulletin*, November 16, 1981, p. C-1.

39. As quoted in Pamela Black, "Abortion Affects Men, Too." *New York Times Magazine*, March 28, 1982, p. 94.

40. See the McCallister essay in Chapter 8.

41. Mary Kay Blakely, "Hers." *New York Times* April 9, 1981, p. C-2. See also Barbara Ehrenreich, *The Hearts of Men: American Dreams and the Flight from Commitments.* New York: Anchor Press/Doubleday, 1983. On the resolution of underlying religious conflicts, see Catholics for a Free Choice, *Catholic Women and Abortion.* Washington, D.C.: Catholics for a Free Choice, 1981. This is an excellent source of many and varied data on the attitudes of Catholic and non-Catholic women toward abortion questions. See also Arthur Shostak, "Catholic Men and Abortion," *Conscience* (January/February 1984): 5–6.

Chapter 14

Clinic Day: A Better Way

A man repressing strong feelings who finds himself confronted with uncomfortable or hostile professionals, and no positive role to play in resolving the pregnancy, doesn't have much incentive to involve himself or make his feelings known. Yet, we know from both women and men that involving the man is important. New avenues and opportunities for involvement of men in pregnancy counseling and abortion need to be adopted. Men will not be a part of what is, in essence, a no-win situation. Men—and women—need roles other than those of victims and villains.

Stephen McCallister (*abortion counselor*)

There are a lot of important struggles going on now in America. But none is more important than this one. In some ways, learning to nuture—whether as fathers, husbands, or friends—is the hardest change for men to make. For men to do this would be a revolution.

James Levine, Director, Fatherhood Project (as quoted in Mark Gerzon, *A Choice of Heroes: The Changing Faces of American Manhood*, Boston: Houghton Mifflin, 1982, p. 261).

241

Discussions we have had with scores of waiting room men, clinic staffers, family planning specialists, and others eager to upgrade clinic options for men impress us with the progress that can soon be made in seven areas: needs assessment research; clinic ambience; male groups; counseling; counseling context; joint participation; and back-up aids.

    1. *Needs Assessment Study.*   Clinics that want to improve their male-oriented services might begin by inviting an outside researcher (perhaps a local, low-cost graduate student specializing in evaluation research or clinical psychology) to complete a sophisticated needs assessment study.

    As modeled here by Michael C. Finley's 1978 work for Preterm (Brookline, Massachusetts),[1] the project could have two research populations and several different goals and tools:

Type of Participant	Goals and Tools
Male partners	Assess their felt needs, emotional states, and behavioral changes
	Tools: Use of a questionnaire, personal observations, and participation in counseling situations of several kinds.
Clinic staffers	Gain the personnel's perceptions of male needs, as conveyed by the female patient and, less frequently, by the couple together.
	Identify logistical problems, patient flow, "discrepancies" between staff perceptions of male needs and the expressed needs of men themselves, and the present level of skills available in dealing with various types of counseling situations.

Tools: Elicit feedback from all
clinic personnel by attending
staff meetings, holding private
conversations, and observing
counseling situations.

Fortified by this approach, a researcher could help clinic decision
makers clarify and quantify the situation. As well, of course, he
or she could offer tentative recommendations for a new male-
oriented counseling program, one that is consistent with the real-
world budgetary and staffing constraints of the clinic.

2. *Ambience.* Given the critical importance of first impressions,
it was helpful to visit waiting rooms of clinics in Baltimore, Maryland; Buffalo, New York; Chester, Pennsylvania; New York City;
Minneapolis, Minnesota; Paoli and Pittsburgh, Pennsylvania;
Boston, Massachusetts; and San Rafael, California, to experience
what our 1,000 men knew much more directly in our 30 cooperating clinics.

Considerable care had commonly gone into making waiting
room areas as pleasant and comfortable as possible. Pastel-hued
wall colors, well-cushioned couches, and low tables covered with
(dogeared) magazines of recent vintage were staples. (A few clinics
even had one or two electronic arcade games, carefully cordoned
off in a small separate room heavily used by otherwise restless
young men.) Naturally, most of the clinics had coffee, soda, and
canteen snack machines on the premises or close by.

For all of this conscientious effort at creating a caring environment, however, there were some easily remedied shortcomings.
Wall posters, for example, offered comfort and advice to female
onlookers, but never included a male in the artwork—as if somehow abortion was only a woman's business. Magazines often were
dog-eared leftovers from previous male clinic attenders or gener-
ous staffers, and none were from the men's movement, such as
American Man, M, or the like. Nor did many clinics have popular
male fare like *Sports Illustrated, Car and Road, Rod and Gun, Inc.,
Money,* etc.

Especially vexing was finding many clinic waiting rooms serving as "mixed purpose" areas, i.e. those that combine the clientele of the abortion unit with the clientele of a pregnancy care unit
(expectant mothers, new mothers with infants, women seeking gy-

necological exams, etc.). Their sights and sounds could and did stir the fatherhood instincts of certain waiting room males—often painfully, and unnecessarily.

As long ago as 1973, after only three years' experience with legalized abortion in New York state, an organization of concerned clergy criticized the mixing of different patients by unfeeling hospital bureaucrats:

> ...if abortions were done in ordinary hospitals...the woman who was terminating her pregnancy would be placed in a room with women delivering babies. The psychological trauma resulting from that situation would be cruel treatment for the abortion patient.[2]

And, we might add, the analogous situation is cruel for the male who may accompany her. Clear physical demarcation between abortion and childbirth-seeking patients, by portable screens if necessary, might help relieve the psychic toll of this insensitive proximity.

Another source of stress involved the part played in a male's initial "reading" of the situation by a clinic receptionist. Unfortunately, a small number behaved in very strange ways.

> When I went into the clinic, I was talking with the receptionist. I asked if abortion really messed up women for having kids, and she said it doesn't, but *she* wouldn't advise it, because if you start, you might as well finish. So, that means if she gets in the bed, "slam bang, and thank you, ma'am," and she gets pregnant—go through with it. The receptionist didn't believe in abortion. It was just a job to her, and I agree with her. If you start, finish. Don't go half way and say, "Whoa!"

> A receptionist told me when I phoned and asked if counseling was available, "It's the woman's pain, and not the man's, so you can't get any counseling here, even if you want it...unless your partner is willing to have you sit in, while *she* is being counseled."

Much more common were tales we heard of sensitive and relaxing greetings, often deeply appreciated by awkward and apprehensive males:

> The woman at the front desk was very nice and took our names and told us to go to a specific floor. I'm glad she was nice because

we both felt like sleazy degenerates, first, for having premarital sex and just being there; second, for getting pregnant; and, third, for having to go to a place which I thought was geared to lower-class, poverty-stricken, and uneducated people. But just the fact that the building was clean and semi-new-looking made it a little easier to be there.

Little wonder that the vast majority of our respondents were pleased with their reception, though a very few had been hurt in ways they had not expected or deserved.

As for reforming this matter, a researcher who focused on one Massachusetts clinic in 1978 advised it later in its consultant's report that:

> ...the reception desk seems to be a focal point for a number of *ad hoc* counseling sessions. Men go to the reception desk three or four times during their stay. They come to get information, coffee, directions, etc, but, many end up discussing their problems with one of the reception counselors. Greater male visibility and availability in the reception area, as well as in the waiting room, would likely generate more counseling contacts with men. Reception counselors do not have adequate time to devote to counseling.[3]

Tips of this sort can be gathered by any clinic through its own unsparing self-examination, especially if aided by a clinic-designed survey of its waiting room men.

3. *Male Groups.* We asked our waiting room men if they would use the following types of male-only group discussion options:

	"Yes"
Small-group discussion (with other males from the waiting room) to give you a chance to discuss abortion-related issues and feelings with a clinic staff member.	51%
Educational group session to discuss birth control methods, their safety, and their effectiveness with a clinic staff member.	56%
Some combination of the two above.	74%

Note: These data were drawn from only the last 505 of our 1,000 respondents.

When we asked our 30 cooperating clinics if these options were available, we learned that only 38% offered small-group discussions, though 62% offered contraception education sessions. The clinics, however, estimated that less than three in ten men took advantage of these opportunities (estimates ranged from 23% of the husbands to 27% of teenage males and 28% of unwed men).

Why this low rate of participation? And what might concerned clinics do to help bring these rates up closer to the 51% or 74% levels cited above?

Part of the problem can be traced to the reluctance many men have about sharing their feelings with others who have been drawn together only by circumstance, a "mixed bag" of every lifestyle, ethnicity, religion, race, and political and moral philosophy found among American men.

When a distinction, however, was carefully made between a group counseling session and a birth control education session, the approval rate for the latter went up (Marsiglio found only 31% of his 126-man sample endorsing the counseling approach, but 41% approved of the education option).[4] Male preference for straightforward, information-exchange meetings, as opposed to let-it-all-hang-out encounters, would seem deep-reaching and decisive.

A sensitive accommodation was pioneered in 1979 by an Oakland, California clinic:

> Using slides, the counselors gave the men a tour of the clinic and a detailed description of the abortion procedure itself. The counselors then urged the men to discuss their relationships with their partners and how they had arrived at the abortion decision. The men were encouraged to talk about any pains or disagreements that had occurred along the way with their wives or girlfriends. The program included a segment on birth control, with the aim of involving each man in the method used by his partner, thereby reducing the chance of another unwanted pregnancy.... The emotional aftermath of the abortion was the final topic.... The counselors suggested that to ease the transition back into sexual life, the man initiate a conversation about contraception with his partner before they had intercourse. That way, the counselors pointed out, the man would be letting the female know that he didn't want her or himself to have to go through another abortion.[5]

Evaluations by Oakland waiting room men had 86% persuaded the birth-control education component above would make a valued difference, and 60% were grateful for guidelines for emotional support after the abortion.[6]

Another variation on the theme was offered in 1979 by the Significant Other program at Reproductive Health Services in St. Louis, Missouri. Waiting room men were invited to join others also in the anteroom (mothers, sisters, and girlfriends of the patient) in a special hour-long program. They learned exactly what would happen in the procedure room, its possible aftereffects, and what they could do to help. Much time was spent rebutting the propaganda of the anti-abortionists, and discussing any worries or concerns they might have had about the abortion. Above all, the attendees received a "dose of education about existing threats to abortion rights—the women at Reproductive Health are emphatically and openly political."[7]

Certain counselors worry that mixed-sex groups like the St. Louis Significant Other program inhibit male disclosure and full participation:

> ...most men either remain silent, feeling that the counseling is really for the women, or, given their own undiscussed and unresolved fears, try to dominate the counseling session.[8]

Chan, in 1978, raised two reservations about *any* type of counseling—groups or couple in character—that draws the sexes into *one* discussion:

> First, a man may not want to appear weak before a woman. Therefore, he may not reveal emotions he is actually experiencing.

> Second, he may not feel able to speak honestly in front of the woman he accompanied. He may fear any negative statements of his will be misconstrued by either or both of the two women in the office with him, especially, by his partner.[9]

Clinic staffers of this persuasion urge colleagues to offer *every* waiting room male *his* own choice of counseling setting.

Ideal here would be a clinic that offers the options of a *visitor's group*, an informational meeting to learn about abortion and aftercare; a *"for men only" group*, a session where males can talk in a relaxed environment and hear one another's feelings; *individual counseling*, where specific concerns about the abortion and relationship issues are discussed; *postabortion counseling*, both for individuals and couples; a *men's support group*, for individuals who need the help of like-situated abortion "veterans;" and, *family planning counseling*, available to men on a walk-in basis.

4. *Counseling.* We asked 500 waiting room men if they would use the following types of clinic counseling options:

	"Yes"
Private meeting alone with clinic counselor to discuss questions, concerns, and feelings.	62%
Private meeting, involving partner, waiting room male, and a clinic counselor.	74%

When we asked why they wanted this option, some of our men answered:

Just to understand what a girl has to go through.

Need counseling on how to be supportive.

I would like to know exactly what is going to happen, and how to support my partner afterwards, both physically and mentally.

Wish I could understand or believe that a fetus is anything different than a baby.

Confused as to who is right (anti- or pro-?). I wish I could have drawn a conclusion from hard facts.

Men need to be more informed about the abortion procedures and women need to know more about practicing birth control.

To notice us as an entity of the conceptual act of sex, and thus being responsible for the child.

Talk to us about our feelings about it.

Knowing how to handle it and not feel ashamed of having had an abortion.

One respondent spoke for many when he wrote, "It would have been much worse for us if we hadn't gone to counseling, which helped us communicate much better."

When we asked our 30 cooperating clinics if they offered counseling, 96% answered ''yes,'' provided the male requested it. But,
when we asked them to estimate how many waiting room males
actually took advantage of this opportunity, the figures were much
lower than the 62% and 74% endorsement votes we had gotten:
Only 11% of teenage males, 18% of singles, and 20% of the husbands were thought to have sought and used clinic counseling
services.

Why such a low level of male response? What might clinics
do to help more males try the counseling option?

Perhaps 20–25% of the nonusers insisted they knew what they
were giving up, and denied having any interest in counseling,
reformed or otherwise.

> Everything was up front. I was not coerced or tricked. We talked
> it all out. If I had been in the clinic, and someone had come out and
> asked if I wanted to talk about it, I wouldn't have. I'd done my talk-
> ing. But maybe some other guys would need it or take advantage
> of it.

Another very small number claimed to be too distracted to take
advantage of the opportunity.

> The clinic experience left me edgy. I wanted to see her before she
> went in, but I went to make a phone call and when I got back, she
> had gone in already. We didn't have any counseling. I would have
> wanted counseling, but we didn't ask. We were preoccupied with
> the decision, and with just being there.

Counselor Peter Zelles would *require* the participation of such men
in some sort of counseling (solo, couple, group-same sex; group-
mixed sex), as he explained in Chapter 8. Many other staffers,
however, hesistate to use compulsion here, fearing a backlash and
considerable rejection from offended males.

As for the remaining 70–75% (of whom only 10–20% appear
to be asking now for counseling), much of their resistance can be
traced to rigid role requirements that have men pretend to be self-
contained and emotionally controlled:

> The male role is so rigid that many men are reluctant to ask for
> directions at a service station much less ask for help or information
> about more sensitive areas like contraception or sexuality.[10]

Many shy from any clinic service with mental health connotations, anything that might suggest to others sitting around that they couldn't take it, were less than "real men," or, in some other revealing way, needed the attention of a counselor.

Sensitive to this learned prejudice and role constriction, a West Coast innovator, counselor Bruce Rappaport, had his clinic drop the use of the term "counseling" and the job title of "counselor." Instead, as each male partner entered the clinic he was asked to fill out a short registration form similar to his sex partner's. A male staffer later called out the man's name from the form, and the two of them went off to a separate room for what amounted to, but was not designated, individual counseling:

> Staff are careful not to imply that any man is being singled out because he needs help: there is no requirement that he asks for help.

Rappaport's clinic considers this innovative tact "quite a success. Not one man has ever mentioned feeling manipulated. Consistently, the men are extremely glad to be given information about the procedure."[11]

A second hindrance to male utilization concerns the common absence of *male* staffers. While no reliable statistics could be found, our contacts in clinics across the country estimated that 98% or more of all personnel are female. If the men who wait are to surmount learned resistance to asking for help, at least some of them may require the availability of male role models, or "real-man" types operating as clinic staffers and available for counseling sessions.[12]

A third hindrance involves a rare, but costly prejudice that surfaces in certain clinic settings. Typical is this account from a 26-year-old respondent of ours:

> The clinic staff...were completely ignoring me. Maybe it was part of the economy of how many people there were, but at the same time, there was a lot of insensitivity toward the guys who were there that cared.... I went to the clinic twice, for counseling and scheduling. I sat next to my lover and the counselor acted as if I were not in the room. It's as if the one who carries the fetus also carries *all* the emotions, and that's a lot of bullshit. At the same time, I can see how they get hardened by their work, and the number of women who must show up without guys or emotionally beaten and burdened.

Later in the same interview, the young investment banker added:

> The clinic thing got under my skin. It bothered both of us. I mean,
> all men are not wife beaters, uncaring people. They spend a few
> minutes with her, and she comes out into my arms, maybe for the
> rest of her life. Yet, the clinic totally ignored either helping me be
> better support or any needs I might have had.

Journalist Judith Patterson traces much of this to "a certain lack
of sympathy for men—even hostility," an example of where
"much-needed advocacy of women's rights has hardened into a
stance that is almost 'anti-man'."[13]

Counselor Stephen McCallister concurs, and explains that "the
compassion and empathy of the counselors for the women they
serve can make it difficult for them to view men without suspicion or distrust." Similarly, Counselor Roger Wade suspects that
"even some of the most liberated of our staff somewhere in their
minds held the men culpable for the pregnancies...lingering about
is the old image of the man as culprit in matters sexual."[14]

Earning the reform of these obstacles to male use of the counseling option may not be easy. Opposition is persistent, and even
forthright on occasion. Typical is the position taken in 1982 by a
director of counseling and fertility at the Women's Medical Center in Washington, D.C. This staffer "insists most men do not
want counseling: like others among abortion clinic workers she believes many men would try to prevent the abortion if they were
included in the decision-making...."[15]

Advocates of male counseling reforms urge detractors to ponder research on female patients that affirms the desire of most
women to see clinics do more here for their men. A majority of
clients consider their male partner integral to their own counseling experience. These women indicate a "marked willingness to
share more aspects of their sexual relationships, not just the physical one, with their male partner."[16] Where both halves of the
couple, in short, want better male counseling opportunities, their
availability should soon be more widespread.

5. *Counseling Components.* Almost regardless of whether the
session is held one-on-one, in a couples' format, or a same-sex or
mixed-sex group, a case can be made for an updating of its
content.

Historically, a counselor sought to help clients in four major
ways:

- Aid the patient in clarifying feelings and motivations;
- Assist in implementing the decision;
- Help the client control future fertility; and,
- Aid the client in overall development (as with the sexual maturity of teenagers).

Nowadays, clinic staffers are urged to add two further items—aid in understanding the moral reasoning of the opposite sex, and aid in mourning the loss of the fetus and of fatherhood.

Moral reasoning education builds on the new field research and theoretical work of Carol Gilligan (see Chapter 11, "Men: What Do they Want?"), feminist writer Barbara Ehrenreich, psychologists Arthur and Libby Colman, men's liberation writer Mark Gerzon, psychologist Arnold Medvene (also in Chapter 11), and other comparable pathbreakers. Abortion counselors can learn much from their insights into different ways of reaching moral judgments: Males, for example, are reared to respect absolute rights and to search for the "game rules." Females, in contrast, are reared to fear hurting others and to facilitate intimacy and caring.

Empowered by a new grasp of these distinct moral domains, clinic staffers can help both parties better "decipher" the moral reasoning of the other. Down the hall in the (female-only) recovery room, and elsewhere in the (male-only) waiting room, skilled counselors can help replace the distrust each sex has of the other with insights into where each partner is coming from, with a set of gender-specific ideas that might help couples achieve a finer post-abortion adjustment.

If we are to achieve soon such abortion counseling for *both* sexes, all the parties involved—staffers, as well as clients—will have to secure a "changed understanding of human development and a more generative view of human life."[17]

Grieving during and after an abortion can be aided by counselors strong and sensitive enough to undertake the task. More and more authorities are recommending inclusion of "bereavement counseling" in a thoroughgoing range of abortion clinic aids. An experienced psychologist, for example, contends that abortion is "undeniably a death experience, a loss and a separation experience with immense reverberations for everybody. If all of that gets blocked and is not resolved, it is bound to have a dramatic and destructive impact on the relationship."[18] Two other members of the same profession similarly warn that men who are not helped to mourn over an abortion "are learning how to be even less involved as nurturant parents in the future."[19] A third and especially prominent psychiatrist, John Bowlby, urges counselors to understand that the most compelling emotions in adult mourning are commonly disguised for fear of embarassment and shame. As such, they usually go unrecognized and untreated—to no one's lasting benefit.[20]

6. *Joint Participation.* We asked 500 waiting room men if they would prefer to stay with their partner during the abortion procedure, provided, of course, that she desired this: 69% answered "yes." But only 12% of our 30 cooperating clinics approved of this option.

We next asked the men if they would prefer to join their partner in the clinic recovery room, provided, of course, that she desired this: 91% answered "yes." But only 12% of our cooperating clinics allowed this practice.

When we asked for explanations, clinic staffers assured us they knew of some vague interest that some unknown number of waiting room men had in these options: As best they could recall, between 3% (teenage males) and 10% (husbands) asked to accompany a female through the entire process—though 69% to 91% of our men seemed so inclined.

Objections to having male partners in the procedure room were almost identical to those used for many years to exclude expectant fathers from the hospital delivery room; for example,

- the men were too squeamish to watch the medical process without passing out;

- the men would merely be in the way and serve no good purpose;

- the men might overreact to a rare sound of discomfort from the female patient, and interfere in the proceedings;

- the men would take up valuable space in quarters already crowded and cramped to the limit; and,

- the men would violate the sterile environment.

Happily, nearly 80% of husbands can now be with their wives during childbirth, compared with only 27% in 1972—a development that raises hope where relief of comparable bans in abortion clinics are concerned.[21]

This desire to help one's partner through the entire experience is *not* a new, or faddish, or short-lived interest of waiting room males. Quite the contrary! Rothstein's pioneering 1974 research found 80% of her 60 men convinced they should have the option to go along as far as their partner wished.[22] Finley, in 1978, found 48% wanted to be with their partners during the procedure.[23] Marsiglio, in 1983, found 75% willing to be involved in the actual abortion experience, provided that their partners and the clinic agreed (95% wanted to be with their partners in the recovery room).[24] Hill-Falkenthal found 56% eager to comfort their partner during the abortion procedure (72% of them wanted to do so to provide support; 50%, from concern over the partner's safety; and 16%, from curiosity about the procedure).[25]

Why did many of our waiting room men want to accompany their partners throughout the entire abortion appointment? Several wrote cogent and compelling explanations:

> I saw my first baby born, and I should be here now, too!

> I don't like letting her go through this *alone*! Up until walking through this door, this has been a shared problem. Suddenly it becomes entirely hers to deal with. Somehow, I think my support would be better than that of a counselor.

> There is no way for it to be better unless, perhaps, I could be with my companion before, during, and after the procedure.

> We feel support throughout the whole procedure allows us to grow together, rather than feel punished or guilty.

During our interviews, respondents could, and did, expand on their pro-bonding motivation:

> Half of the guys waiting with me wanted to go in with their partners. You could see worry in their faces. I mean, if they let you go in and see your baby born, I don't see why we can't go in for our own abortion. You're just there to be with her, to comfort her.

> I would liked to have gone back there in the procedure room with

her. I didn't inquire, but I wish I could have joined her. In the recovery room, she should not be interrupted in her rest.

The clinic was the worst part of the whole deal. They tried to be very helpful, but after it was performed, you should be able to go in with her. They tell you to go for a walk after three and a half hours that seem like days, and all you can think of is being with her. . . . I felt like I was in left field. . . . I had a lot of feelings, and I wanted to be with her during the procedure, and especially in recovery. That's the part that wasn't satisfying.

I would worry much less about my partner if it was not a situation where she went in the door at one time and came out an hour and a half later with nothing but mystery in between not knowing what she is going through and not being with her as soon as possible creates resentment.

My biggest bitch about about the whole thing and one of my wife's, too, was not being allowed in the procedure room or the recovery room. They like to pay lip service to giving emotional support, but it's clearly emphasis on the physical part of it and not the emotional or psychological. I spent as much time with her as I could, because I didn't want the whole thing to go up in smoke.

Similarly, a 30-year-old restauranteur hoped to reduce some post-abortion stress:

When we found out about the pregnancy and started to discuss the option of abortion, I was determined to go through it with my wife. I'd gone through the delivery of our two kids; so, why not this?

For this man, sharing the procedure as part of the reality was "one of the best things" that ever happened to his marriage.

There was no gainsaying the fact that going along is not a wise choice for every couple or for every man. The freedom, therefore, to say "Thanks, but no thanks," is a precious one that clinics should preserve with dignity. Nor is any good purpose served by glossing over the emotional pain an onlooking male *may* experience, like this one:

I was so scared when they said I could sit with her if I wanted to. When we went into the abortion room I was incredibly nervous. I can't even think of how scared my girlfriend was.

I was in a small room, with a table and stirrups on it, and a large medical-looking machine with tubes connected to a plumbing system overhead. They told her to lie down, and told me to sit next to her facing the wall in back of her. The nurse cleaned her up, and the doctor came in. He was young, very pleasant, and told us everything he was doing. I was holding her hand, thinking I was the reason she was losing my child right now.

When he started the procedure, I could tell she was in pain. I would have done anything to trade places, if it were possible.

Even the relatively calmer atmosphere of the recovery room can trigger very deep emotions:

After the abortion, the nurse let me come in to be with her. I held her hand tight and we cried. She was groggy, and I was worn out and exhausted. We both fell asleep, her on the stretcher and me on a stool behind her. I never want to see or feel the situation again.

Sensitive educational preparation of males *before* they decide—with their partner's prior consent—to join her in *either* the procedure and/or the recovery room would seem an indispensable component in this particular reform.

Some clinics will oppose a male presence in the recovery room as much as, if not more than in the procedure rooms. They will insist, quite soundly, that certain patients want their privacy protected from male eyes. As well, some patients seem to recover best in a female-only atmosphere. These clinics, however, could use screens, wall dividers, cubicles, partitions, and other such devices to segregate distinct sections of the recovery room, and thereby accommodate the different wishes of all of their clients.

Overall, the case for offering this option *must* include sensitive protection of the female's prior consent, the male's prior (educational) preparation, the male's right to decline (without loss of esteem or honor), and the patient's right to a recovery room atmosphere of her own choosing. Given the apparent desire of a large majority of waiting room men to offer comfort and reassurance throughout their clinic stay, to promote the kind of bonding possible in this context, these qualifications seem well worth the clinic effort entailed. Men merit more than mere seat-warming in a clinic anteroom, and the women they accompany deserve much better than that throughout (see Table 14-1).

Table 14-1. Reform Preferences of Waiting Room Men (1974–1983)

	Shostak and McLouth (1983/1,000)	Hill-Falkenthal (1983/106)	Marsiglio (1983/126)	Finley (1978/193)	Rothstein 1974/60
Would like to join partner in counseling	74%	53%	64%	68%	75%
Would like some form of counseling	N.D.†	77%	54%	49%	75%
Would like solo meeting with counselor	52%	13%	60%	N.D.	20%
Would like group session with other men	54%	4%	31%*	25%	5%
—with other men and women	N.D.	12%	N.D.	N.D.	N.D.
Would like to join partner in procedure room	69%	56%	80%	48%	42%
Would like to join partner in recovery room	91%	N.D.	96%	N.D.	N.D.

*37%: Birth control education. †N.D. = No Data.

7. *Additional Aids.*   When we asked our respondents what they remembered had been valuable, several cited videotape presentations, slideshows, Super-8 format or 16-mm films as part of their clinic orientations. Similarly, when 126 men in two Midwest clinics were asked in 1980 what method they would prefer for learning about abortion and birth control, they chose "viewing a short film" as their most desired medium.[26] One researcher suggests waiting room males be shown a film *before* being invited to participate in any single or group discussion: "By establishing a knowledge base, subjects might then feel better prepared for joining and participating in a discussion group."[27]

Unfortunately, only 15% of our 30 cooperating clinics offered this engaging and instructive option. As well, a film viewed by us in a Midwest clinic centered around a question-and-answer discussion between a female counselor and three patients: Although shown many times daily to waiting room males, the Super-8 format production excluded any attention whatsoever to the men who watched and waited. Fortunately, a low-cost and practical plan for preparing new video tape material was drafted for this book by concerned specialists (and appears in the book's appendix).

A second novel *and* valuable item applauded by respondents involved the pamphlets distributed by 62% of our clinics. Authored by counselors Wade and Zelles, and by a female counselor, Anne Baker, these low-cost items satisfy a need many males have for something concrete to take with them, something more substantial than dialogue with clinic counselors, or the single sheet of postabortion medical tips routinely offered by certain clinics. Until more clinics in America help circulate these highly readable, brief, and instructive publications, many more men will leave with less to rely on than the situation warrants.

A third item clinics might pay fresh attention to involves clinic imagery per se. Wherever we traveled we took special notice of clinic ads on billboards or on the back of park benches, clinic ads in local newspapers, and clinic ads in the phone company's yellow pages: Not once in hundreds of such displays did we see a representation of a male partner. Only females were pictured or profiled, and the intimated message—"For women only!"—could not have been clearer!

If we are soon to earn the attendance of more than 50% of

eligible males in clinic waiting rooms, a rapid change in clinic PR artwork would seem a strategic consciousness raising contribution. For, as educator Warren Bennis reminds us, "it is not so much the articulation of goals about what an institution *should* be doing that creates new practice. It's the imagery that creates the understanding, the compelling moral necessity that the new way is right."[28]

Finally, the clinics might want to help revise the content of the current (1981) version of the *Standards* booklet published by the National Abortion Federation. Since NAF is the only organization of its kind, it is a major force in the field. All the more regrettable, therefore, is the fact that its otherwise comprehensive 15-page booklet says nothing at present about a clinic's professional responsibility to waiting room occupants. Nor is any recognition paid in the two-page section, "Counseling Standards," to the appropriateness of couples' counseling (*after* the female has first given her consent).[29]

Summary

When we are asked what we are after, what we want the nation's abortion providers (clinics *and* private physicians *and* hospitals) to offer men, we think of a passage in the 1981 abortion *Handbook* addressed to female readers:

> Abortion should not be an assembly-line process, but one in which each individual is made to feel unique, special, and cared for. This means answering questions, explaining, and allowing time for relaxation, talking, sharing, and recovery.... Relaxation is the key. You are not going to a motel room. You are not meeting an abortionist in a warehouse. You are receiving a medical service, to which you are entitled, in a safe, welcoming environment staffed by competent, empathetic personnel—people just like yourself.[30]

Men in the waiting room merit much the same, no more and certainly no less.

We have heard much that has given us encouragement from clinic directors and staff members—and also have heard much praise for ongoing clinic care from men who have felt well-served.

> I believe this clinic has an excellent staff, and in a delicate situation, they run a class act.

The clinic was responsive, my presence was noticed. At my college health center, I felt ignored. My presence was not noted, and twice I had the door almost shut in my face when I accompanied my girl-friend with the nurse.

The staff at the clinic was extremely supportive and, I believe, made the experience as positive as possible, considering its inherent psychological and emotional negativeness.

I was pleased and impressed with the professional attitude and atmosphere of the clinic.

With all of this, however, few who know the scene would deny that more can be done—if the other half of the clinic's responsibility, the caring male, is soon to feel unique, special, and cared for.

. . . all that we know of psychological functioning suggests that active involvement of a person in his own life planning fosters mastery. While we cannot say that every man who is thus engaged will be more active in subsequent family planning, that he will become more supportive of his partner at the time of the abortion, or that he will be a better father in years to come, it is possible that some small movement in these directions could take place. The abortion experience considered as a whole might well serve to perpetuate or suggest alternatives to a man's proclivity for active or passive modes of dealing with stress, thus potentially influencing further development.

Arden Aibel Rothstein, "Men's Reactions to Their Partners' Elective Abortion." (*American Journal of Obstetrics and Gynecology,* **128,** 8 August 1977, p. 837).

Men, Women, and Abortion: A Clinic's Perspective*

From the first day that Preterm opened its doors in 1971, people who have come here for medical and counseling services have been treated holistically

*This article results from the collaborative efforts of Bonnie Falbo, Ellen Godwin, Jeanne Hoppenfeld, and Wayne Pawlowski, all staff of Preterm.

and with compassion and caring. We believe now, as then, that the ultimate decision about whether to terminate a pregnancy lies with the woman; however, we have always recognized that the feelings and concerns of 'significant others' are important and worthy of attention. Further, we believe that whatever increases the comfort and understanding of the man will inevitably be of value to the woman.

Our experience over the past 13 years has confirmed these beliefs. Preterm is convinced that high quality services can be provided to couples who desire them, without placing undue financial stress on facilities, like ours, that are non-profit. Following is a description of our services; we hope it will be useful to providers and consumers alike.

As a privately owned non-profit reproductive health center, Preterm must balance the benefits of offering services to men against the additional costs for those services, the added caseload of staff members, and the protection of patient confidentiality. We have found that the most important factor in enabling male comfort is the attitude of our staff members, and this costs nothing to a clinic.

Beginning with the initial patient telephone contact, where all pertinent information is provided to the woman, we also extend an invitation to bring a friend, relative, or partner when she comes for her appointment. No further emphasis is placed on involving the man at that time to insure that the feelings of women who will be going through the abortion experience alone are protected. If a woman should request more specific information on partner involvement, it is then discussed at greater length.

Upon arriving at Preterm, the waiting room is designed to let men know they are welcome. Literature is available that is of interest to men. A copy of the "Informed Consent" booklet, which outlines the procedure, its risks and complications, is provided to the man. Another handout, "Your Day at Preterm," which outlines each step of patient care that day is available, as well as the "Condom Quiz," a contraceptive information sheet comparing various methods of birth control. Literature on other Preterm services for men, such as vasectomy, herpes, and other sexually transmitted disease checks and short-term counseling is displayed. A men's bulletin board containing recent articles and pamphlets is prominent. The overt message is that men are welcome and that we consider them to be interested and important. The subliminal message we want to convey is that men share in the responsibility for the woman's circumstance that day as well as in subsequent decisions they will be making about their reproductive futures.

On Saturdays, our busiest day and the day when the only service offered is abortion, we have a volunteer male counselor who holds group sessions for people waiting for women who are in individual counseling, the abortion procedure or in the recovery room. This counselor, who is well-versed in the subject matter and sensitive to feelings, reviews the details of what each woman will experience during her time at Preterm: lab work, the structure of the counseling session, the abortion procedure, the format of the recovery room, etc. Information is also provided about birth control methods. Questions are welcomed. Minimally, it is an information-giving session; optimally, dialogues and discussions develop between and among the counselor and the audience. Because those waiting represent a wide variety of needs and concerns, age groups and relationships, interesting and constructive interchange often takes place.

One of our greatest areas of emphasis is encouraging male participation in counseling sessions. To give greater life to our commitment to enabling male participation in the abortion process, we have hired a man to serve as our director of counseling. While he was not hired because of his gender, his very presence in our center serves to increase the awareness of all staff members to the concerns of men. He actively works with his counselors to increase their level of confidence and improve their skills in working with men. His professional background in social work has given him the ability to work effectively with individuals; his unique personal skills enable him to view the needs of others within their social contexts.

When applied to abortion counseling, this means relationships and partner input are seen as parts of a woman's decision. The counseling session, mandatory for the woman, is a time for clarification of feelings and facts that go into the decision-making process. Male involvement, when desired by the couple, benefits not only the man, but also increases the woman's clarity in making a decision and can be a bonding experience for the couple in general.

Pragmatically, from an organizational point of view, joint sessions are also beneficial to counseling staff members. Much like the theories about workers' satisfaction increasing when they are allowed to work on a product through to completion, counselors are rewarded by the knowledge that the man will carry on as a resource for the woman, and, vice versa. Hopefully, the quality of the relationship will be enriched by the couples' realization that they have created, acknowledged, and made responsible choices together about a difficult circumstance.

Although our experience has shown us that most men have found joint sessions satisfactory, we would like to be able to offer individualized counseling to men. At present, if a counselor becomes aware of a man's need for one-on-one counseling, either by observing him in the waiting room or in a joint session, she will offer to talk with him alone as soon as her regular caseload allows. Practically, this is not ideal as it could be a relatively long time until she can get back to him. Although we could not afford to hire a counselor to work exclusively with partners, we have applied for private funding specifically for this purpose. If secured, we could then offer this service to men without having to increase the medical fees.

Additional counseling options are available for couples and individuals in our short-term therapy program, and for these sessions we charge a minimal fee. These sessions relate to pre- or postabortion conflicts, as well as a host of other issues.

When the time for the actual procedure arises, the decision as to whether the man may accompany the woman is up to her, her partner, and her physician. If a couple requests to be together, every effort is made to accommodate them. If the man wishes to join his partner during the procedure but the woman wishes to be alone, her decision is paramount. The foregoing notwithstanding, there are times in every medical facility when prevailing circumstances make it necessary for as few people as possible to be in the medical area (i.e., an emergency). If we must refuse a couple the opportunity to be together, the man is kept informed of his partner's status at regular intervals.

Similar constraints exist in the recovery room. Not only must the desires of the couple be taken into account, but also the needs of the other women present. The atmosphere in the recovery room varies with the personalities of the patients present and their medical status. If women are in varying states of undress, or if a woman is having a difficult postoperative course, it would be inappropriate to allow any visitors. One needs to be sensitive to the environment in recovery as a whole, and the decision to allow partners, friends, and family is up to the nurse in charge. If we must refuse admission to anyone accompanying a woman, we make every effort to either let them see each other briefly or talk on the telephone between the waiting room and recovery. We have found if we take the time to explain to patients and partners what the circumstances are, they respect the decision and are appreciative of our efforts.

Our final encounter with each woman is during her two-week postoperative visit. At this time she is examined, counseled, and advised again about birth control choices. As always, her partner is welcome if she so desires his presence.

Summary

The central thesis of this piece is merely this: most non-profit abortion facilities are caring places with professional staff members who have made choices about their professional lives—most care deeply or they wouldn't be there.

Recognizing the reality of continually rising costs and expenses, facilities make choices about how, when and where to react to the financial pressures. Humane and considerate service rarely costs more. We all wish to aid the woman through a particularly difficult decision and experience—we must learn to expand the definition of 'aid' to allow others whom she desires to share in the process.

It costs nothing to be considerate, welcoming, well-informed, and caring. Special services, such as individualized male counseling or support groups do require a financial investment. They will be meaningless, however, if the foundation of caring, personified in each staff member, is inadequate. That is the place to begin.

Notes

1. Michael C. Finley, "A Male Counseling Component for Aborting Fathers at Preterm," op. cit. See also Alison J. Lubman, "Assessment of an Intervention Program for Partners of Abortion Patients" (Unpublished Ph.D. dissertation, University of Colorado at Boulder, 1980).

2. Arlene Carmen and Howard Moody, *Abortion Counseling and Social Change*, p. 87. Valley Forge, Penn.: Judson Press, 1973.

3. Finley, op. cit., p. 6

4. William Marsiglio, "Evaluation Study: Assessment of Males' Needs for Abortion-Related Services." Columbus, Ohio: Ohio State University, 1983. Unpublished report. See also Robert H. Gordon, "Efficacy of a Group Crisis-Counseling Program for Men Who Accompany Women Seeking Abortion," *American Journal of Community Psychology*, 6 (1978): 239–246.

5. Linda Bird Francke, "Abortion and Men," op. cit., p. 60.

6. Ibid. See also Linda Bird Francke, *The Ambivalence of Abortion*, op. cit.

7. Carol Lynn Mithers, "Abortion: Are Men There When Women Need Them Most?" op. cit., p. 250.

8. Bruce M. Rappaport, "Family Planning: Helping Men Ask for Help," op. cit., p. 26.

9. Janet Chan, "Right Now: Abortion and Men," op. cit., p. 93.

10. Rappaport, op. cit., p. 24.

11. Ibid., p. 26. The entire paragraph draws on this source. See also Robert H. Gordon and C. A. Vilpatrick, "A Program of Group Counseling for Men Who Accompany Women Seeking Legal Abortions," *Community Mental Health Journal* 13 (1977): 291–295.

12. Only a small minority of males (5% in our sample; 13% of Marsiglio's 126 men) expressed a preference for a male counselor. When we discussed this with certain male counselors they linked it to the novelty of the idea, the expectation males are reared to have of nutur-

ing roles being filled by females, and the general absence of males in counseling roles elsewhere in the lives of waiting room men. Marsiglio, "Evaluation Study," op. cit.

13. Judith Patterson, "Whose Freedom of Choice?" op. cit., p. 44.

14. See, in this connection, the contributions of these men to Chapter 8.

15. Ibid. "She admits, however, that every case is different and that some men *do* support partners who seek abortion." (p. 44)

16. Karen Brosseau, "Utilizing Male Partners of Adolescent Abortion Patients as Change Agents," op. cit., p. 28.

17. Carol Gilligan, *In A Different Voice*, op. cit., p. 174.

18. Arnold Medvene, as quoted in Patterson, op. cit., p. 44.

19. Arthur and Libby Colman, *Earth Father, Sky Father*, op. cit., p. 128.

20. John Bowlby, *Attachment and Loss*, New York: Basic Books, 1969.

21. Anonymous, "Most Hospitals Allow Father to View Births." *Philadelphia Inquirer*, November 11, 1983, p. 20-D. "Dr. Michael W. Yogman of Harvard Medical School said research indicates that it is beneficial to later family life to involve fathers in the deliveries of their children."

22. Arden Aibel Rothstein, "The 'Would-Have-Been Father.' " New York: Columbia University, pp. 229–233. Unpublished doctoral dissertation, 1974.

23. Finley, op. cit., p. 4.

24. Marsiglio, op. cit., p. 10.

25. June Hill-Falkenthal, "Counseling Needs of Men about Abortion," op. cit., p. 29

26. Kristine L. Rotter, "Men and the Abortion Experience," op. cit., p. 67.

27. Ibid., p. 91.

28. As quoted in Thomas J. Peters and Robert H. Waterman, Jr., *In Search of Excellence*, p. 105. New York: Harper and Row, 1982.

29. National Abortion Federation, *Standards*. Washington, D.C.: NAF, 1981.

30. Carole Dornblaser and Uta Landy, *The Abortion Guide*, op. cit., p. 149. For an informative exploration of conditions elsewhere, see Colin

Francome, *Abortion Freedom: A Worldwide Movement*, London: George Allen & Unwin, 1984. Note, however, that this 224-page book regrettably makes no reference to males or men, a practice that cannot end soon enough.

Epilogue

If we begin to use the abortion drama to help men become better contraceptors, better communicators, and better partners, we may begin to reduce the number of abortion first-timers and repeaters. We may also lower the frequency of post-abortion breakups. We may even assuage the worst of the ethical and moral aftermath, for even the right decision is not necessarily easily made or lived with.[1] Above all, we may help strengthen the nation's commitment to preserving legal abortion services.

Buoyed by the support we've received from clinic staffers, some of whom first told us of the need for reform, we are convinced that improvements in clinic services for men *can* be secured in the very near future. Far more difficult will be winning related gains in home and school sex education, contraceptive education, media attention, and mass-movement endorsement. If, however, we understand the fundamental interrelationship of all of these, if we understand the need for a comprehensive overhaul in the male's *entire* approach to the conception *and* termination of life, we will persist, despite the odds.

Something at the center of us all understands that men are not doing as well as they could, as well as many earnestly want to, and that, until they feel better about the men they are before, during, and after an abortion experience, we will continue to have more losses and less love here than is good for any of us.

What captures us, sends us, mobilizes our commitment and draws upon our deep experience, is an idea
of how things might be, an image of a way of life and
a pattern of social organization that seems to us workable, possible and good, or, in the context of our time,
better than what we have.

[Robert A. Solo, "Values and Judgments in the
Discourse of the Sciences" (In *Value Judgment and
Income Distribution*, R. A. Solo and C. W. Ander-
son, eds. (New York: Praeger, 1981, p.40).]

PROFILE

Our interviews and profiles have been selected for their applicability to
emerging points of interest and emphasis in our research. They give articulation and tone and texture. Most importantly, they say what we could not
possibly say as well.

Geoffery and Joseph offer similar impressions of committed love. Even
though their backgrounds and stations in life are as different as possible (one
is a 27-year-old account executive, the other, a 19-year-old Marine), they both
discovered similar empathetic ties with their lovers.

Geoffery shares the complex concerns of a man doing his best to negotiate potentially treacherous emotional terrain. There was no time for a dry run,
no dress rehearsal. Geoffery speaks ably for men at the brink of loss. His concerns and behavior may define love and support as fully as his clinical critique explains the disadvantages love and support have to endure.

Joseph simply asks if there is any other way but love. We think not.

Geoffrey:

I live in New York, she lives in Boston. She's a nurse and works at night.
She's trying to save money to go back to school.

The experience was positive because we showed a lot of faith toward
each other.

It was handled in an almost militant feminist way. The clinic staff was
handling the woman, who is supposedly their friend and comrade, very
coldly, and they were completely ignoring me. Maybe it was part of the econ-
omy of how many people there were, but at the same time, there was a lot
of insensitivity toward the guys who were there that cared.

My girlfriend is Roman Catholic. It's one thing in her life she regrets having to have done. It was tough on her morally. . . not as tough on me in that
way.

You get in the position where you did something with no intent. Helpless. . .that was my response, but it was not my decision. I would have been happy to marry her to keep her from going through the abortion, but we probably did the right thing.

It's half your child, but in terms of ultimate say, you have nothing because it's not your body. I would have been happy to have the kid and if things don't work out between us at some time, my major regret will be not having the child. It's tough to divorce my love for her from the experience of having the kid.

It's not rational, but having the kid would have been a terrific thing. I feel less that way now than I did then.

We talked about it for quite awhile. We were not at the stage to consider marriage, and pregnancy was not a reason to, but on the other hand, we could have married because of it and I don't think it would have been a bad thing.

Before the whole thing developed, I don't think I ever saw a fetus at that point in development as a child, but when it's your own, it becomes a child, I guess. You're talking about a little redheaded kid.

I have friends who have kids that were being born at that time and that brings home the notion that it is not a piece of tissue.

The toughest thing is loving someone and causing them such problems because of your love for them. You care so much about somebody. . .that contradiction is tough, love and pain. We haven't talked about it very much since. It's not a matter of avoidance, but a matter of not bringing it up. Sometimes I'm at a loss. You don't want to bring guilt back on her, but you don't want to be calloused and cold either. She says the one thing in her life she regrets is having had to do it.

She found out Christmas Eve. We've never lived in the same town. She had just graduated and was trying hard to get a start on work. It would have been very hard, given her ambition, for us to get started in life together like that.

She had doubts about spending her life with me then and still has them. If you're going to make a commitment to marrying, it should not be based on other circumstances like a baby. The abortion hasn't driven any apparent wedge into the relationship.

I talked with my parents, because I'm close with them. It was fine from my perspective. She found out later and was a little uncomfortable, but it's not a problem. I talked to some close friends and a couple women I knew, who had been through the experience. It was important for me, because I didn't know much about the process. My parents gave me emotional support. The women gave me information about how they went through it and felt, so I could help Joan out. . .make sure she didn't feel that I was deserting her.

There must be a line there somewhere when you've talked to too many people. You have emotions you don't know are there. Since, I wouldn't do it differently. It brought us closer together. The key is being sensitive to the woman.

In the waiting room some of the guys sitting around seemed to be bored or unsensitive. One guy was asleep when his wife came down. She had to wake him up. That is clearly not the way to do it.

I went to the clinic twice for counseling and scheduling. I sat next to Joan and the counselor acted as if I were not in the room. It's as if the one who carries the fetus also carries all the emotions and that's a lot of bullshit. At the same time I can see how they get hardened by their work and the number of women who must show up without guys or emotionally beaten and burdened.

The only advice I have is that you have to be open with the woman, but that's my viewpoint, because I'm tremendously in love with the woman I'm talking about. It can't be otherwise than to be her decision. You can't dictate somebody's life for them. Like if the guy wanted the kid, there is no way he should be able to make the woman have the kid and turn it over to him.

The clinic thing got under my skin. It bothered both of us. I mean, all men are not wife beaters, uncaring people. They spend a few minutes with her and she comes out into my arms, maybe for the rest of her life. Yet, the clinic totally ignored either helping me be better support or any needs I might have had.

I almost feel an obligation to speak to you to try to pay back something. It's such a serious situation and yet we're all amateurs at it. There are a lot of questions I have. The funny thing about the clinic is that, here are professionals and they only reach out to one side of the equation.

At times I've had a tough time looking at little kids. Some of my friends have beautiful kids. . . Joan would be due just about now.

There's a sense of sadness about the whole thing. This woman I love is going to carry a scar deep inside for who knows how long. A sense of relief or satisfaction doesn't even apply to me. If I'd gotten some girl I'd just met at the beach pregnant, I guess I'd be relieved.

I'm not for participating in group discussions about something this private and personal. I don't want to show my feelings with a bunch of strangers necessarily. I would want to be with my girlfriend and a professional or in a mixed sex group. A bunch of guys sitting around just exacerbates the problem.

I had studied a lot of biology. I'm a very liberally educated person, but I knew nothing of birth control. It was a woman's responsibility. Clearly, if you are 26 years old and have had relationships with a number of people, and know as little as you can, something is wrong with the way you're educated.

My biggest bitch about the whole thing and one of Joan's too, was not being allowed in the procedure room or the recovery room. They like to pay lip service to giving emotional support, but it's clearly emphasis on the physical part of it and not the emotional or psychological. I spent as much time with her as I could, because I didn't want the whole thing to go up in smoke.

If anything happens to her, I'm never going to forgive myself. I felt like I'd hurt her enough already . . . complete helplessness and nothing you can do to unmake it.

I knew she had a diaphragm, but I didn't know how it worked. Maybe I didn't want to know. I do now.

We were picking among options, all not good, because there's nothing you can do to make it better. No way not to cause pain. It's just how much you cause. The whole idea of loving someone and having sex with them is supposed to be a joyful thing and all of a sudden you've got two people going crazy.

Joseph:

The abortion pulled us closer together, made us understand each other better. I know how much she needs me and how much I need her.

We don't let it bother us. She didn't want to go through it, really. It was mostly her decision and I supported her and gave her all the love I could. We're not prepared now for children. Maybe in a few years, because I'm studying computers and I want to get a master's, so we can start a family.

For a while, just thinking of being a father made me feel proud. But then, I'm only 19, and not ready. She's 17. Most people look at us like we're just young, but we're not like any other couple. Our love is there.

I was the only guy in the clinic with my wife. It made her feel better that I was there. I wanted so bad to be in the room to hold her hand or something. It made me mad because she wanted and needed me. I don't understand why I wasn't able to be there, as her husband. The nurses didn't give her much support. They didn't calm her down or help her out. They just did it. I felt I should have been in there.

I went to one counseling session with her. It was supposed to be just for her, but she wanted me to go and we went together.

Right now, we're at my parents, but we're moving to our own place. We're getting along fine. I'm positive with myself and we're positive about our relationship and our love. . . . That's the way things should be, right?

Notes

1. Lindsey van Gelder, "Cracking the Women's Movement Protection Game," *Ms.* (December 1978): 101.

APPENDIXES

A

Men and Abortion in Retrospect: A Methodological Evaluation[1]

Joan Z. Spade

The purpose of this appendix is to evaluate the processes by which data were gathered for the book, specifically, the survey of 1,000 men in abortion clinics. While data collection and analyses have been discussed throughout the text, I will summarize as well as examine the procedures. Additionally, I will include suggestions for a future study which could build upon the innovative research which is the basis of *Men and Abortion.*

An evaluation should be impartial, with little vested interest on the part of the evaluator. Thus, it is appropriate that I begin by defining my association with this research. My initial contact with the authors, Art Shostak and Gary McLouth, was toward the end of the data collection process. I did not participate in the organization of the research nor in the design of specific instruments. I did analyze the data and, as part of that process, designed the two indexes used in the book.

Let us begin by examining the methods used in the survey of men in abortion clinic waiting rooms. The sample of 1,000 men was collected from 30 abortion clinics across the country. An obvious caution is that this sample cannot be considered a representative sample of all men whose partners choose to abort a pregnancy, since not all men accompany their partners to the abortion clinic. In the sample, those men who for whatever reason did not chose to go to the abortion clinic with their partners are not represented, nor are those men who are unaware of the abortion. Additionally, the sampling does not include those men whose partners go to a private physician. Because women who seek out a private physician are likely to have a higher social class background, their partners are probably underrepresented in this sample.

Attempts to locate clinics willing to participate in this study began with a letter mailed to all abortion clinics listed in either the 1980–1981 or 1982–1983 National Abortion Federation Directories. Over 3,000 questionnaires were sent to the 40 abortion clinics who responded to the initial mailing, although only 30 clinics actually participated. Of the clinics that did participate, 21 were located using the 1980–1981 National Abortion Federation Directory, four from the 1982–1983 Directory, and five from other sources.

The reasons why the ten clinics refused to participate vary. For the most part, clinics were concerned about possible biases. Abortion is a very sensitive issue in society today and some clinics felt that their participation would be used for political purposes. A decision by Planned Parenthood to refuse to allow their affiliates to help in the research also reduced the number of participating clinics. Planned Parenthood's reservation was that the project would be used to support more control for men in the abortion process. Therefore, the sample of 1,000 men cannot be considered representative of all men who accompany their partners to abortion clinics.

The clinics participating in the survey, however, are located across the country. The geographical distribution of these clinics is as follows[2]:

New England	7%
Mid-Atlantic	25
East North Central	25
West North Central	7
South Atlantic	19
East South Central	1
West South Central	9
Mountain	3
Pacific	4

While all parts of the country are represented in the study, obviously the largest proportion of respondents are from the Eastern-Atlantic states. The Western states are underrepresented. Nevertheless, men from different regions of the country are similar (less than 5 percentage points) in terms of the personal background data and the two key abortion questions (whether abortion is morally wrong, and whether abortion is the killing of a child). Consequently, the bias of oversampling Eastern-Atlantic states does not seem to affect the types of men in the survey or their attitudes toward abortion.

With these caveats in mind, a strength of this study is that the characteristics of the 1,000 waiting room males are fairly representative of the abortion clinic client as defined by the survey of 30 abortion clinic directors,[3] as well as by national statistics on abortion. Additionally, the personal backgrounds of the 1,000 waiting room males are similar to the U.S. population generally. For example, the racial and religious backgrounds of these men are similar to the distributions of the population. In addition to region of the country, the only characteristic of the sample which differs markedly from the U.S. population is that of age. The younger age of these waiting room males is as expected, since clients of abortion clinics are most likely to be between the ages of 16–40.

While no attempt is made to suggest that the results of the 1,000-man sample is generalizable to the population of men whose partners have had abortions, or even to the men who accompany their partners to an abortion clinic, it is important to pause to consider the value of this sample. Shostak and McLouth have gathered considerable data on a group which has been ignored in social science research. The group—men whose partners are having abortions—is a particularly difficult group to study. Their project is to be commended for the time and energy which went into locating and describing these men.

Another important element in the *Men and Abortion* research is the questionnaire used to survey the waiting room males (see Appendix G). Because the study of abortion from the male perspective is relatively unique, there was little research available to replicate. Therefore, Dr. Shostak developed the majority of the questions himself, pretesting the items on classes at Drexel University and in clinics in the Philadelphia area.[4] The questionnaire is typed on 8½" × 11" paper, and is five pages long (copied on the front and back of three pages).

Areas covered in the questionnaire include general attitudes toward abortion as well as attitudes toward the specific abortion experience; the relationship of the men to their partners; the participation of these men in the abortion itself, including their role in counseling, paying for the abortion, and whether they consulted others regarding the abortion; the effects of the abortion on the relationship between the men and their partners, on men's attitude toward fatherhood, and the risk of future pregnancies; men's knowledge of abortion procedures, laws, and medical dangers; their general moral orientation; and personal data such as age, race, religion, marital status, and education. These questions provide considerable data about the respondents.

The format of the questionnaire is relatively succinct. This is an advantage since the instrument deals with a very sensitive issue—abortion—and fewer words offer fewer cues which might bias responses. There is little in the wording of questionnaire instructions or individual items which would structure respondents' answers. While I found the questionnaire unobjectionable, since the purpose of this appendix is to evaluate, let me include some suggestions for future replications. These suggestions fall under two broad categories: a reorganization of the questionnaire itself, and changes in individual items.

The reorganization of the questionnaire would involve moving the questions relating to personal experiences and background to the end of the instrument. The rationale for this reorganization is to make the questionnaire less threatening to potential respondents and, hopefully, increase the number of people who would respond. The rearranged questionnaire would begin with questions on attitudes and the first item would be on attitudes toward the topic of study—abortion. Thus, potential respondents who are asked to participate in the study instantly recognize the relevance of the questionnaire, but would not be threatened by items which ask for information about themselves or their role in the particular abortion experiences that brought them to the clinic. Following questions on attitudes toward abortion and toward any other relevant issues (e.g., laws, fetal development, moral orientation), it would be good to ask the questions regarding participation in the abortion, reaction to the abortion, recommendations for changes in abortion procedures, and, lastly, requests for personal background data. This format is probably less threatening than beginning by asking for age, race, religion, etc., and should increase the number of potential respondents.

Relative to the rewording of questionnaire items, replications of this study should carefully consider expanding the number of responses on individual questions. That over one-half of the items in the current questionnaire were limited to one of two possibilities is a handicap in analysis. (Most of the dichotomous responses are either a yes/no choice or a check if the respondent agrees with the item.) The disadvantage of using dichotomous categories is that the range of available responses is limited.

For example, a critical question asks whether abortion is morally wrong. If so, the respondent checks that item. Attitudes toward abortion, however, are not always so clear. A preferable method would be to give respondents a range of choices such as always, almost always, sometimes, almost never, or never. Another important question on abortion did include a broader range of response categories. The item asked whether the respondent agreed or disagreed that abortion is the killing of a child using the categories strongly agree, agree, neutral, disagree, or strongly disagree. While the two items measure different aspects of the abortion issue, the broader range of responses elicited much more information than the dichotomous response pattern.

The following comparison of the distribution of these two questions illustrates the need to allow for as much variance as possible when designing questionnaire items.

	Yes				No
Abortion is morally wrong	17%				83%

	Strongly Agree	Agree	Neutral	Disagree	Strongly Disagree
Abortion is the killing of a child	10%	16%	32%	25%	17%

There are several other ways in which questions could be improved. One is to include more closed-ended questions whenever feasible, especially when the possible responses are apparent (e.g., age, race, and ethnicity). Also, the question regarding social class should be expanded. As it is currently worded, the majority of these men consider themselves to be in the middle class (73%). While there has been some research which indicates that respondents' self-evaluation of class is fairly accurate, it would be useful to also measure social class with a scale which includes occupation and educational level of the respondents.

While collecting data, Shostak and McLouth made some minor improvements in the instrument which meant two different versions of the questionnaire were used in the survey. The format of the first version, administered to 495 males, was rearranged slightly (e.g., numbering of questions and spacing), with relatively minor changes in wording for the second version administered to 505 men.

One change, however, altered the responses from the first version to the second. In the first version, the questions pertaining to reactions to the abortion and the pregnancy asked respondents to "imagine that your female sex partner has just told you" she is pregnant or going to have an abortion. The second version of the questionnaire, however, asks "what was your reaction" when your female sex partner told you she was pregnant or going to have an abortion. This is a critical change in wording, and the distributions of the reactions differ when controlling for the version of the questionnaire used. For example, those men who were asked to imagine that their female sex partner has just told them she is pregnant or going to have an abortion were more likely to indicate that they would ask her what she wants to do, offer to marry her, urge single parenthood, offer only to pay for the abortion, pay for the abortion, join in the counseling, seek counseling for themselves, or be less likely to go along with her wishes or recommend abortion. Thus, it appears that possible or imagined reactions are different from actual behavior in these situations. The difference between these two questions is recognized, and they have not been combined for analysis in the text.

While the preceding suggestions may be incorporated into a replication of the *Men and Abortion* survey, they should not be taken as a denial of the value of the research itself. The strengths of the data collected by Shostak and McLouth include ample indicators of critical concepts in the study. The relationships between these multiple indicators support the internal validity of the measures.

Before discussing the adequacy of the measures used in the project, a brief detour is necessary to describe two composite measures drawn on by the researchers. One index summarizes attitudes toward abortion generally, and is the sum of the total number of circumstances where the respondent felt that a woman should be able to obtain a legal abortion. Many of these items have been used in studies of attitudes toward abortion (e.g., if the couple already has as many children as they want, if the pregnancy is a result of incest), and some items have been developed by Shostak and McLouth (e.g., if, for any reason, the male wants this pregnancy terminated, if the parents of this pregnant minor want the abortion). While 17 items may appear to be quite large, the alpha reliability coefficient for the index is 0.87 and is not improved by removing indicators. The correlations between the abortion index and other items support the internal validity of the index. For example, the higher the attitudes toward abortion index, the more likely is the respondent to have agreed that abortion is the killing of a child ($R = -0.33$) and to have checked abortion as one of the items which is morally wrong (Gamma = -0.41).

A second index measuring moral attitudes is the sum of items checked, indicating how many items the respondent felt were morally wrong. Seven items were used: sex between two single persons; homosexuality; pornographic movies; use of hard drugs; smoking marijuana; sex before age 16; and living with someone of the opposite sex. The question asking whether abortion is considered morally wrong was not included in the morality index because it measures one of the principal concepts in the research and would confound any analyses using the morality index with other measures of attitudes toward abortion or the abortion experience. The alpha reliability coefficient for the morality index is 0.68. The internal validity of the morality index is supported by its relationship with whether a respondent checked abortion as morally wrong (Gamma = 0.63), attitudes toward abortion ($R = 0.14$), and whether abortion is the killing of a child ($R = 0.21$).

The interrelationships between single measures of orientation toward abortion and other concepts in the study also bolsters the internal validity of the research. For example, the single measure indicators of orientation toward abortion, "abortion is the killing of a child" and "abortion is morally wrong," are correlated (Gamma = 0.62). Relative to options considered, there is a relationship between seriously considering marriage as an option and offering to marry the partner (Gamma = 0.79). Also, considering adoption and recommending adoption are related (Gamma = 0.56). Additionally, paying half the cost of the abortion is related to the questions asking if the respondent is helping with the costs (Gamma = −0.70) and if he is paying all of the cost of the abortion (Gamma = −0.76). The indicators of participation in the abortion are also correlated. Whether the men joined in counseling is related to whether they offered to accompany their partner to counseling (Gamma = 0.73); sought counseling for themselves (Gamma = 0.64); and accompanied their partner to counseling (Gamma = 0.83). And, whether they sought counseling for themselves is related to whether they turned to an abortion counselor for counseling (Gamma = 0.55) and accompanied their partner to counseling (Gamma = 0.67).

The strength of the associations between similar indicators of a concept provides strong support for the internal validity of the questionnaire items. However, as noted in the beginning of this appendix, the external validity of the survey is impossible to assess. The survey was not a random sample, using only those men who were willing to fill out questionnaires at the 30 participating abortion clinics. Shostak and McLouth considered this and conducted surveys of participating clinics (once using a questionnaire and later by phone) to assess the representativeness of the men who answered as opposed to those who refused to participate. As noted in the text, the number of teenage males participating in the survey is considerably lower than those who accompany their partners to an abortion. The other characteristics, however, appear to be fairly representative of the men in these 30 clinics.

Shostak and McLouth are very careful never to suggest that these findings extend to all men who accompany their partners to abortion clinics. Their research is exploratory. They ask—What are the issues surrounding men and abortion? and What patterns exist around these issues? The final question in this evaluation must be did they adequately address these questions? My response is an unqualified yes. Certainly more research is needed, but that research will rest upon the exploratory work done in *Men and Abortion*.

Notes

1. I want to thank Art Shostak and Gary McLouth for asking me to contribute this evaluation. They not only provided me with all their data and documentation, but they also gave me free rein to criticize their efforts in any way I saw fit. I also want to acknowledge the support of Beth E. Vanfossen who read, discussed, and offered valuable suggestions on earlier drafts of this appendix.

2. The coding categories are those used in NORC Surveys (NORC, 1980).

3. The abortion clinics that filled out the clinic survey are the same clinics that participated in the waiting-room sample.

4. The pretest data is reported in an article by Shostak entitled "Abortion as Fatherhood Lost." *The Family Coordinator* (October 1979): 569–574. The data gathered in these pretests are not used in the survey of 1,000 waiting room males.

5. Any comparisons using the items asking "What did you do...." (Section IV, questions 1 and 2) use data from the second version of the questionnaire only (505 respondents) because of the change in wording between version 1 and version 2, as discussed earlier in this appendix.

B

Sharing Some of the Pain: Men's Response to Mastectomy

Donald F. Sabo, Jr. and
L. Robert Paskoff

Throughout our research we have tried to find an analogous situation to men passing through abortion. When Dan Sabo contacted us and discussed the findings of "Men's Response to Mastectomy," we knew we had found a rare comparative experience.

The remarkable similarity between the male role in abortion and mastectomy experiences made clear by the Sabo-Paskoff study lend very helpful and welcomed perspectives to Men and Abortion. *We have included a synopsis of the study for the benefit of our readers and our abortion veterans.*

To describe men as unfeeling is to fall prey to social myth. Like women, men have a rather complex emotional makeup. However, many of the roles that society has constructed for men to play—unlike those for women—do not allow for the expression of very much feeling. A soldier who cries in battle might sacrifice his life; the executive who freely expresses personal misgivings may lose credibility. Most of men's roles, moreover, are underpinned by cultural stereotypes which call for men to be tough, objective, stoic, and emotionally inexpressive. The end result is that many men play a complicated game of masking or denying inner emotions in order to conform to the expectations attached to many traditional male roles. Like seeds in an apple, men's feelings lay inside their core, hidden from public view but present and vital nonetheless. Nowhere is this more evident than in men's reactions and adjustments to mastectomy.

One in 13 American women will develop breast cancer some-time in her life. Breast cancer is the largest single cause of cancer deaths among women. Its treatments, and aftercare, involve con-siderable psychological and emotional problems. Researchers tell us that, for many women, mastectomy* is apt to result in a ma-jor disruption of body image, depression, fears of rejection and death, and deep-seated concerns about sexual identity and be-havior. For these reasons, therapy is usually aimed at helping the mastectomy patient herself.[1]

Very little is known about how men react to a partner's mastectomy since most research has focused on female patients. Moreover, husbands are usually excluded from counseling or ther-apy designed to meet the needs of the female patient. This is dou-bly regrettable. To begin with, a few studies show that the psy-chological effects of mastectomy upon a husband are often severe. Anxiety reactions, depression, feelings of inadequacy about his ability to help his spouse through the crisis, and concerns about sexual intimacy are common. Also, researchers find that husbandly support and empathy play a large part in the emotional recovery of wives. The husband's adjustment, therefore, is often critically important to the mastectomy patient herself.[2]

In order to learn more about men's adjustments to a spouse's mastectomy, 24 married men were recruited and interviewed in depth. Six of these men participated in a support group which met weekly for almost one-half year. The 24 men had an average age of 46, and included laborers, salesmen, managers, and profes-sionals. Interviews and observations of the support group revealed that they experienced a number of common difficulties adjusting to mastectomy.

First, the men's emotional reactions to mastectomy were quite intense. The initial diagnosis and surgery triggered disbelief, alarm, and painful feelings of isolation. One man compared his emotional state at this time to "being hit across the gut by a two-by-four." Others, alone in offices, bathrooms, or automobiles, cried "like ba-

---

*The term mastectomy refers to a variety of surgical methods that remove the breast(s) and/or associated tissue. For example, one common surgical procedure, the Halsted radical mastectomy, entails removal of the entire breast, skin, ma-jor and minor pectoral muscles, the axillary lymph nodes, and fat. [See *The Breast Cancer Digest*, U.S. Dept. of Health, Education, and Welfare (1980).]

bies." They shared their spouse's chief anxieties surrounding breast loss and the threat of mortality. However, whereas wives underwent mastectomy with at least minimal social and emotional support (e.g., women friends, nurses, relatives), husbands made the trek from diagnosis through surgery and hospitalization essentially alone. Many felt pushed aside to a "waiting room" position as events unfolded around the wife's bedside. Some had a chance to talk over sensitive issues with women friends and relatives; only two found other men to talk with openly.

The statement below reflects most men's sense of isolation and emotional turmoil:

> I'd go to work and be in a daze. I didn't know what to do. I wanted to do something, but didn't know where to begin. I didn't know what the next person was thinking. I didn't know what my wife was thinking. Should I cry with her or be strong? Should I talk or should I shut up? Should I take her in my arms or would this make her feel worse than she already did? I felt extremely isolated. No one knew, or really cared to know, what I was going through.

After the initial shockwave of diagnosis and surgery began to fade, the men began to define their primary role as that of protective guardians of their wives' physical and emotional well-being.

A second major impact of mastectomy upon a husband, therefore, is to challenge him to effectively meet the responsibilities of supporting, loving, and reassuring his spouse that she and the marriage will survive. Husbands readily understood that their wives must cope with considerable emotional stress and build a new self-image fragmented by illness and disfigurement. Yet the men only vaguely realized that their own emotional makeup and self-concept was also being affected by the surgery and resulting changes in their marital lives.

As time progressed, the men pushed awareness of their own feelings into the background and placed their wives' feelings in the foreground. Almost all the husbands said they had discussed their wives' emotions and attitudes about issues such as the breast loss or fears of dying, but none of the men reported talking about his own feelings around these concerns. Indeed, the most typical male response was to flatly and ardently assert that the breast loss "made absolutely no difference" to them, that their "feelings and attraction had not changed at all.'' Similarly, the men would declare that they were "completely confident" that the doctors "had got it all" and the "cancer would not return again." We call this coping pattern the "denial role."

Making a wife's adjustment and feelings the priority and keeping their own feelings at bay, therefore, is a third common experience among the 24 husbands. For husbands to take on the role of protective guardians meant developing a capacity to deny their own feelings. On a conscious level, this denial is designed to allay a wife's fears of rejection and further illness. Indeed, during the months immediately following surgery, men's denial of their own worst fears and their facade of optimism is probably necessary in that the physical and emotional needs of the patient herself are most pressing. At a deeper emotional level, and in terms of its longer-range effects on the marital relationship, however, playing the "denial role" led to several problems worthy of comment.

First, denial often intensified the husband's own anxieties. As time passes, maintaining a calm, confident, "on stage" posture with his wife becomes increasingly more difficult. Inner life becomes more stressful. Most husbands reported increased moodiness, loss of energy, and gnawing fears about their own health and death. Clearly, the energy put into denying feelings and maintaining the masculine posture of the protective guardian is not without psychic costs.

Second, despite his good intentions, a husband's protective silence makes communicating about important issues such as breast loss and fears of recurrence difficult for the couple to pursue. As one man confided about his fears of losing his wife, "Sometimes I'm terrified, and I try not to let her know it but I'm sure she's aware of it." Furthermore, it seems unlikely that wives actually found their husbands' performance totally believable, thus opening a door to distrust and, perhaps, resentment. As one man put it,

> My wife asked me how I deal with worrying whether she'd get cancer again. I told her that I put it out of my mind, that I just have to push it out. She thought that this was terrible because it means that I wasn't supporting her, and that I don't love her. Then she gets angry!

Third, sexual adjustment after mastectomy may be complicated by the man's denial role. Virtually all husbands reported experiencing some type of sexual problem including: wife's rejection of husband's advances; husband's loss of sexual interest; impotence; concerns about inflicting pain due to the sensitivity of the surgical wound; reduction of coital frequency; fears of potential pregnancy which, for chemotherapy patients, physicians had warned could prove dangerous both to wife and fetus. Eventually, 20 of the 24 husbands reported making satisfactory sexual adjustments. We speculate, however, that less denial and more open communication between spouses would have enhanced and accelerated the overall process.

Finally, early psychological denial can soon take on a pattern of fervent and conscious desire for the postmastectomy marital relationship to return to the old, premastectomy status quo. One obvious problem with this longing, however, is that it belies the facts. The breast is gone. Cancer has struck a medical and personal blow. Misgivings about recurrence and mortality are real—for both wives and husbands! The emotional core of wife and husband has been altered and, fundamentally, the marital relationship is changed.

For the 18 men we interviewed who did not participate in the support group, it is our feeling that many had not come to grips with the complex ways that mastectomy had affected themselves and their wives. For them, in varying degrees, denial had become a way of life; illusions of safety and sameness had taken root. We suspect that a marital relationship built upon mutual denial inhibits self-expression, interpersonal flexibility, and personal growth. Denial is too strong a filter for marital communication to pass through and receive clarification. In short, we speculate that some men's denial, with or without the complicity of a spouse, may prevent or hinder the creation of a new relationship after mastectomy.

For the six men who did participate in the support group, the experience helped them recognize and explore the denial process. Perhaps the most critical impact of a men's support group experience is its power to cut through the psychological and social barriers that have traditionally barred open and honest communication, empathy, and emotional support between men.

In traditional social settings, when men get together to plan community events, watch a sports contest, or celebrate one another's good fortune, the ground rules are familiar and comfortable. Male role expectations are fairly clear; the handshakes, jokes, backslaps, and questions about work and relationships come easily.

In contrast, the surface assumption holding a support group together is that the situation somehow calls for intimacy, self-disclosure, and warm acceptance of others. An atmosphere of trust and closeness develops and, simply put, men become closer to one another and themselves. Group members learned how denying and hiding their own feelings often kindled anxiety or depression in themselves, and anger and vague dismay in their spouses. Insights and discussions within the group spilled over into their marital relationships. Communication at home increased. With issues like love, sexuality, and fears of future cancer out in the open, they reported that somehow their marital lives had been made better.[3]

Thoreau's often-quoted declaration that "the mass of men lead lives of quiet desperation" accurately describes many of our husbands' experiences with mastectomy. We learned that men definitely meet with much inner turmoil in the face of mastectomy, though role demands and personal notions about masculinity often keep them from more freely expressing these feelings. We came to understand that mastectomy is not something that happens to the woman, and not the man. Just as women's and men's social lives are inexorably intertwined, so also are their psychologies in the wake of mastectomy.

We saw that denying feelings and taking on the role of protective guardian produces both positive and negative consequences for husbands, wives, and marriages. And, finally, we learned that, given the opportunity to meaningfully communicate with one another in a nontraditional setting, men can find a more healthful balance between strength and vulnerability, and courage and dependency, which helps them to more effectively meet the challenges of adjustment to mastectomy.

Notes

1. For useful reading, see: Sandy Hotchkiss (1976), "After Mastectomy," *Human Behavior.* 5:40–41; Peter Maguire (1975), "The Psychological and Social Consequences of Breast Cancer," *Nursing Mirror and Midwives Journal, 140:54–57; Tina Morris (1979), "Psychological Adjustment to Mastectomy," *Cancer Treatment Reviews,* 6:41–61.

2. James G. Joiner and Joan Z. Fisher (1981), "Postmastectomy Counseling," in Elizabeth Howell and Marjorie Bayes (eds.), *Women and Mental Health*. *New York*: Basic Books, pp. 411–418.

3. The effectiveness of a men's support group experience for helping male partners of mastectomy patients healthfully adjust to the surgery is more fully demonstrated by a research study conducted by the authors. The project was funded by the S.U.N.Y. Research Foundation. Clinical observations are combined with a repeated measures analysis of questionnaire data comparing support group members to a control group. Several key hypotheses concerning husbands' adjustment were verified. (Publication forthcoming; contact authors for further information.)

C

Working Through Abortion
Leslie M. Butterfield

To consider abortion a simple matter is to denigrate its possible impact upon the woman who chooses it and the individuals who contribute to, or are affected by, her decision. To deny its complexity is to also deny the complexity of human experience; the inextricably interwoven patterns of life and death, joy and sorrow, and the choices we must make regarding them.

In order to create a setting in which the psychological meanings of abortion could be fully explored, I have established an on-going program of postabortion therapy groups for women in the Richmond, Virginia area.[1] While the general purpose of these groups is to aid women in resolving their abortion experiences, the group format has been specifically designed to:

1. Provide a sense of social support and shared experience;

2. Teach clients how to recognize and cope with loss in a constructive manner;

3. Educate clients about the stages of grief and mourning, and aid in the resolution of conflicts arising in these stages;

4. Develop skills in initiating and maintaining individualized support systems;

5. Improve information gathering and decision-making skills;

6. Increase clients' sense of self-esteem and efficacy as they relate to situations of personal or social stress; and

293

7. Utilize the abortion experience as a step toward personal maturity and increased self-knowledge.

In the groups, as well as in the abortion-related literature, the themes of loss and isolation arise repeatedly. These appear to be figural themes for both aborting women *and* their partners. Unfortunately, because they are so rarely discussed, their impact tends to be destructive rather than constructive, carrying many couples to a point of emotional detachment and despair, rather than to a sense of emotional maturity and enhanced intimacy.

A deeper understanding of loss, and of the psychological meanings people derive from it, inevitably becomes a topic of major concern in postabortion groups. Learning to grieve the tangible and intangible losses resulting from abortion is probably the most essential aspect of working through abortion-related conflicts, and plays a large part in the prevention of additional unplanned pregnancies.

The ambivalence of abortion, while painful to experience, is a necessary part of our ability to derive meaning from the experience. It is difficult to assimilate, within the single context of abortion, both its destructive and life-affirming qualities; yet both are clearly present. Such assimilation, with the deepened understanding it brings, depends to a large degree upon our willingness to share our feelings and perceptions with one another; and to mourn together rather than alone. An inability or unwillingness to communicate may be harmful, establishing emotional and behavioral patterns that not only hurt men and women individually, but preclude their ability to engage in loving relationships with one another.

Delayed or distorted grieving can result in exaggerated feelings of hostility toward others, emotional withdrawal, social isolation, somatic complaints, chronic depression and a noticeable decrease in one's ability to initiate or maintain loving relationships. It seems, therefore, that if we are to emerge from the abortion experience with our ability to love intact, we must share with others our questions, our fears, and our desires to maintain affectionate and respectful relationships.

Listed below are some suggestions for facing the pre- and postabortion time periods together in a constructive and loving manner:

D

Feedback from 521 Waiting Room Males

Peter Zelles

Abortion providers in this country are asked by local boards of health to maintain statistics about the patients they see such as age, ethnicity, marital status, religion, education, social class, and pregnancy/contraceptive history. These records are used to help understand family planning trends and to target special programming to populations which are at an especially high risk.

Statistics describing male partners of abortion patients are conspicuously absent, an omission that reflects an attitude of the abortion and family planning community to ignore almost all aspects of male involvement. This failure in record keeping parallels a lack of services for men, from the educational (e.g., teaching contraceptive use) to the emotional (e.g., counseling male partners of abortion patients).

Without adequate hard data, the case for male family planning services is little more than wishful thinking. Public awareness of male family planning issues (especially abortion related issues) is limited; the general public views abortion as a *woman's* dilemma, and almost exclusively a woman's *solitary* crisis.

Since 1977, Midwest Health Center for Women in Minneapolis, Minnesota has provided family planning and counseling services for male client-partners of abortion patients. Approximately 1,000 men annually are seen by this service for contraceptive education and abortion counseling. After participating in the program—which consists of both individual and group counseling—all men are asked to complete a one-page questionnaire for record keeping/evaluation purposes.

The data outlined in this article comes from a sample of 521 cases seen between January 1982 and January 1983 at the Midwest Health Center for Women (MHCW). All information comes from the post-session questionnaire, and is gathered on the day of the visit.

A glance at the data collected in this study dispels any myths about a stereotypical male involved with an abortion; the ages, careers, relationship styles and lengths all vary a great deal. The biological realities of conception (along with the tendency for involvement with a same-age partner) however, result in the largest percentage of clients (65.6%) being between 18–25 years of age (client ages range from 14 years into the fifties). Reflective of this age group, the most frequent type of relationship is a dating couple, not living together (63%). Twelve percent are married, and nearly 20% live together outside of marriage.

Just over half of the sample (53.4%) were involved with their partners for less than a year; interestingly, a large increase is seen in couples together for 3–5 years (perhaps these are families between children, who are not yet ready for sterilization and not prepared for another child). Eighty-eight percent predicted their relationship would continue past their abortion experience.

All but 13.2% had completed high school, 20.1% were college graduates, and 32.6% had attended but not completed college (this includes undergraduate students). The smallest educational subgroup was clients with graduate degrees (1.3%); as age and level of education increases, abortions decrease—we can hypothesize that the decision to parent reflects age and education.

Examining the contraceptive history of these clients exposes a laxity of use; in the six months previous to their appointment, over half (58.7%) had not used contraception, or had used an ineffective method such as withdrawal or "rhythm." Twenty-three percent reported they always use contraception, 39.9% state they use it "most of the time," and 8.1% state they rarely use any form of contraception. When asked what form of birth control they plan to use in the future, 49.1% didn't answer, but of those remaining, over half reported their partners would use oral contraceptives, and almost 14% stated their partners would use the diaphragm. Condoms, which were the most frequently used method prior to the abortion, were the postabortion contraception choice for only 3.8% of men (4.5% chose condoms and contraceptive foam together). Sixty-six percent stated they were "very comfortable" talking with their partners about birth control.

Several items on the questionnaire addressed emotional aspects of the abortion experience. The most frequent responses when hearing of their pregnancy were surprise (33.4%), disappointment (25.5%), and "mixed emotions" (20.2%). Other reactions were primarily negative, with only 2.1% feeling "good" about the pregnancy. Fifty-seven percent stated they had "positive feelings" about the abortion, 13.4% reported negative emotions, and 18.6 felt "mixed emotions." The majority of men agreed with their partners decision to abort (88.1%), and only 1.9% stated disagreement.

One of the major issues in male abortion counseling is isolation; in the counseling session most men say they haven't sought support other than from their partners. The data confirm this: while 92.7% had discussed the abortion with their partner, 63.3% had not spoken with anyone else about their crisis.

In evaluation of counseling services received, 59.9% rated their experience as "very useful," 34.7% found it "somewhat useful," and only 1.9% responded with a negative rating. In rating the various aspects of the male counseling program, receiving information about abortion was considered to be most significant, followed by hearing about the feelings of other men (in group session), having a chance to talk about feelings, and, finally, learning about birth control.

In view of the goals of short-term counseling, the data presented here have great significance. Breaking down isolation, reducing anxiety, and allowing for ventilation of emotion are all priorities in acute interventions, and it was precisely these areas that the clients identified as most crucial. In this light it is interesting to note that while 88.1% were in agreement with the abortion decision, and 92.7% had discussed the situation with their partner, well over half found it significant or very significant to have a chance to talk and hear the feelings of other men. In total, 94.6% of the men questioned stated the counseling experience was useful.

While the validity of self-report as a research design is frequently called into question, it is difficult to competely ignore the anonymous responses of these 521 men. The argument for male abortion counseling has few active proponents, and it is data of this sort which point to the strong need for counseling directed toward male client partners. Despite its necessity and constitutionality, abortion is a tremendously difficult experience for *both* partners, and it is the responsibility of the professional community to assure that patients and client-partners alike are provided with appropriate emotional support services.

STATISTICS

Age group	Percentage
14–17	6.7
18–21	39.5
22–25	26.1
26–29	15.0
30–34	6.0
35–39	3.6
40+	2.3
No answer	0.8

Relationship to partner

12.7%	Husband
63.0	Boyfriend (not live-in)
19.6	Boyfriend (live-in)
2.1	Friend (not sexual)
0.6	Acquaintance
0.6	Brother
1.2	Father
0.4	No answer

Length of relationship

7.3%	0–3 months
19.4	3–6 months
26.7	7–12 months
8.6	13–18 months
10.9	19–24 months
3.6	25–36 months
12.1	3–5 years
3.3	6–10 years
2.7	10+ years
5.4	No answer

Will relationship continue past abortion?

88.7%	Yes
1.5	No
4.6	Don't know
5.2	No answer

Feelings about pregnancy

33.4%	Surprise
25.5	Disappointment
20.2	Mixed emotions
2.1	Frustrated
2.1	Good
1.7	Concern
0.6	Angry
13.8	No answer

Kind of work

29.8%	Blue collar
27.3	Student
10.7	Sales/Service/Clerical
9.3	White collar
6.9	Working student
6.3	Unemployed
3.5	Working but category unknown
0.6	Professional
5.2	No answer

Education

32.8%	High school graduate
32.6	Some college
14.6	College graduate
13.2	Some high school
4.2	Some graduate school
1.3	Graduate degree
1.2	No answer

Discussed abortion with partner

92.7%	Yes
1.7	No
5.4	No answer

Spoken to person (other than partner) about abortion

31.9%	Yes
63.3	No
4.8	No answer

Feelings about abortion decision

57.0%	Positive
13.4	Negative
18.6	Mixed
10.9	No answer

Do you agree with abortion decision

88.1%	Yes
1.9	No
10.0	No answer

STATISTICS

Are you comfortable talking with partner about contraception

0.6%	1) Not comfortable
3.3	2)
11.1	3)
11.9	4)
66.4	5) Very comfortable

Types of birth control used in past six months (may choose more than one type)

25.0%	Condoms
21.1	None
20.9	Rhythm
19.8	Oral contraceptives
16.7	Withdrawal
13.4	Diaphragm
8.1	Condom + foam
6.7	Foam
1.5	IUD
5.8	No answer

Type of birth control chosen for after abortion

49.1%	No answer

Of those remaining:

56.2	Oral contraceptives
14.7	Don't know
13.5	Diaphragm
7.2	Vasectomy
5.7	IUD
4.5	Foam and condom
3.8	Condom
1.1	Foam
0.8	Natural Family Planning

How often is birth control used?

39.9%	Most of the time
23.2	Always
8.1	Hardly ever
28.8	No answer

Was the counseling useful?

59.9%	Very useful
34.7	Somewhat useful
1.9	Not useful
3.5	No answer

Significant aspects of counseling
Receiving information about abortion

77.7%	1) Very significant
8.1	2)
4.0	3) Not significant
10.2	No answer

Hearing feelings of other men

41.5%	1) Very significant
15.2	2)
26.3	Not significant
16.9	No answer

Having a chance to talk

38.2%	1) Very significant
19.6	2)
27.1	3) Not significant
15.0	No answer

Learning about contraception

34.0%	1) Very significant
20.0	2)
30.7	3) Not significant
15.4	No answer

E

"Videotape Proposal"
Glen Muschio and Anja Dalderup

This is a project proposal for the production of a video tape and a counseling brochure on abortion. The tape is intended for a male audience comprised of individuals who have accompanied their partners to an abortion clinic or hospital for the purpose of abortion. The running time of the tape will be 25–32 minutes. The counseling brochure will serve as reinforcement for information presented in the tape. It will also provide information on counseling services available in specific geographic areas.

The video tape will be divided into three sections; the objectives of each section are as follows: First, to help alleviate the anxiety associated with the event of abortion. Second, to highlight the fact that the abortion process continues beyond the event of abortion; to provide information that the emotions being experienced by the male are common feelings which are shared by a number of other men who have gone through the process; to suggest possible courses of action which may be taken by the male and his partner to lessen the trauma of the post-abortion experience. Third, to provide information regarding birth control devices including the condom, foam, IUD, sponge, and diaphragm.

Outline and Explanation of the Video Scenario

Section One

Through reenactment the viewer will be informed of the process through which his partner is now going. This section of the tape is intended to help relieve the anxiety of a male who accompanies his partner for an abortion and is often left to wait for hours in a waiting room with no inkling as to what his partner is experiencing. By relieving some of the anxiety associated with "not knowing" it is maintained that the viewer will be in a better psychological state to receive the information which follows. Section One will run 5–7 minutes. It will be recorded in a cooperating clinic.

Section Two

This section will be composed of interviews with men who have gone through the abortion process. The upshot is abortion is a trying psychological experience which will not end with the abortion itself. Men will discuss their experiences in the abortion process. The interviews will stress that abortion is a shared responsibility, that the strong emotions and mixed feelings which accompany the event of abortion need not be a destructive experience. Through continued open communication with their partners the relationship will survive and grow. It will be mentioned that the couple or individual need not go through the process alone; counseling is available. The interviews in this section will be reenactments, the scripts will be written based upon interviews conducted with men who have gone through the abortion process. This section of the tape will run between 12 and 15 minutes.

Section Three

This section of the tape will graphically present information on how fertilization of an egg can be prevented. Voiceover narration will present the viewer with information regarding the effectiveness of condoms, IUDs, sponges, and diaphragms. Since many of these devices are designed for women, men are often not familiar with the effectiveness of each device. Voiceover narration will suggest that the male and his partner discuss which birth control device is best suited to their needs. This section of the tape will make use of previously made films concerning fertilization. To this material video and computer graphics will be designed to illustrate how the various mechanical devices prevent fertilization. Running time of this section is 8–10 minutes.

The Brochure

The brochure is designed to reinforce information presented in the tape. Photographs of still frames from the tape will act as visual reminders to paragraphs containing information on counseling services and birth control devices. Whereas the videotape will not contain information on the whereabouts of counseling services, the brochure will provide this needed information. As counseling services become more readily available updates can be made to a brochure at a fraction of the cost of making changes to an edited videotape.

F

Comparison of Samples of Waiting Room Males, 1974-1983

Demographic Characteristics	Researcher(s); Date; Sample Size; Site			
	Shostak and McLouth, 1983 (N = 1,000; 18 states)	Hill-Falkenthal, 1983 (N = 106; California)	Marsiglio, 1983 (N = 76; Ohio)	Dimock, 1982 (n = 66; Wisconsin)
Race	87%, White; 10%, Black; 2%, Hispanic; 1%, Asian	69%, White; 10%, Black 6%, Asian; 4%, Spanish; 8%, Other	88%, White; 8%, Black	86%, White; 8%, Black
Marital Status	60%, Single; 12%, Living Together; 5%, Separated; 6%, Divorced; –1% Widowed; 18%, Married	77%, Single; 1%, Divorced; 1%, Divorced or Separated or Widowed; 20%, Married	79%, Single; (70%, dating more than 6 months); 20%, married	61%, Single; (14%, engaged); 21%, married
Age	5% Under 18 30% 18-21 30% 22-25 18% 26-30 10% 31-35 5% 36-40	1% 17 and under 58% 18-24 32% 25-34 7% 35 or older	11% 16-18 28% 19-20 27% 21-25 16% 26-30 18% 31+	Mean—25 yrs. Mode—22 yrs. Std. deviation—7.1 yrs. Range—17-55 yrs.

Demographic Characteristics

Demographic Characteristics	Researcher(s); Date; Sample Size; Site			
	Zelles, 1982–1983 (N = 521; Minnesota)	Rotter, 1980 (N = 126; Missouri, Nebraska)	Smith, 1979 (N = 91; Iowa)	Brosseau, 1978 (N = 42; Colorado)
Religion	N.D.	26% Catholic 27% Protestant 9% Jewish 45% Other	N.D.	27% Catholic 52% Protestant 14% None 9% N.D.
Education	11% Less than High School 45% High School Graduate 27% Some College 12% College 6% Graduate School	N.D.	12% Less than High School 29% High School Graduate 37% Some College 12% College 11% Graduate School	8% 23% 38% 9% 13%
Race	N.D.	83%, White; 16%, Black; 1%, Other	90%, White; 4%, Black; 6%, Other	100% White
Marital Status	87%, Single (20%, Living Together; 63%, Boyfriend); 13%, Married	72%, Single; 28%, Married	54%, Single; 45%, Married	100%, Single
Age	7% 14–17	2% Under 18	4% 15–17	9% 15–17

	Finley, 1978 (N = 192; Massachusetts)	Lees, 1975 (N = 73; Michigan)	Milling, 1975 (N = 400; New York City)	Rothstein, 1973 (N = 60; New York City)
Age	40% 18–21 26% 22–25 15% 26–29 6% 30–34 4% 35–39 2% 40+	34% 18–21 24% 22–25 19% 26–30 10% 31–35 6% 36–40 5% 41+	51% 18–24 31% 25–34 12% Over 34	80% 18–24 11% 25 and over
Religion	N.D.	28% Catholic 53% Protestant 1% Jewish 12% Other 7% None	28% Catholic 39% Protestant 0% Jewish 8% Other 15% None 10% N.D.	N.D.
Education	13% Some High School 33% High School Graduate 33% Some College 15% College Graduate 1% Graduate Degree	8% Less than High School 42% High School Graduate 30% Some College 8% College 13% Graduate School	18% Less than High School 31% High School Graduate 36% Some College 15% College Graduate and Higher	22% Less than High School 57% High School Graduate 21% Some College
Race	N.D.	88%, White; 11%, Black; 1%, Asian	67%, White; 25%, Black; 7%, Hispanic	33%, White; 30%, Black; 27%, Puerto Rican; 10%, other

Demographic Characteristics

Demographic Characteristics	Researcher(s); Date; Sample Size; Site			
Marital Status	73%, Single; (15%, Living Together; 11%, fiancé; 45%, lover; 2%, other); 17%, Married	92%, Single; 4%, Divorced; 2%, Married (as dictated by the study's design)	60%, Single; −1%, Widowed; −1%, Separated; −1%, Separated; 35%, Married	63%, Single; (37%, not engaged; 27%, engaged): 37%, married
Age	2% 17 and under 25% 18–21 28% 22–25 24% 26–30 14% 31–40 5% 41 and over 3% No answer	32% 18 and under 45% 19–22 16% 23–26 7% 27 and over	6% 17–19 30% 20–24 26% 25–29 21% 30–34 14% 35–39 5% 40 +	7% 17 and under 50% 18–24 35% 25–34 8% 35–44
Religion	39% Catholic 19% Protestant 4% Jewish 17% Other 21% No answer	40% Catholic 56% Protestant 0% Jewish 5% Other, None	50% Catholic 30% Protestant 10% Jewish 8% None 2% Other	65% Catholic 18% Protestant 17% Other
Education	39% High School or less 46% Some College 8% Graduate School 7% No Answer	33% Less than High School 33% High School Graduate 27% Some College 7% College or more	N.D.	N.D.

*N.D. = No data

G

Questionnaire

Men and Abortion Questionnaire

We are writing a book about the experiences of men involved in abortion situations. Please answer our questions as accurately as possible. Your answers will be kept confidential. Many thanks for your help and cooperation.

> Art Shostak, Professor, Drexel University, Philadelphia, PA
> Gary McLouth, Teaching Fellow, SUNY Albany, Albany, NY
> Lynn Seng, Counselor, Temple University, Philadelphia, PA

* = See supplement   Bold type = actual percent answer of 1,000 respondents

PART I: ANONYMOUS PERSONAL DATA
(please fill in or check the appropriate answer)

(1) Age *   (2) Race *   (3) Religion *
(4) Importance of your religion: Very **21**   Somewhat **47**   Not
Very **19**   Not At All **14**
(5) Marital Status: Married **18**   Single **60**   Divorced **6**   Separated **5**
Living Together **12**
(6) Last year of schooling completed *   (7) Occupation or College
Major *
(8) Social class of family *   (9) Today's date

PART II: ACTUAL EXPERIENCE
(please fill in or check the appropriate answer)

(1) Who favored this abortion?   **4** You only
5 Female only   **85** Both   **6** Neither
(2) Before the abortion, how many options did you seriously

313

consider? **18** Adoption **25** Remain single, provide child
. support **42** Marry and keep baby
(3) With whom did you consult before reaching your
decision? **75** Sex partner only **8** Parents
17 Other (please explain)
(4) Are you helping with the costs? **57** All **29** Half **6** Some
8 None
(5) Did you accompany your partner to any counseling
sessions? **40** Yes **58** No
(6) What was your relationship with your sex partner:
* At the time of conception? * Now?
(please use the following)
1. very casual   3. steady date   5. living together   7. separated
2. frequent date   4. engaged   6. married   8. divorced
9. other (please explain)
(7) How is having the abortion influencing this relationship?
(please check ONE)
31 Helping to bring us closer together   **47** Do not know at this time
 3 Contributing to our break-up   **19** Makes no difference
(8) Will you be more careful about risking pregnancy after this
abortion? **93** Yes **2** No **3** Don't know
(9) How is the abortion influencing your ideas about fatherhood?
58 No special way   **24** Am more eager than ever for that experience
17 Am more uncertain now about wanting that experience
(10) Since your decision to have the abortion, have you had any
thoughts about the fetus?
19 None **52** Occasional **29** Frequent
Were these thoughts generally:
21 Sad? **35** Curious? **25** Troublesome?
Other (please explain)
(11) How could this entire experience be a better one for you? (please
explain)

(12) How many abortion experiences have you been involved in
personally? *
(13) How many of your experiences do you regard, on balance, as more
distressful than positive for you personally? *

PART III: ATTITUDES

(1) Which of the following are *morally wrong*? (please check)

314

7 Sex between two single persons   17 Abortion
63 Homosexuality   21 Smoking marijuana
24 Pornographic movies   32 Sex before age 16
61 Use of hard drugs   8 Living with someone of the
opposite sex

(2) When do you think a fetus becomes a human being?
(please check ONLY ONE)
20 At conception (when sperm meets egg)
19 When fetus' nervous system begins to function
21 When fetus can survive outside the mother's womb
15 When baby is actually born
25 Cannot be determined one way or the other

(3) Do you feel you presently know all the facts you need concerning
abortion (check if YES)
52 Medical risks involved?   74 What it costs?   46 Local laws?

(4) Under what circumstances, if any, do you feel that a woman should
be able to obtain a legal abortion? (please check those you agree with)
a.   82 If the couple cannot support a child
b.   69 If the pregnancy is the result of a "one night stand"
c.   60 If the couple already has as many children as they want
d.   64 If the female is physically handicapped
e.   56 If this pregnancy may cause a marital breakdown
f.   18 If, for any reason, the male wants this pregnancy terminated
g.   48 If the couple has just ended their relationship
h.   81 If the fetus has serious genetic defects (deformity; mental
handicap)
i.   91 If the female's health is put at risk
j.   31 If the parents of this pregnant minor want the abortion
k.   37 If the couple is on the verge of breaking up
l.   79 If the pregnancy is the result of incest
m.   62 If the female wants the abortion, for whatever reason
n.   79 If the pregnancy may cause the female mental harm
o.   13 If tests reveal that the sex of the fetus is not what the prospective
parents want at this time
p.   65 If, for any reason, the couple wants the abortion
q.   63 If the female is a pregnant unmarried teenager

(5) How much say in the decision to have an abortion should a husband
have? (check ONE)
80 As much as his wife   19 Less than his wife   1 More than his wife

(6) How much say in the decision to have an abortion should an
unmarried male have?
58 As much as his pregnant sex partner   41 Less   1 More

(7) How do you feel about these matters? (please check each one using SA for *Strongly Agree,* A for *Agree,* N for *Neutral,* D for *Disagree,* and SD for *Strongly Disagree.*)

a. Abortion is the killing of a child

10	16	32	25	17
SA	A	N	D	SD

b. Males involved in abortions generally have an easy time of it.

5	16	11	44	24
SA	A	N	D	SD

c. The fact that abortions are now legal actually encourages people to have more.

8	32	22	28	10
SA	A	N	D	SD

d. Adolescents should get more information about birth control at school.

58	33	7	1	1
SA	A	N	D	SD

e. Females involved in an abortion generally have an easy time of it.

1	2	6	34	58
SA	A	N	D	SD

f. Government funds should be provided to help poor women pay the cost of an abortion.

21	30	28	14	7
SA	A	N	D	SD

g. Males involved in an abortion generally have disturbing thoughts about it afterwards.

9	38	39	12	3
SA	A	N	D	SD

h. A female under 18 should have to notify her parents before she can have an abortion.

8	18	22	28	24
SA	A	N	D	SD

i. Males who are sitting in a waiting room during an abortion should be offered counseling and/or education about abortion and contraception.

25	42	26	6	2
SA	A	N	D	SD

j. Abortion clinics should be required to notify a husband before performing an abortion on his wife.

28	28	20	15	9
SA	A	N	D	SD

(N =)

(8) If a woman has decided to have an abortion, but her husband is against it, do you think she should go ahead and have it, or not? (please check ONE)
59 Have the abortion   **40** Not have the abortion
(9) Do you think abortions will soon (next 5 years) be made illegal?   **19** Yes   **75** No

316

(10) If a federal law is passed which declares that life begins at conception, therefore making abortion a crime of murder, would you **9** FAVOR or **83** OPPOSE such a law?

(11) In what situations, and to what degree, should a male share responsibility for abortion decision-making? (Please rate the *degree of involvement* using COMPLETELY, VERY, MODERATELY, SLIGHTLY, or NONE for each situation listed.)

Engaged: *   Broken engagement: *
Married: *   Repeat abortion: *
Steady date: *   Single encounter: *

(12) Should the law require that the man be consulted before a woman decides to have an abortion?   **36** Yes, if they're married **28** Yes, whether or not married   **34** No

(13) Should a man be required to pay child support if a woman has refused his request that she have an abortion and she bears the child?   **51** Yes   **48** No

PART IV: REACTIONS

(1) When your female sex partner told you that she was pregnant, what was your reaction? (please check YES or NO for each one)

DID YOU:	YES	NO
a. Ask her what she wanted to do about it?	**86**	
b. Offer to marry her and have the child?	**35**	
c. Urge childbirth followed by adoption?	**9**	
d. Go along with whatever she wanted?	**66**	
e. Urge her to have and keep the baby?	**11**	
f. Recommend she have an abortion?	**51**	
g. Deny paternity?	**5**	
h. End the relationship?	**2**	
i. Offer to pay for the abortion, but no more than that?	**16**	
j. Discuss it together until an agreement was reached?	**94**	

(N = 505)

(2) When your pregnant sex partner told you she was going to have an abortion, what did you do? (please check YES or NO for each one)

DID YOU:	YES	NO
a. Offer to pay all the costs?	**69**	
b. Offer to pay half or some costs?	**43**	
c. Offer to join her in preabortion counseling?	**56**	
d. Offer to join her while she alone receives preabortion counseling?	**52**	
e. Seek preabortion counseling yourself?	**10**	
f. Offer to accompany her to the abortion?	**97**	
g. Refuse to have anything to do with the abortion?	**2**	

h. Decline to have anything more to do with her? **2**

(N = 505)

(3) If you wanted counseling before or during this abortion, to whom did you turn? (please check as many as apply)

29 Male friends	**4** Clergy	**10** Brother(s)
17 Female friends	**11** Parent(s)	**10** Sister(s)

30 Abortion clinic counselors (**5** male or **10** female?)

11 Other (please explain)

(4) Would you participate in any of the following clinic options if they were available to you now? (please check YES or NO for each one)

	YES	NO
a. Small group discussion (with other males from the waiting room) to give you a chance to discuss abortion-related issues and feelings with a clinic staff member?	**51**	**49**
b. Educational group session to discuss birth control methods, their safety, and their effectiveness with a clinic staff member?	**56**	**44**
c. A combination of the two above options?	**54**	**46**
d. Private meeting involving your partner, yourself, and a clinic counselor?	**74**	**26**
e. Private meeting alone with clinic counselor to discuss your questions, concerns, and feelings?	**62**	**38**
f. Opportunity to be with your partner during the abortion procedure, if your partner approved?	**69**	**31**
g. Opportunity to be with your partner in the recovery room after the abortion, if your partner approved?	**91**	**9**

(N = 501)

(5) What can this clinic do to be more responsive to men's needs with respect to counseling, facilities, information, procedures, etc.?

Offered ideas = **46%**

No idea = **54%**

(6) We are very interested in personal interviews to add more depth and reality to the information you have shared with us. If we can interview you, please give us your name and a phone number where you can be reached.

Name: **Yes = 21%; No = 79%**   Phone:

(area code)

Again, thank you very much for your help with this. If you have any additional thoughts you want to share with us about your experience, or about this questionnaire, please feel free to do so in the space below.

Supplemental: Men and Abortion Questionnaire

I.   ANONYMOUS PERSONAL DATA

   (1)   *Age*

            Under 18— 5%
               18–21— 30
               22–25— 30
               26–30— 18
               31–35— 10
               36–40— 5
               41–50— 2
               50 + —.05

   (2)   *Race*

            White—87%
            Black —10
          Hispanic — 2
           Asian — 1
           Other — 1

   (3)   *Religion*

          Protestant—45%
           Catholic—33
            Jewish— 2
           Muslim— 1
            Other— 4

   (4)   *Importance of Religion*

             Very—21%
          Somewhat—47
           Not very—19
          Not at all—14

   (6)   *Last Year of Schooling Completed*

        Less than 8 years—.05%
           8 years—.05
          8–11 years – 10
          12 years—45
        13–15 years— 27
          16 years— 12
        over 16 years— 6

   (7)   *Occupation or College Major*

           Student—28%

Blue-collar—35
White-collar—20
Professional— 6
Unemployed— 3
Other— 8

(8)   *Social Class of Family*
Lower— 3
Lower-Middle— 8
Middle—73
Upper-Middle—13
Upper— 4

II.   ACTUAL EXPERIENCE

(6)   *Relationship with your sex partner:*

	At the time of conception	Now
Very casual	4%	5%
Frequent date	6	5
Steady date	41	37
Financee	15	17
Living-together	18	17
Spouse	16	17
Separated	——	1
Divorced	——	——

(12)   *How many abortion experiences have you been involved in personally?*
1—75%
2—18
3— 4
4 or more— 3

(13)   *How many of your experiences do you regard, on balance, as more distressful than positive for you personally?*
0—51%
1—34
2—10
3 or more— 4

320

III. ATTITUDES
   (11)

	Completely Involved	Very much Involved	Moderately Involved	Slightly Involved	No Involvement
Engaged	47%	41%	10%	1%	1%
Married	65	28	6	1	1
Dating steadily	28	37	27	6	2
Broken en-gagement	20	27	26	15	13
Repeat abortion	30	30	19	11	10
Single encounter	13	14	19	19	34

H

Cooperating Clinics*

1. Albany Women's Medical Center, Chicago, IL
2. Alternatives, Inc., Silver Spring, MD
3. Atlanta Center for Reproductive Health, Atlanta, GA
4. The Aware Woman Clinic, Inc., Melbourne, FL
5. Birth Control Institute, Inc., Anaheim, CA
6. Boulder Abortion Clinic, P.C., Boulder, CO
7. Bread and Roses Women's Health Center, Inc., Milwaukee, WI
8. Cleveland Center for Reproductive Health, Cleveland, OH
9. Dallas Women's Center, Inc., North Central Women's Center, Dallas, TX
10. Doctors Family Planning Medical Groups, Inc., Tustin, CA
11. EMW Health Services for Women, Louisville, KY
12. Erie Medical Center, Buffalo, NY
13. Family Planning Alternatives, Inc., Sunnyvale, CA
14. The Fleming Center, Inc., Raleigh, NC
15. Gynecare Center, Glen Burnie, MD
16. Hagerstown Reproductive Health Services, Hagerstown, MD
17. Harrisburg Reproductive Health Services, Inc., Harrisburg, PA
18. Hillcrest Clinic, Norfolk, VA
19. Hope Medical Group for Women, Shreveport, LA
20. Mayfair Women's Clinic, Aurora, OH
21. Metairie Women's Medical Center, Metairie, LA

---

*All of the above clinics except 3, 7, 25, and 26 also participated in the Clinic Directors Survey.

22. Midwest Health Center for Women, Minneapolis, MN
23. Preterm Cleveland, Cleveland, OH
24. Preterm, Inc., Brookline, MA
25. Reproductive Health & Counseling Center, Chester, PA
26. San Vincente Hospital, Los Angeles, CA
27. Sigma Reproductive Health Center, Wheaton, MD
28. Summit Medical Center, Milwaukee, IL
29. Women's Center for Reproductive Health, Jacksonville, FL
30. Women's Community Health Center, Inc., South Portland, ME

Name Index

Subject Index

About the Author

Arthur B. Shostak has been an applied sociologist since earning his Ph.D. in 1961 at Princeton. Dr. Shostak previously earned a Bachelor's degree in industrial and labor relations from Cornell University (1958). After teaching for the Wharton School at the University of Pennsylvania (1961–1967) he moved to Drexel University where he has taught ever since. He also serves as an adjunct Professor of Sociology at the George Meany Center for Labor Studies, an adult education program run by the AFL-CIO in Silver Spring, Maryland.

Principal author of *Men and Abortion* (Praeger: 1984), he has also written *Blue-Collar Stress* (Addison-Wesley: 1980), *Blue-Collar Life* (Random House: 1968), and *America's Forgotten Labor Organization* (Princeton University Industrial Relations Section: 1962). Dr. Shostak has edited *Our Sociological Eye* (Alfred: 1977), *Modern Social Reforms* (Macmillan: 1974), *Putting Sociology to Work* (David McKay: 1974), *Sociology and Student Life* (David McKay: 1972), and *Sociology in Action* (Dorsey: 1966). He has co-edited *Privilege in America: An End to Inequality* (Prentice-Hall: 1974; with Jon and Sally Von Til), *New Perspectives on Poverty* (Prentice-Hall: 1965; with William Gomberg), and *Blue-Collar World* (Prentice-Hall: 1964; with William Gomberg).

Dr. Shostak has had over 80 essays published in various journals and edited volumes, and is presently working on new manuscripts concerned with the lives of former air traffic controllers since the mass firing of over 11,000 in 1981, and, the technological challenges ahead for older Americans.

Gary McLouth, born in Batavia, New York, holds graduate degrees from Syracuse University and Western Michigan University in Social Studies Education and English. He is completing the Doctor of Arts in English degree at SUNY Albany where he has taught American Literature and creative writing.

McLouth has worked in college administration and teaching and is the former Director of The University Without Walls in Providence, R.I. He has also been associated with Rhode Island College's Urban Education Center and SUNY at Oswego. McLouth has led a number of creative writing workshops in Newport, R.I. and Albany, N.Y.

In addition to *Men and Abortion*, Gary has published poetry in a variety of small magazines including, *Blueline, The Small Pond*, and *Nadir*. He has also published feature articles in *The Providence Journal Magazine, Playboy*, and others. He is currently finishing a collection of short stories and collaborating on a screenplay.

39·901